52 Weeks in the California Garden

By Robert Smaus

GARDEN EDITOR OF THE LOS ANGELES TIMES

Los Angeles Times

PUBLISHER: John P. Puerner
EDITOR: John S. Carroll

BOOK EDITOR: Linda Estrin
BOOK DESIGN: Tom Trapnell
COVER AND INSIDE ART: Catherine Deeter

Library of Congress Catalogue Number
96-076061

ISBN 1-883792-11-8
Copyright © 1996 Los Angeles Times

Published by the Los Angeles Times
202 West First St. Los Angeles, Ca. 90012

FIRST PRINTING APRIL 1996

FIFTH PRINTING APRIL 2003

Printed in the U.S.A.

Acknowledgments

Many avid gardeners have contributed to this book. From nursery people, botanic garden personnel and designers to longtime home gardeners, they have given valuable information to the *Los Angeles Times* through the years, and much of that has found its way into this book. In gardening, there is no substitute for firsthand experience. These real gardeners have made our articles more useful and accurate, and California gardens have benefited, mine included. Thank you.

Linda Estrin, who carefully edited the manuscript, is an enthusiastic gardener, growing all sorts of succulents and Southern California-only plants in her Westside garden. I can't tell you how wonderful it is to work with an editor who understands gardening and likes what you're writing about. I've always been fortunate that way. Dick Barnes, editor of the Real Estate section, where some of this information first appeared, is also a gardener, with a passion for fruit trees and tomatoes (he holds an office tomato taste test at *The Times* each summer). I'd also like to thank Bobbie Justice and Carol Powers, former editors of mine at *The Times*, who were always encouraging and made room for garden columns.

For the illustrations, artist Catherine Deeter didn't need to see photographs of all the flowers and plants because she grows many of them in her Central California garden. Unfortunately, when asked to draw one of our worst weeds, she discovered that it too was growing in her garden. Like many (including me), she had thought it was a nice little ornamental allium. Art director Tom Trapnell has a fondness for roses and daylilies, and director of book development Don Michel, who put this book together, grew up on a Fillmore citrus ranch. You can see that this book has been in good hands, and all have a little California dirt under their nails.

One reason gardening is such an adventure is that you can never know it all. It is my hope that gardeners will continue to share what they have personally discovered while gardening in this unique climate of ours. If you read something here and think, "Well, that wasn't my experience," let me know. Growth is what gardening is all about.

Contents

INTRODUCTION:

Why We Begin in September

MY GARDENING YEAR BEGINS IN LATE SUMMER, when I fish out some weathered redwood flats and sow seeds of broccoli, calendulas, delphiniums and other things I plan to plant in the fall. In the warm weather of August, seeds don't sit, but sprout like a rocket lifting off, and six weeks later they're large enough to go out into the garden. By then, it's October, probably the best time to plant just about anything in Southern California, and the only time to plant the "cool-season" flowers and vegetables. In our climate, fall is spring, at least as far as planting is concerned, and autumn, not spring, should be our busiest time in the garden.

This is one distinct difference between gardening in Southern California and gardening elsewhere. There are lots, enough to make gardening books that originate elsewhere misleading, if not entirely useless. Heaven help the Californian who follows the frequently encountered advice to add lime to the soil! It would be a disastrous mistake. Even Northern California is on a different timetable, and England or our own East Coast are in another world, with acidic soils, hard frosts, summer rain and other climatological events we can only imagine, or remember from some previous place of residence. Starting in late summer doesn't mean that our gardening year is any shorter. It's still 52 weeks long. If anything, it's longer than in other places, because there are very few weeks when there is nothing you could be doing in the garden, or when the weather keeps you inside. Even in August, it's nice enough outside in the early morning or late evening for a sit-down job like seed sowing.

This book suggests at least one significant thing you can do in the garden, or one job you should be doing, for each of the 52 weeks. Though we have a nearly seamless garden year—divided only by the rainy season and the dry season, the cool season and the warm season—a book must begin somewhere, so I'll begin this one, as I have begun most of my gardens, in autumn. Just remember that one month earlier, in the unlikely month of August, is the best time to sow seed, if you like starting gardens from scratch.

AUTUMN

I N SOUTHERN CALIFORNIA'S MILD, MEDITERRANEAN-like climate it's possible to plant in any season, but fall is the best time to plant almost anything, from a few pansies to an entire landscape. In autumn, planting is surefire and much, much easier. The urge to garden may be more primal in the spring, but fall is the better time, with only a few exceptions. After a long, hot summer, gardeners here should look forward to fall the way snowbound easterners look forward to spring, champing at the bit by August, anxious to begin gardening again.

It is far easier to list the exceptions than it is the opportunities: Tender subtropicals—such as citrus, bougainvillea, hibiscus, mandevilla and banana—are better planted in early summer when the soil is quite warm and there is no immediate danger of frost. Roses, berries and deciduous fruit trees are a real bargain purchased bare root in winter. And there are those annual flowers and vegetables, such as marigolds and tomatoes, that must be planted in spring because they flower or fruit in summer's warmth. Everything else, from ground covers to trees, does better planted in fall.

Research shows that roots grow quickly in autumn soils warmed by months of summer weather. You may see little above-ground growth, but down below roots are growing furiously. When spring arrives plants are well established and rooted fast, able to support astounding spring growth.

Remember how often you must water new plants, and you'll appreciate all the help winter rains provide. And the sun is lower and less intense in winter so plants experience little stress and take longer to dry out. These factors combine to make a powerful argument for fall planting.

The bulk of my own gardens have been planted in the fall, and I

WHAT TO PLANT DURING THE COOL SEASON (OCTOBER TO MID-DECEMBER)

FLOWERS

🍃 *These are annuals best started from seed:*

African daisy
Alyssum
California poppy
Clarkia and
   godetia
Linaria
Sweet pea
Wildflowers

🍃 *These are annuals and bedding plants best started from nursery packs:*

Bells-of-Ireland
Calendula
Candytuft
Canterbury bell
Chrysanthemum multicaule
Chrysanthemum paludosum
Cineraria*
Columbine
Cyclamen*
Delphinium
Dusty miller
English daisy
Forget-me-not*
Foxglove*
Hollyhock
Iceland poppy
Larkspur
Nicotiana
Pansy and viola
Phlox
Primrose*
Ranunculus

Blue bedding
   salvia (*Salvia farinacea*)
Schizanthus
Snapdragon
Stock
Sweet William

PERENNIALS

🍃 *You can plant almost any perennial flower, from four-inch pots or gallon cans.*

BULBS

🍃 *Purchase these early in the season, and refrigerate (in the vegetable crisper) for six to eight weeks:*

Garden tulips
Hyacinth
Spring-blooming
   crocus

🍃 *These can be planted right away:*

Allium
Amaryllis
Anemone
Babiana
Brodiaea
Calla lily*
Crocosmia
Cyclamen
Daffodil
Dutch iris
Freesia

Homeria
Ipheion
Ixia
Lachenalia
Leucojum
Lily*
Muscari
Ornithogalum
Oxalis
Ranunculus
Scilla*
Sparaxis
Species, or wild,
   tulips
Watsonia

VEGETABLES

🍃 *These are best started from seed:*

Beet
Carrot
Endive
Fava bean
Kale
Kohlrabi
Head and leaf
   lettuce
Peas
Radish
Spinach
Swiss chard
Turnip

🍃 *These are best started from nursery packs, bulbs or bare root:*

Artichoke
Broccoli
Brussels sprouts
Cabbage
Cauliflower
Celery

Garlic
Onion
Rhubarb

LAWNS

🍃 *Plant cool-season grasses, including annual rye over Bermuda grass, perennial rye, bluegrass and tall fescue.*

LANDSCAPE PLANTS

🍃 *You can plant most shrubs, trees, ground covers and vines, including all California natives, though this is not the best time of year to plant citrus, subtropical vines and shrubs, deciduous fruit trees such as apples and apricots, roses (best planted bare root in winter) and subtropical lawn grasses such as Bermuda and St. Augustine.*

* *will grow in a fair amount of shade*

don't think I have ever lost a plant put in then. That is not to say I haven't killed my share of plants, but it has always occurred much later on, or when I've tried to fill some hole or void in the garden at other times. I now go so far as to buy plants whenever they strike my fancy—say, at the Huntington Botanical Garden's big sale in May—and then keep them in a makeshift nursery alongside the house until fall arrives.

While planting is the major autumn opportunity, it is by no means the only one, and accomplishing everything you set out to do takes some planning. Begin in September with jobs that must be done early, such as killing off weeds or portions of the lawn. Then plant any fall-blooming bulbs, such as saffron crocus, and move on to the vegetables and flowers that need the longest growing season, such as Brussels sprouts and cabbage, and any cool-season annual flowers you want blooming by the winter holidays. The Arboretum of Los Angeles County has found that calendulas, pansies, Iceland poppies and stock do best planted in September, even in Arcadia, surviving the occasional week or two of sizzling weather.

When the weather begins to cool in October and November, you can plant any new trees, shrubs or ground covers. That's also the time to plant perennials, spring-blooming bulbs and any other cool-season annuals. Late in November, I like to plant drought-resistant things including California natives and wildflowers, though this usually drags on into December and even January because days become so short.

That's the downside of autumn—days grow shorter and shorter, so the later in the season it gets, the less time you have. Shadows also get longer as the sun drops ever lower, so be sure you're not planting something that needs sun in an area that will soon be shady. And be prepared for the first Santa Ana winds, which can make gardens very messy but, in most areas, really don't do much to plants despite their ferocity and extreme dryness.

September

FALL-FLOWERING BULBS

A S MENTIONED IN THE INTRODUCTION, IN Southern California the gardener's year really starts in September, with Week 36. You can begin it with a bang by planting some special bulbs that bloom almost immediately. This is as close to instant gratification as you get in the garden, especially when planting bulbs, where patience is not only a virtue but usually a necessity, while you wait for their leaves to push out of the ground.

One of these bulbs may never get into the ground. Colchicums are perhaps the best-known fall-flowering bulb, but most people never plant them. You don't really need to because they'll bloom almost anywhere—in the box at the nursery, on the potting bench, or sitting in the middle of the kitchen table. All they need is light from a window. The flowers are crocus-like, but bigger and usually pink. Later they'll make leaves and roots if they're planted in the ground, though snails and slugs relish the bulbs, which, unfortunately, must be planted part way out of the ground. Snails

WEEK
36

peel the exposed bulbs like an onion and eat the leaves as they appear, so most people enjoy the novelty of bulbs flowering out of the ground, then toss them out.

Much more satisfactory in the garden are the saffron crocus, from which the precious spice is made. The flowers are a lovely lilac and large for a crocus, and flopping out of the petals are several bright, burnt orange-red stigmas, a bonus. Save these, and you'll have homegrown saffron, and, as any cook knows, it doesn't take much to season and color a dish. The flowers last for only two days, so simply pick the stigmas at the end of the second day, air dry, then seal away in a little jar.

I should be clear on this point—none of the fall-blooming crocus blooms for long, and they hardly make a dazzling show. But discovering a patch of them at your feet one dry autumn morning is a thrill nonetheless. Because crocus are so small of stature, they should be planted in a protected place, such as at the edge of a path, where they will not be overwhelmed by larger plants. But be sure to remember where the little bulbs are so you don't accidentally dig them up while they're dormant.

All of the fall-blooming crocus should be planted twice as deep as they are tall. Space them about three to six inches apart, in full sun, and in soil that can dry out a little in the summer (which is true for all of the bulbs mentioned here). Autumn crocus are native to the Mediterranean region, with a summer-dry climate like our own, where they flower in fall, grow in winter, then go completely dormant for the summer, returning the following autumn. The trick to growing them is to keep the dormant bulbs reasonably dry in summer so they do not rot.

With a little searching, you can find some of the other fall-flowering crocus, though you may have to go to some of the more adventurous nurseries or order them from bulb catalogues. *Crocus speciosus*, perhaps the prettiest—with dainty, deep violet-blue flowers and a darker veining in the petals—is native to Iran and Turkey, though, like all the other bulbs you buy, they are commercially raised in Holland. 'Conqueror' is a clear deep blue form developed by the Dutch. These crocus grow four to five inches tall.

The crocus with pale lilac flowers and a yellow throat sold as *Crocus zonatus* or *Crocus kotschyanus* is a native of Lebanon. It too is considered easy to grow, though *Crocus karduchorum*, with a white throat, is even easier.

And, easier to grow than it is to pronounce, *Crocus goulimyi* was discovered only in 1955, growing on a Greek island. It has soft lilac flowers and multiplies quickly in our gardens.

Lycoris bulbs are usually at nurseries in late summer or early fall. Dan Davids, of Davids & Royston Bulb Company, one of the suppliers, says that if you want flowers the first year plant the bulbs early in September, or even in late August. Wait too late, and you'll get leaves

Found on a Greek island in 1955, *Crocus goulimyi* has soft lilac flowers, blooms in autumn and naturalizes here.

SPRING BULBS TO PLANT IN EARLY SEPTEMBER

While tulips and daffodils and a few other common bulbs are best planted in a cooler soil a little later in the fall (or a lot later, in the case of tulips), several of the spring-flowering bulbs from hot climates like our own can go in the ground right away. Here are some, with how deep and far apart to plant them, and how tall they get.

All of these should be at nurseries now, or soon, and many are being grown in California, not Holland, so they need no acclimatization. All should return year after year with no digging or other special care.

Babiana: Cover with 2" of soil, spaced 6" apart; grows 12" tall.

Freesia: Cover with 1" of soil, spaced 3" apart; grows 12" tall.

'Grand Duchess' oxalis: Cover with 1" of soil, spaced 6" apart; grows 4" tall. Watch out, these spread rapidly in good soil.

Sparaxis: Cover with 1" of soil, spaced 3" apart; grows 12" tall.

Tritonia: Cover with 1" of soil, spaced 3" apart; grows 12" tall.

Watsonia: Cover with 4" to 6" of soil, spaced 6" apart; grows 36" tall.

but no flowers, at least not until the following fall, which is probably true for many of these bulbs. Its common name, spider lily, refers to the delicate, spidery flowers on some kinds (and shouldn't cause alarm). *Lycoris aurea* has golden-yellow flowers and is the easiest to grow, according to Davids. *Lycoris radiata* is a fiery red and the most spidery; *Lycoris sanguinea* is a salmon color; *Lycoris squamigera* is a pink, and *Lycoris albiflora* is white.

All grow about one to two feet tall, tall enough for the front of a flower bed, though they do best in areas that won't get too much summer water. The leaves that come in winter "are just kind of there," as Davids puts it, nothing to write home about. Plant the bulbs three to four inches deep and six inches apart. Slugs and snails often search them out, so be sure to bait.

Nerines, from South Africa, are similar-looking plants in shades of pink, red, orange and white, with petals that actually glisten in the sun (little crystalline structures in the petals refract light like tiny lenses). Nerines are hard to find at nurseries, but you might come across bulbs grown in quart pots. Gardeners find them easier to grow in pots, which should be small, than in the ground. A single bulb in a six-inch-diameter clay pot will live contentedly for a number of years and multiply into a small clump.

Bulb expert John E. Bryan, in the two-volume "Bulbs" (Timber Press, Portland), considers *Sternbergia lutea* "the best of all fall-flowering bulbs." Native throughout the Mediterranean, this bulb has been unavailable for several years because it was being collected from the wild, a practice now frowned on. Now it is being grown in Holland and is again showing up at a few nurseries.

Mary Brosius, a horticulturist at Descanso Gardens, who has grown many fall-blooming bulbs, agrees they're the best. The flowers are a bright golden yellow, like a daffodil in color, but "shiny like a buttercup," she says. She plants the bulbs just under the soil surface, and inland, she says, they do better with a smattering of midday shade.

If you plant enough of these autumn-flowering bulbs, fall will seem more like early spring than the smoggy end of summer.

QUICK AND TANGY MESCLUN

That very fancy, decidedly delicious and pricey mix of French salad greens called mesclun (or field salad in some fine restaurants) may be the easiest thing you grow in your garden, especially now. From seed to salad bowl takes about six weeks, and the seeds are unusually easy to sprout. It can be grown almost all year, even in containers if you haven't a garden or the room.

In the dialect of Nice, *mesclun* more or less means "mix." Though gardeners and gourmets don't always agree about what's in it, tangy arugula and soft lettuces are mainstays in traditional mesclun. But almost anything goes, as long as it can be called a green.

Put any in a salad bowl and drizzle a little olive oil and vinegar with a couple teaspoons of Dijon mustard mixed in, and you have a zesty and colorful salad. The zest comes from the greens other than lettuce, such as endive, chicory, dandelion, cress, mustard, mâche, chervil, purslane and, of course, arugula. The color comes from the various red and green lettuces, and texture is provided by the traditional roundish leaves and pointed and deeply lobed leaves.

Seedsman Shepherd Ogden, of The Cook's Garden, thinks that many of these true European mixes are too bitter for most Americans, so the company developed its own milder mix, called Tangy and Mild. The Cook's Garden [*P.O. Box 535, Londonderry, VT 05148 (800) 457-9705*] and Shepherd's Garden Seeds [*30 Irene St., Torrington, CT 06790 (860) 482-3638*] have the largest selection of mesclun mixes.

Though the contents may vary, one thing never does: You must harvest mesclun when the plants are small and tender. Wait too long, and a touch or, in the case of arugula, a truckload of bitterness awaits you. Plants are typically harvested when they are less than six inches tall. Three inches is considered ideal, and plants get there in about six weeks.

And don't plant too much at a time, or you'll find the plants going over the hill before you can use them. Waiting even a week will allow the leaves to grow larger than you want for true mesclun. Successive plantings are the answer. Though a seed packet may contain several thousand seeds, plant only a pinch or two.

Rows don't suit mesclun. Planted in wide beds, the ingredients are as pretty in the garden as they are in the salad bowl, maybe more so, when the sun is low and the various shades of green and red seem to glow.

I've grown two different mixes in a three-by-four-foot space at the Ocean View Farms community garden in Mar Vista. In one part I tried a mix from the Niçoise region of France that contained endive, chicory, dandelion, cress and arugula. In another was a Provençal mesclun with lots of lettuce as well as other greens (chervil, arugula and endive). If you're already growing lettuce, the Niçoise mesclun can be added to salads to spice them up a bit, or, for a really tart, teeth-clattering salad, eat them alone, as done in Nice. The Provençal mesclun is a stand-alone salad—you don't need to add anything but dressing.

If you garden in a clay soil, make a mesclun bed by mixing in organic matter with a spading fork or tiller, so it is loose and well aerated. If your soil is silty or sandy, you can add a little organic matter, though it isn't really necessary. But do add a mild fertilizer, such as cottonseed meal, and spade it into the soil.

At first, you may not be able to tell the weeds from the mesclun, since some of the ingredients are close cousins of garden weeds. If you suspect there might be weed seeds in the soil, before sowing the mesclun, water the beds every day to bring them up, then hoe or pull them out.

Make sure the soil is still moist, or water it again and wait a couple more days. After it dries a little on top, lightly pull a garden rake over the bed, making very shallow furrows with the tines. Sow seed sparingly—scatter so it is about one or two inches apart—and then lightly tamp the soil with the flat end of the rake. Make sure the seed is either uncovered or barely buried, then water with a fine spray.

At first, you may not be able to tell the weeds from the mesclun, since some of the ingredients are close cousins of garden weeds.

MAKINGS OF MESCLUN

These greens might be in mesclun (in addition to lettuce):

Arugula (roquette or rocket): Deep green lobed leaves, reminiscent of dandelion. Some say peppery flavor, others sesame.

Chervil: Ferny dark green leaves. Anise flavor.

Curly endive: Curly, lacy light green leaves. Mild, but with some bite.

Dandelion and **chicory:** Look like the weeds in your lawn. Tangy.

Garden cress (pepper grass): Very different from watercress. Broad or curly leaves. Peppery.

Mâche: Looks like tiny dark green lettuce plants. Mild taste some call buttery, others nutty— definitely delicious, even alone. Slow, so better planted by itself.

Mustard: Usually broad leaves, often red or purple. Spicy mustard taste.

Purslane (*verdolaga, carti-choy, pourpier* and portulaca are other, international names): Small, oval, somewhat succulent leaves. Acidic nip.

Keep the soil moist until seeds sprout.

Because the mesclun grows so quickly, pests won't be a problem, except for slugs and snails. Watch out for these on the lettuce. Some high-tech fabrics can help speed germination and keep slugs and snails out. Try covering the mesclun bed with a floating row cover such as Reemay, Agryl or Tufbell—one source is Harmony Farm Supply [*3244 Hwy. 116 North, Sebastopol, CA 95472 (707) 823-9125; www.harmonyfarm.com*]. These woven plastic fabrics let in the light and water but keep out pests (though they also raise the temperature underneath so don't use them in summer). You'll find that the seeds sprout rapidly because of the added warmth. Fit them loosely to the bed right after sowing, tuck the edges into the soil, and the greens will push the covers up as they grow. Lift an edge to harvest.

No garden or short of space? You can also grow a few salads' worth in large containers filled with commercial potting soil. Try the seed mixes that contain greens other than lettuce, since you can always buy lettuce at the market, then liven it up with your own mesclun.

Mesclun likes the cooler times of the year, from fall into early summer. Coastal gardeners should have no trouble growing mesclun even in mid-summer, but inland gardeners may have to move their beds into a little shade.

To harvest, use scissors to cut the leaves about an inch above the ground. Tear in half and soak in the sink to wash off any dirt. To dry, use a lettuce spinner, or roll the greens loosely in a dishtowel, take the towel outside and swing it sharply back and forth—the water flies off the greens and is absorbed by the towel.

Once you've cut your first mesclun, more leaves will push up, and you can usually get a second or even third cutting from the same plants, though the first is always the best, so you may want to turn the soil and simply plant more. Keep planting every few weeks, and you'll never run out.

PREPARING THE SOIL FOR PLANTING

D o you remember the saying about the $5 hole? "It's better to plant a $1 plant in a $5 hole," it goes, "than a $5 plant in a $1 hole." The point is: Soil preparation is everything. Beneath every good garden is a very good soil, at least where flowers and vegetables are concerned. When it comes to trees, shrubs and most native plants, there is gathering evidence that these do better without soil amending—just dig the hole and make sure the soil that goes back into it is completely pulverized, with no clods.

But for lawns, flower beds—especially those containing perennials and roses—and vegetable gardens, it's worth heeding this advice by diligently preparing the soil in advance of planting. That means getting rid of weeds, adding organic amendments to make the soil more manageable and putting in fertilizer to make it more nutritious.

WEEK 38

If you are thinking of shrinking the lawn to make room for more interesting or useful plants, say, more flowers or a vegetable patch, or if you are going to plant where there were only weeds before, it's time to get started while the weather is still hot.

Begin by thoroughly watering any areas you plan to plant. Water with some kind of sprinkler (not with your thumb clamped over the end of the hose, as fun as that may be) for a good hour, to make sure the water soaks deep into the soil. Water again the next day and again the next, then wait two weeks for seeds of annual weeds to sprout or for perennial weeds to begin actively growing. The idea is to get all the weeds up and growing.

If it turns out that all you have are annual weeds, you can simply hoe all the new sprouts out on a day that promises to be hot, so they wither quickly. More likely the weeds are going to include some of the same spreading grasses that make up our lawns, such as Bermuda grass (also appropriately called devil grass), the coarser Kikuyu or St. Augustine. These grasses are our most common weeds, and they are easily recognized by the white rhizomes that travel deep underground as well as along the surface.

In September, you can easily kill the above and below portions of these invasive grasses with glyphosate, commonly sold as Roundup. This herbicide works systemically and so does nothing harmful to the soil, and so far, anyway, it has an excellent environmental record. Spray it on the foliage, and it travels inside the plant to the roots, killing them as well. You can plant as soon as the grass or weeds turn completely brown.

Read the label carefully. The herbicide works best in hot weather, so choose a day that promises to be hot, which, in September, is just about any day. To prevent the spray from drifting to plants you intend to keep, apply it early in the day.

With weeds dealt with, it's time to turn the soil. The best way is with a flat-bladed garden spade, perhaps the gardener's most valued tool. In a soil that, ideally, is still barely moist from that watering you gave the weeds, dig the spade, straight down, as deep into the soil as you can and turn the spadeful of soil on its side, right back into the hole you just made. Don't try doing this in a dry soil or in a wet soil—always work in a soil that is just moist. Work in rows so you don't lose track of where you've already dug.

Break up the soil with a flat-bladed spade (it's not a shovel!), and mix in amendments with a spading fork.

This first turning of the soil is done simply to loosen it. Now you want to improve it by mixing in organic amendments. This can be homemade compost or any of the products sold in bags as planting mixes (don't confuse them with *planter* mixes, used in containers) made from organic materials, such as rice hulls and ground bark. Some have fertilizer value, but their ability to make a soil more manageable is their true worth.

Spread a two- to four-inch layer over the already-dug soil. Two inches will work on most soils, but if you have a heavy clay and are trying to grow fussy things such as azaleas, you may want to add four inches, or even six.

This is a lot of amendment. To cover 1,000 square feet (25 by 40 feet, a typical front yard, not counting the driveway) two inches deep, you'll need about six cubic yards, or one truckload, which makes a very big pile.

At this point, if you've got a heavy clay soil, you can also spread

---

RECIPE FOR A GOOD SOIL

For every 100 square feet of garden (an area 10 by 10 feet, or 4 by 25 feet), add the following ingredients:

- A 2" layer of organic amendments (about 4 three-cubic-foot bags)
- 2 pounds of an all-purpose fertilizer (a 1-pound coffee can holds 2 pounds of fertilizer)
- 10 pounds of gypsum (for clay soils)

Water thoroughly to bring up weeds. Wait two weeks, then dig out weeds or use the herbicide Roundup. Once weeds are eliminated, dig soil, then spread organic amendments, fertilizer and gypsum on surface. Mix ingredients into soil, lightly compact, and water one last time. Wait a week, check for weeds, then plant.

---

around gypsum, available at nurseries, since it helps to separate soil particles, breaking up the clay structure. Sprinkle 10 pounds over every 100 square feet, or follow the directions on the bag. On top of all that, sprinkle some balanced fertilizer, such as an all-purpose kind with numbers like 8-8-8 or 10-6-6 on the label. This is a good opportunity to get organic fertilizers down into the soil, where they work best, so you might want to use something like blood and bone meal or one of the other organics.

With all these ingredients on the soil surface, mix them in, with the spade, a spading fork or a tiller. Though tillers do not do a good job of breaking up soils (they often don't dig deep enough), even the smallest does a great job of mixing in amendments and fertilizer once the soil is broken. Whatever tool you use, make sure the amendments and dirt become thoroughly mixed together, breaking up all clods as you go. When you're finished, you should be able to squeeze a handful of moist soil together and, when you loosen your grip, the ball of soil ought to fall apart with just a gentle push. If it remains a hard ball of clay, more of a weapon than a handful of good soil, you may want to add more amendments, though, with time, it will get better, especially if you add your own organic mulch after planting.

With the soil prepared, walk it all down, slightly compressing it (kids like this job), then thoroughly water one more time, to bring up any more weed seeds and to further settle the soil. A week or so later, with all new weeds hoed out, you have more than a "$5 hole," you have an entire bed ready for intensive gardening.

PEST PLANTS

S everal years ago I asked readers of the *Los Angeles Times* to send me the names of garden plants that grew out of control. The subject came up because several things I had planted were suddenly trying to take over the place. We're not talking about weeds here, but things planted on purpose that soon begin behaving like weeds—invasively spreading underground or everywhere sprouting from seeds.

As an example of such as plant, I nominated a pretty thing with  red and yellow tubular flowers named *Lobelia laxiflora*. It took only minutes to plant, but months to get rid of, after I realized how aggressive it was. In my opinion, nurseries should have a large warning sign posted next to it—similar to those at gas stations, paint stores and other places that dispense potentially hazardous chemicals—"Warning: May Spread Everywhere." It moves on fat white roots that can grow as deep as 14 inches underground, which puts them almost beneath the reach of a spade. As you dig, you can't help but break off little pieces of root, and all of these proceed to grow new plants. If this is sounding like bad science fiction, then you have the idea. I suppose this plant has its place—on dry slopes where little else will grow—but I will never let it back into my garden.

You can try and cage plants like this, growing them inside bottomless buckets or tubs sunk into the soil, but I once tried this with a European ornamental grass named *Elymus* and it managed to escape. Nevertheless, some bamboo growers surround their spreading kinds (there are clumping bamboos that don't spread) with sheet metal buried at least 14 inches deep, and claim this works. But I suspect it has a lot to do with your soil. Plants aren't likely to send their roots too deep in a hard clay soil, but in good garden soil they might. I once grew a black bamboo that contentedly lived in one corner until I redid the neighboring lawn. Somehow it sensed all the great new soil nearby and took off. Weeks later, I found sprouts coming up 15 feet away, smack in the middle of my new lawn. It took days to get it out.

I think the worst offenders are those that spread widely underground, unnoticed by the gardener. But many who wrote were equally upset by plants that scatter seed a little too freely. Here, then, is a list of menace plants suggested by *The Times* readers. Each was mentioned in at least several letters, so it is not just one person's condemnation.

Japanese anemone (*Anemone hybrida* or *Anemone japonica*): One of the most reliable and pretty fall-blooming perennials for somewhat shady parts of the garden, it spreads deep underground, though slowly. In the right place it's great, but make sure you want it there for a long time, as it's nearly impossible to get rid of and will spread more than a few feet. One reader in Palos Verdes wrote, "While it was doing its thing above ground, it was much more active below ground."

Asparagus fern (*Asparagus setaceus*): "Just plain sneaky," wrote one Whittier reader. Seedlings spread by birds are surprisingly hard to pull out in one piece.

Night jessamine (*Cestrum nocturnum*): Powerful, almost sickly sweet scent in summer and seeds everywhere. As one reader described: "By the next day, what was bare dirt was now covered with two-inch seedlings."

Cashmere bouquet (*Clerodendrun bungei*): "It seems to sprout from ridiculously small pieces, and, worse yet, the crushed foliage smells like dirty socks," complained a Fullerton reader.

Pampas grass (*Cortaderia selloana*): A Santa Monica reader wrote that it has "nasty sword-edged leaves and a tough and horrid root system." Many conservationists suggest not planting it near wild areas since it may escape, like its cousin, *Cortaderia jubata*, which has become a noxious weed along the coast, scarring roadsides all through Big Sur and other formerly pristine areas.

Montbretia (*Crocosmia crocosmiiflora*): A beautiful, brilliant orange bulb that one reader said multiplies too fast so is "not worth the beauty."

Indian mock strawberry (*Duchesnea indica*): "It chokes out everything in its way," wrote a Santa Monica reader. "Seedlings spring up everywhere and the roots spread like wildfire," which is probably why this strawberry look-alike was such a popular ground cover for a while.

Horsetail (*Equisetum hyemale*): Without a doubt, this plant, which looks like a bunch of spreading sticks, got the largest number of bad marks from readers. Keep it in a container, out of the ground, as it spreads wildly and is tough enough to have survived from the Carboniferous Age.

Female shamel ash (*Fraxinus uhdei*): A Corona reader wrote: "Its seeds are more prolific than rabbits."

Algerian ivy (*Hedera canariensis*): "My neighbors on four sides

"Cashmere bouquet seems to sprout from ridiculously small pieces, and, worse yet, the crushed foliage smells like dirty socks," complained one reader.

have it, and I am constantly fighting to keep it out," wrote a Covina reader, though at least it doesn't root deeply, so isn't that hard to remove.

Morning glory (*Ipomoea tricolor*): "I was warned by the nursery that I'd be sorry," wrote a Huntington Beach reader. "And they were right. It seeds everywhere."

Giant Burmese honeysuckle (*Lonicera hildebrandiana*): "I found it growing in flower beds 100 feet from the original plant," said a Palos Verdes reader.

Japanese honeysuckle (*Lonicera japonica*): "You think you have it all out and there it is again," said a reader in Carpinteria.

Four o'clock (*Mirabilis jalapa*): "They drop hundreds of seeds," a Cardiff reader said. "And the seeds are hard-shelled enough to survive time and chemical agents"—which is why it is seen growing in so many vacant lots.

Sword fern (*Nephrolepis cordifolia*): "Takes over everything," said a Santa Monica reader.

Mexican evening primrose (*Oenothera berlandieri*): "I find it a nuisance," wrote a Palos Verdes Estates reader, "but the flowers are very pretty," which is probably why it survives as a popular, pink-flowered spreading perennial in drought-resistant designs.

Ornamental oxalis (*Oxalis purpurea*): "It spreads by bulbs, seeds, runners—you name it," said a Costa Mesa reader. And though it grows only a few inches tall and completely dies down for the summer, it is very hard to get rid of because it has so many tiny prodigy, the white form of the 'Grand Duchess' strain particularly so.

Virginia creeper (*Parthenocissus quinquefolia*, sometimes still sold as *Ampelopsis*): In Lancaster, a reader "filled eight bags with roots that had taken over the rose garden." Also seeds about.

Passion vine (*Passiflora*): Said a reader in South Pasadena: "I have seen it grow to the top of very tall pines and completely smother large shrubs in a jungle-like tangle. We found the little seedlings everywhere." A butterfly named the Gulf Fritillary likes it, though.

Fountain grass (*Pennisetum setaceum*): A Palm Springs reader wrote to tell us that "it's been banned by the city of Palm Desert." 'Nuff said.

Golden bamboo and **black bamboo** (*Phyllostachys aurea* and *Phyllostachys nigra*): One reader said these running bamboos are as "bad as Bermuda grass, but a whole lot bigger." Some other bamboos clump and don't run.

Obedient plant (*Physostegia virginiana*): Another handsome

One reader said the running golden and black bamboos are as "bad as Bermuda grass, but a whole lot bigger."

perennial that spreads a bit fast and far, or as a Costa Mesa reader put it: "A misnomer for certain."

Pincushion flower (*Scabiosa atropurpurea*): "Never let the dried flowers go to seed!" cautioned one reader in La Cañada Flintridge.

Cape honeysuckle (*Tecomaria capensis*): "Our landscaper put this in," one reader wrote, "and I could wring his neck! It has taken over a 400-square-foot area [from one plant]!" Another said, "Its tenacious tentacles are well on the way to an unfriendly takeover of our garden," and added that "tin snips are required to trim it back." Numerous readers complained about this common landscape shrub with the bright orange flowers and shiny foliage.

Rice paper plant (*Tetrapanax papyiferous*): "It is a real sorcerer's apprentice," wrote one reader. "I got rid of it by moving from Hawthorne to Northridge." This was another frequently mentioned pest; it also has a reputation for causing rashes.

Sweet violet (*Viola odorata*): A Los Angeles reader said, "My parents used to make me pull them up instead of writing sentences." Nothing sweet about the way it spreads.

Periwinkle (*Vinca major*): A Santa Monica reader cried: "It's taking over my whole garden!"

Though I would be suspect of any plant in this list, it is important to realize that not all people feel the same about these plants. For instance, one reader actually wrote and asked where he could buy the lovely lobelia I was having such trouble with! He thought it just the plant for his tough slope.

COOL-SEASON VEGETABLES

Sometime in fall, the tomatoes come out and turnips go in. This seasonal change doesn't happen overnight, because many summer vegetables linger well into November. But as the fruiting vegetables of summer fade, they should quickly be replaced by things like broccoli, lettuce, onions and peas. Beginning as far back as August, vegetable gardeners begin planting what are called the cool-season crops, those crunchy vegetables that do best in fall, winter and early spring.

For some, fall, winter and early spring are the best times in a vegetable garden. Veteran gardener Ginny Mackintosh thinks so. "It's a wonderful sea-

WEEK
40

son because you don't have all the insects to contend with," she says—and virtually no diseases, or the heat of summer, or the constant watering.

A couple of crops, Brussels sprouts and cabbage in particular, take a long time to mature, so many gardeners sow seed late in August and then transplant the seedlings into the garden in September. Janie Malloy, who runs a business called Home Grown in Pasadena that installs and plants vegetable gardens, is one who begins the switch then. She starts these two slow-growers early so they are mature before the heat of spring and summer arrives in the inland valley areas.

The cabbage worm is the larva of that flitting white butterfly so common in gardens.

Nearer the coast, timing isn't so critical, because the cool season is so much longer. At the Ocean View Farms community garden in Mar Vista, Mackintosh may start that early but she keeps planting right through February. "I don't pay too much attention to planting times of cool-season vegetables," she says.

The cole crops—broccoli, cabbage, cauliflower, kale and kohlrabi—are the anchors in a cool-season garden, big, heavy and slow. All are best transplanted into the garden as seedlings, purchased at a nursery or homegrown in little pots or recycled nursery packs. They are seldom sown directly in the ground, even by commercial farmers. Try this trick: When transplanting, bury the seedlings deep—like you would a tomato plant—so the stem is covered and the plant stands up straight and sturdy. As a group, these vegetables tend to have crooked, weak stems. Mackintosh snips off the two bottom leaves and makes sure seedlings get planted deep enough to cover the crook in the stem.

About the only pest you'll encounter all winter happens to favor the cole crops, especially cabbage. The cabbage worm is the larva of that flitting white butterfly so common in gardens. As soon as you plant, take preemptive measures against the worm by dusting the plants with a biological control called *Bacillus thuringiensis*, or simply BT, since it works best on young larvae. Don't wait to see holes in the leaves. Reapply from time to time through the winter months, because rain and irrigation wash it off. Safer Vegetable Insect Attack is one brand of BT that comes in a cleverly designed squeeze bottle that makes it easy to dust under the leaves when you hold it upside-down.

You might also see cutworm damage. If seedlings disappear overnight, suspect this fat larva. Malloy surrounds new seedlings with sections of milk carton that effectively fence out the invaders. Snails are also fond of the cole crops, so protect against them.

Beets, carrots, parsnips, radish, turnips and onions are cool-season root vegetables that also can be planted now.

You can start onions from little bulbs called sets, or sow seed as Malloy does. Sow now and onions will be ready in June or July. Malloy cautions that, if the plants try to flower before that time, break off the blooms; otherwise, the bulbs will begin to shrivel. She also grows garlic from cloves bought at the market and shallots from seed.

Potatoes are another cool-season crop. Mackintosh plants hers from what are called seed potatoes, actually little baby potatoes. Seed potatoes show up at nurseries in winter, or order from Ronninger's Potato Farm [*Star Route Rd. 73, Moyie Springs, ID 83845, (208) 267-7938; www.ronningers.com*]. Malloy uses seed potato starts and plants as soon as the tomatoes come out of the garden. Her favorite variety is 'Yukon Gold'.

And don't forget peas. You can grow them on the same trellises or cages you use in summer for tomatoes and snap beans. Malloy, who grows them on the trellises she uses for summer's cucumbers, plants two crops, one now and then one in February, when the first is finished.

This is also the best season for all the leafy greens, which are the easiest cool-season crops to sow and grow. All the various lettuces can be grown now, as well as spinach, chard and more exotic greens such as mustard, chicory, mâche and arugula. Don't plant too much at one time—make successive sowing throughout the year so you're never overwhelmed by greens. Plant a short three-foot-long row now, another in several weeks. Or sow seed in wide swathes, a small bed at a time, and harvest the thinnings as the plants grow. This method gives you lots of tender young leaves. Harvesting tends to start within four weeks and continues for four to six months, if only the outer, mature leaves of plants are cut.

ALL ABOUT LETTUCE

Lettuce is one edible every Southern California gardener should be growing. Lettuce is a cool-season crop, growing right through our winter and growing fastest in fall and spring. Because of our long cool growing season, California became famous for its lettuce early on, especially after Los Angeles seedsman H.L.

Musser introduced a heading type from France, about 1902, that later became known as "iceberg" lettuce, though it was first called 'Los Angeles Market' (the true 'Iceberg', introduced in 1894, is still sold by W. Atlee Burpee & Co.).

Because this lettuce grew as a compact, cabbage-like ball, it was easy to ship east in refrigerated railroad cars, and, since we could grow it in almost any season, it soon dominated eastern as well as western markets.

For a while, iceberg-type lettuces were just about the only lettuce you could buy in stores, though in the last few years other types have begun to compete with it (it still commands 80 percent of the market) and eclipse it in the garden.

Lettuce hybridizer William Waycott, formerly with the USDA and now Petoseed, broadly divides lettuces into six different categories—leaf, romaine, butterhead, crisphead, latin and stem.

Stem lettuce, also called celtuce, is an Asian kind where the leaf is discarded and the stem eaten ("Lettuce leaves are for geese," a Chinese friend told Waycott). Latin lettuces (one strain is named 'Gallega') are for South American climates that are warmer even than ours in winter. Seed for both may be difficult to find.

By far the most popular in home gardens are the leaf lettuces, because they are the easiest to grow, though they are also the most prone to bolt (when the weather gets too hot, the plants divert all their energy to seed production and send up seed stalks; old leaves shrivel, and new leaves become bitter). One of the oldest varieties is 'Black-seeded Simpson', introduced in 1879. It's still the most common in seed racks because it is one of the tastier varieties. 'Simpson Elite' is an improved version that takes up to a month longer to bolt so it seldom becomes bitter. 'Salad Bowl' (an All-America Selections winner), 'Red Salad Bowl', 'Prizehead' and 'Red Sails' are common ruffly loose-leaf varieties. 'Oak Leaf', with the deeply lobed leaves, is one of the most heat-resistant of the leaf lettuces, a good choice for late-summer harvesting. 'Selma Lollo', or 'Lolla Rossa', is an extremely frilly variety with red-tinged tips (this one will amaze your friends).

Leaf lettuces are also called cutting lettuces because you don't wait for them to mature, but cut the leaves as you need them. For this reason alone, you should always have some coming along. Most are full grown in fewer than 50 days—then they will produce seed stalks, so you should plant a little (say a three-foot row) every few weeks throughout the year.

There's little point in buying packs of already-planted lettuce. The seed germinates very surely in a few days and barely needs to be covered with soil. In fact, sowing lettuce seed should restore any lost confidence in growing things from seed. If there is any secret to growing lettuces, it is to grow them quick, watering frequently but not fertilizing much, if at all (to avoid nitrate buildup in the leaves). Invest any time and money in preparing the soil, which should be loose and fluffy with organic amendments. Those lucky few who garden on a sandy or silty soil will find growing lettuce ridiculously easy. Those who don't can get similar results by growing in mounded or raised beds.

Seed may germinate poorly out in the garden in August and September. The way around this is to save those little six-packs that flowers come in and refill them with potting soil. Then sow seed in them, keep them in partial shade while they sprout, and transplant several weeks later into the garden. This way it's possible to plant lettuce in August, even in San Bernardino.

Some gardeners in hot inland areas always grow their lettuce in partial, midday shade in late summer. Do this in the partial shade of a tree or make a small shade structure, which is what some gardeners do where it gets really hot (over 100°). But at this time of the year, you needn't bother. Days will be cool by the time the lettuce is maturing.

Some gardeners in hot inland areas always grow their lettuce in partial, midday shade in late summer.

Though leaf lettuces are easy to grow, there are much tastier lettuces, starting with the Butterheads and Bibbs (or Limestone, as they're sometimes called back east). These form loose heads, very loose and creamy colored in the case of the Bibb types. 'Bibb' and 'Buttercrunch' are the standard Butterhead varieties, but a favorite of many gardeners (including me) is the French variety named 'Merveille des Quatre Saisons', or just 'Four Seasons' lettuce. Succulent, tasty and very pretty, it is a maroon-blushed lettuce that can be harvested like a loose-leaf, or left to sit and form a small soft buttery head that melts in your mouth. It takes a little less than two months for the heads to mature. Just as its name conveys, it's good in every season. I am never without it in my West Los Angeles garden.

Romaine is the lettuce of the ancients. Sometimes called Cos, which is an island off the coast of Greece, it was grown by the Egyptians. It is, of course, the lettuce with the stiff, crunchy leaves, longer than they are wide, that are used to make Caesar salads. Romaines are usually harvested when mature, which takes about 75 days, when they make a tall loose head.

True tolerance to bolting is found in the crisphead kinds. According to Waycott, this comes from their Batavian blood (the Batavians are the European ancestors of our crispheads). Burpee's

'Iceberg' and 'Great Lakes' are traditional strains of this crunchy head-forming lettuce.

Waycott considers crispheads the pinnacle of hybridizing, at least for commercial growers, and they certainly add a delightful crunch to salads. Plants have more bolting and disease resistance and more bred-in qualities than do other lettuces. Waycott says that there are as many as 20 different genetic types sold at the market, each developed specifically to ripen during a certain period in the year, in differing locations. In other words, the iceberg lettuce you buy at the market might actually be a different variety every couple of weeks, with names like 'Salinas', 'Vanguard' or 'Empire'. Pay attention and you can spot the changes in color and taste throughout the year.

The crisphead lettuces we gardeners can get seed for tend to be those with the most tolerance to extremes. Three that should do well in Southern California, and that can be grown at almost any time, are 'Summertime', 'Mission' and a miniature called 'Mini-Green', which makes a baseball-sized head. All resist bolting but take time to mature (75 or more days). Space most of the crispheads about a foot apart. Waycott says that the last three weeks are the crucial time for crispheads. Most of the head is formed then and daytime temperatures should be about 70° to 75° at that time, though 'Summertime', 'Mission' and 'Mini-Green' can stand more heat (85° to 90° in the case of the latter). Near the coast, this means you can grow crispheads all year; inland, where summers are really hot and winters colder, the traditional planting months are late July through September, and then again in late February and March. Seedlings can stand the heat, and 60 to 90 days later, when heads form, the temperature should be right.

The similar Batavian types can be planted at about the same times inland, at any time nearer the coast. Their heads are less dense and crunchy than those of the other crispheads, but delicious nonetheless. 'Nevada' is one French Batavian I've grown that makes crunchy, flavorful heads and never seems to bolt. 'Sierra' is another variety I've heard gardeners go on about.

If you haven't grown lettuce in a while, or at all, this is the season to start. Just be sure to plant a little at a time, and then keep doing so—so you don't get too much in one week, or run out later just as the tomatoes ripen.

The iceberg lettuce you buy at the market might actually be a different variety every couple of weeks.

October

PLANTING PANSIES

THE MOST ENDURING, AND PERHAPS ENDEARING, of fall-planted flowers are pansies and violas. Pansies are the ones with the charming faces of contrasting colors, and violas are the more plain-faced ones (but just as pretty), though this distinction has blurred in recent years. If planted now, they will flower until the first hot days of summer. "Even in the San Fernando Valley," says Los Angeles garden designer Sandy Kennedy, "I've planted them in October and had them last through April." That's seven months.

Near the coast, they can last even into July, according to Lew Whitney, of Roger's Gardens in Corona del Mar. That's an incredible 10 months. "Pansies give you the most mileage of all fall-planted annuals," says Whitney, an obvious fan.

Pansies have been a part of California gardening for a long time. Back in 1908, John McLaren, creator of San Francisco's Golden Gate Park, and author of one of the earliest books on California gardening, had this to say of the pansy: "This popular plant is a favorite of rich and poor alike, everyone, who has a garden, growing a few pansies. This is deservedly so, in view of its wonderful variety of color and its free-flowering habit together with the ease with which it may be grown."

At that time, much attention was being given to hybridizing and crossing, with the goal being bigger and bigger flowers. As E.J. Wickson noted in his 1915 "California Garden Flowers": "Pansies are a

WEEK
41

25

great delight if well grown from choice strains of seed, of which a number of seedsman are making a specialty. A pansy specialist is coming to be regarded as a very high class horticulturist."

The culmination of all this was the strain called 'Majestic Giants', which won the first All-America Selections award for pansies. According to Whitney, these are still the best of the big-flowered, long-stemmed, pretty-faced pansies, and the most common at nurseries. Those long stems, for a pansy anyway, were developed so they could be cut, something modern gardeners seem to have forgotten. Whitney remembers his mother having had a special shallow bowl just for these pansies, and old seed catalogues make quite a point of their use as a cut flower.

In the last few years, another flurry of activity has introduced new colors and forms. 'Imperial Antique Shades' is a series that one catalogue states is "difficult to describe" but "fashionable." Call them dusky, decidedly nonprimary colors, and a hit with gardeners who prefer pastel tones. In this series there is also a separate 'Pink' and a 'Lavender', which go beautifully with stock, larkspur and other pastel spring flowers. Other pansy colors include good strong oranges, apricots, deep maroons, even black (actually, a deep, deep maroon, but it looks black as soot). There is a screaming-orange and purple pansy named 'Jolly Joker'—this, definitely no shrinking violet—and there are pansies with ruffled petals (one strain is named 'Rococo'). In the 'Bingo' and 'Rally' series of pansies, the flowers stand up straighter because they have a stronger joint between flower and stem. Nowadays, there are even violas with faces and pansies as plain as violas.

Violas are descended from *Viola cornuta*, but so much crossing has gone on that most violas are now a mix of pansy and viola, which is why some seed catalogues invented the terms *viola-flowered pansies* and *mini-pansies*. You would be pretty safe if you called a plain-faced pansy a viola. The best of these is a strain called 'Crystal Bowl', sold as a mix or as separate colors. It is the longest blooming of all, flowering for what seems like forever—you are likely to tire of it before it gives up. Some gardeners think the faceless pansies and the new violas take spring heat better in the interior valleys (especially the new 'Maxims' and 'Happy Face' series).

The Johnny-jump-up is the least civilized of the viola clan and is so easy to grow it will naturalize in gardens (some consider it a weed). Its botanical name, *Viola tricolor*, is a reference to the lilac, purple and yellow petals. There are fancier Johnny-jump-ups, such as 'King Henry', a deep velvety purple.

Lew Whitney remembers his mother having had a special shallow bowl just for the long-stemmed pansies.

Some people, particularly those who garden in heavy clay soil on the east side of town, have had the maddening experience of their pansies suddenly wilting and dying, especially during wet winters. One gardener, and his father before him, grew hundreds of pansies each year in their San Marino garden. A few years ago, though, the plants started dying out, and the two tried all sorts of things from mounding the soil to growing their own from seed. They have finally given up.

The culprit is a fungus named *Rhizoctonia* that thrives in soggy soil. It attacks the very base of the plant and literally severs it from the roots. If you've had this problem in the recent past, you probably will again, says Frank Burkard, of Burkard Nurseries in Pasadena, because the disease is now in your soil.

Never bury the base, or crown, of a pansy. Leave a little of the rootball sticking out of the ground.

Try planting in a different location and leave that part of the garden pansy-free for a couple of years, like a farmer who rotates crops. You should also make sure that the pansies are planted so that the crown (the top of the rootball) ends up about half an inch out of the soil, and go easy on the watering.

Or try switching to the smaller violas. "Have you ever heard of a Johnny-jump-up rotting?" asks Burkard. Violas are close kin to Johnny-jump-ups, though not as surefire. Or plant pansies in containers using fresh bagged potting soil. Naturals in containers, they are perfectly proportioned to pots and will spill gracefully over the sides. In a pot pansies are virtually problem-free, unless you plant them with the crown buried. Never try to straighten a floppy plant by pushing soil up against the base; it will rot in a matter of days. As you would in the ground, plant them so the base of the plant is a little higher than the surrounding potting soil.

This suggestion comes from Roger's Gardens: If you have had problems in the past, spray plantings with Ortho Multipurpose Fungicide, which contains the active ingredient Daconil, as soon as they go into the ground, and then follow up with a second spraying a few weeks later. This will not bring back plants already infected, but—in the nursery's experience—it prevents the fungus from attacking newly planted pansies and violas. The fungus lives only on the soil's surface, so there's no need to drench the soil—just get the surface good and wet, especially around the bases of the plants.

Pansies and violas can get long and leggy—straggly—and you

27

certainly want to avoid buying them when they look like this. Find tight, compact plants that have not begun to lean or topple. This is especially true of plants in packs and flats, but it's also true of those in four-inch pots that are already flowering.

Should they become leggy in the ground, here's another trick passed along by Whitney, though it sounds drastic. Whack off two-thirds of the growth, fertilize and water. He promises they will bounce right back.

The reason they become long and leggy is most often not enough light. Heed the advice given by a Mr. W.M. Bristol, quoted in the 1915 "California Garden Flowers," by E.J. Wickson: "Don't believe the threadbare and absurd statement that 'pansies like a shady place.' Set them where they will receive full sun but no reflected heat from buildings.

"Remove all blossoms as they wilt," continues Mr. Bristol. This advice is seconded by Mr. Whitney. If they are allowed to go to seed, the flowers will not last nearly as long. Whitney goes so far as to let his thumbnail grow a little longer in winter, so he can use it in true nurseryman fashion to nip off faded pansy flowers.

> ### PANSY TIPS
>
> *If you've had no luck with pansies—if they wilt and die for no apparent reason . . .*
>
> - Plant them in another part of the garden.
> - Plant so the crowns are half an inch out of the soil.
> - Immediately spray new plantings with a fungicide that contains Daconil.
> - Try growing them in pots with fresh potting mix.

While pansies and violas might not like shade, what they do like is a cool and moist soil, so it is worth the effort to add organic amendments before planting and to mulch. They must never be allowed to dry out. These plants like moisture, but Mr. Bristol's advice is again as appropriate today as it must have been then: "Don't give them a showerbath with the hose every day or two. It is folly. It hardens and packs the ground while the roots may be suffering for moisture. Once a week or two make holes or furrows among the plants and keep water therein until the ground is thoroughly soaked."

You may not want to irrigate with "holes or furrows," but when you water, do so thoroughly. Old books make quite a point of never letting pansies go completely dry, and of mulching with some organic material.

The time to plant is now. In the ground or in containers, space plants about six inches apart (the large 'Majestic Giants' are better eight inches apart). Remember to plant them a little high and be careful not to overwater. The traditional place to plant pansies has always been along the front walk so their cheery faces can welcome visitors. A landscape plan in the 1908 edition of "California Gardening" shows pansies on either side of the walk and on either side of the front door against the house, at the base of roses.

Pansies, and especially violas, are the perfect companion for spring bulbs. After you plant the bulbs, plant pansies on top. They will flower both before and after the bulbs, and the fading bulb foliage can be bent and hidden under the pansy foliage. A favorite combination mixes yellow daffodils, which can be planted now, with blue violas, especially the one labeled 'Azure Blue', or one of the blues from the 'Crystal Bowl' strain.

OVERSEEDING BERMUDA-GRASS LAWNS

It's not too late to do something about that dying lawn. Bermuda grass, our most common lawn grass (known as devil grass by many), goes dormant as the weather cools and stays brown or nearly brown for most of winter and early spring. It often doesn't green up again until after all of the fall-planted flowers fade in late spring. An unfortunate but common sight in spring here is a garden full of pretty flowers next to a nearly brown lawn.

There is a solution—overseeding. It is an old solution but remains a dramatic one. All you do is thin out and rough up the Bermuda-grass lawn, mow it very short, and then scatter seed on top and water until it sprouts. The result is a bright, *bright* green lawn that lasts through winter and well into spring, when the Bermuda grass comes back to life.

WEEK 42

The traditional grass sown on top of Bermuda is annual rye. It lives only for the season, then dies and fades away in summer, at which point the Bermuda should take over. It is sold in big bags at just about every nursery and building supply store at this time of year.

How much do you need? Before you head for the nursery, measure the area to be overseeded. Burkard Nurseries in Pasadena suggests one pound of ryegrass seed for every 100 square feet of lawn. For a typical, 1,000-square-foot lawn, you'd need 10 pounds of seed, which is the size of most bags.

Some have suggested overseeding with perennial rye instead. The idea is that this grass will return on its own the following fall, being a perennial, without reseeding. However, all ryegrasses need to be mowed quite high, while Bermuda grass is cropped close to the ground, so the rye would have a hard time surviving summer's short mowings. Perennial rye also needs more water than Bermuda does and is prone to getting a disease called rust, which will turn your shoes bright orange.

Annual rye, perennial rye and the new turf-type tall fescues should be mowed so they end up about two inches tall; Bermuda should be only an inch tall, after mowing, or lower if it's a hybrid kind.

The new turf-type tall fescues, some with brand names such as 'Medallion' and 'Marathon', are another possibility for overseeding. But here the idea is to sow seed of a turf-type tall fescue now so that it replaces the Bermuda by summer, though I haven't seen conclusive proof that this works.

> ## INGREDIENTS FOR A WINTER LAWN
>
> *To overseed 1,000 square feet, you'll need:*
>
> - 10 pounds of annual ryegrass seed
> - 4 two-cubic-foot sacks of mulch or manure
> - 10 pounds of 10-6-4 or similar granular fertilizer

Most nurseries and gardeners, however, still recommend annual rye as a temporary winter cover. Here's how you do it:

Begin by thoroughly watering (for as long as 20 minutes) the lawn for a day or two. Then roughly rake it with a steel rake, or even one of the special rakes sold at nurseries that are designed to cut and rip up Bermuda runners. Mow the lawn as close to the ground as possible and then rake it one more time, being sure to loosen any bare patches of soil (you are trying to make sure that the seed comes in contact with the soil).

Scatter a complete granular fertilizer (one with numbers like 10-6-4 or 10-12-10 on the label) over the lawn, following label recommendations. Now scatter the seed as evenly as possible. Don't sow it too thick, or it will rot as it sprouts (from lack of air circulation). Walk over the lawn in one direction scattering seed lightly, then go back over it again in another direction. It's better to make several passes rather than one. Or do the same thing with a seed spreader.

Cover the seed with a light mulch. Steer manure is the traditional favorite because it acts as a mulch and mild fertilizer, and it's cheap. If you object to the strong odor, use a product such as Kellogg's Topper, which is also part fertilizer, part mulch. Whatever you use, you will need a two-cubic-foot bag for every 250 square feet.

Water right away, and then water often enough to keep the seed moist. Make sure the lawn is damp before you go to bed at night. It takes about a week to a week and a half for the seed to sprout into a brilliant, emerald-green lawn that will last all winter. In late May or June, begin mowing the lawn low again, fertilize, and the Bermuda should bounce back for the summer.

WATCH OUT FOR WINTER'S SHADOWS

B y now, most gardeners have noticed that the days are getting shorter. Soon, we'll need a flashlight after work to pick those last few tomatoes of the season, or the first lettuce. Shadows are also getting longer as the sun sinks lower on the horizon, and they will be their longest toward the end of December during the winter solstice. If, at noontime, you stand in the garden at that point, your shadow will stretch some 10 feet in front of you, if you are six feet tall. Compare this to summer when your noontime shadow is but a circle at your feet. (The actual angle of the sun at noon in Southern California is 79° above the horizon in summer, 33° in winter—about half as high.)

Likewise, the shadows of trees and buildings stretch across the garden. This is something to note, for it often effects what you can plant and where. You might even want to make a sketch of your garden when shadows are their longest—it should prove very useful next

At high noon in summer, a 40-foot tree casts a shadow only seven feet long. In winter, the shadow lengthens to 63 feet.

31

fall when it is time to plant winter's flowers because it will show where the sun shines and where it does not. Draw a plan view of your garden and then at noon shade in the areas in the shadows. My front garden, for instance, usually bathed in sunlight, in winter suffers in the shadow of large magnolias clear across the street! You might also notice that the sun gets low enough to creep under trees, so usually shady beds are actually getting a fair amount of sun, though it is dimmer than in summer. So it works both ways. Some parts of the garden get more shade, some less.

Daffodils for Southern California

There are bulbs to plant in the fall that last, and bulbs that don't. Dutch iris, freesia, sparaxis and watsonia are a few that will come back on their own for years. They grow and spread into larger and larger clumps—what gardeners call naturalizing—with little or no help.

Then there are bulbs, such as tulips, hyacinths and even ranunculus, that bloom once in spring and are finished, just like an annual bedding plant. You get one glorious spring and then you pull them out.

WEEK
43

As a group, daffodils fall somewhere in between—some come back, some don't—but the higher up the "hill" you live, the better the chances are. Those lucky few who live, or keep a cabin, in the high mountains where winters are cold and snow not uncommon will find that daffodils grow like true wildlings, needing no care at all. Even in the lower mountains, the Santa Monicas included, and in the foothills, some varieties will live for at least 30 years. Closer to sea level, some daffodils will naturalize, but most must be treated like tulips or annuals and be replanted each fall, especially if you grow them where they are watered on a regular basis in summer.

Near Big Bear, at an elevation of 5,500 feet, Gene Bauer has covered nearly five acres with daffodils. One year she planted an incredible 30,000 new bulbs, and she's not done yet. Once they're in the ground, she never touches them again—no digging them up and storing them in the garage, no fertilizing, no irrigation and no problems with gophers. Gophers actually got Bauer started with daffodils when she found that they were about the only thing the gophers didn't eat (they also won't eat garlic).

At 1,750 feet in La Cañada Flintridge, Polly Anderson grows daffodils that return every year. She does fertilize twice a year, and she irrigates the bulbs in fall, winter and spring. At 800 feet in the Santa Monica Mountains, on a ridge in Topanga Canyon, John Sherwood has had good luck with many daffodils. And he can show you naturalized daffodils in full flower with a gopher's mound right in the middle of the clump, but the rodents haven't touched the bulbs. Other bulbs have disappeared overnight and even before Sherwood's eyes, but gophers won't eat any part of a daffodil.

At 400 feet in Yorba Linda, in a virtually frost-free area where avocados used to grow, Helen Grier, an avid member of the Southern California Daffodil Society, has learned which daffodil varieties return and which don't. In the last 45 years, she has tried more than 700 different kinds in this climate, which is more typical of where most Southern Californians live.

Only Sherwood occasionally irrigates his daffodils in summer, but he lives in fire country and needs the green buffer other plants provide. The other gardeners let their daffodils go dry for the summer, which would seem to be their secret. Those with drought-resistant gardens should take note.

Don Christensen, of Davids & Royston Bulb Company, suggests that the homeowner might be the daffodil's worst enemy. Planting something over them and watering in summer is sure death. "They need to rest in summer," he says, which is why many daffodil aficionados dig up the faded bulbs each summer and store them in a cool dry place until fall.

But, even if they are kept dry in summer, most daffodils will not last long at low elevations. Christensen says they are perfect the first year—just like the catalogue pictures—fair the next, but they disappear by the third.

In the hills and mountains, it's a very different story. Bauer's original planting in the San Bernardino Mountains is now 35 years old. Single bulbs become clumps that produce 25 to 30 flowers after only five or six years in the ground. She can grow just about any daffodil in her high-mountain garden. She plants each bulb in its own hole, covering it with five to six inches of soil (miniatures are covered with only three inches), spaced at least six inches apart so they can spread. Though she adds nothing to the soil, she does turn it with a

Even if they are kept dry in summer, most daffodils will not last long at low elevations.

SURE-TO-RETURN DAFFODILS FOR LOW ELEVATIONS

Dig each hole twice as deep as the bulb is tall, and plant in clumps of three to five bulbs spaced several inches apart.

SMALL FLOWERS	LARGER FLOWERS
'Geranium'	'Arctic Gold'
'Grand Soleil d'Or'	'Gold Court'
'Minnow'	'King's Court'
'Trevithian'	'Ice Follies'
Chinese sacred lilies	'Falstaff'
Paper whites	'Galloway'

spading fork beforehand, removing any rocks. She begins planting in mid-September and continues well into December. Early varieties, such as 'Peeping Tom' and 'February Gold', bloom at the end of February and the last finish up in May. The peak comes in late March and April.

In La Cañada Flintridge, Anderson has a few clumps that are 30 years old, but most of her successes are the smaller-flowered types. It's an impressive list nonetheless, enough to fill anyone's garden with nodding narcissus. Her no-dig, little-care daffodils include Chinese paper whites, 'Cheerfulness', 'Matador', 'Earlicheer', 'Tête-à-Tête', 'Bell Song', 'Hawera', 'Jumlie', 'Quail', 'Silver Chimes', 'Golden Dawn', 'February Gold', 'Thalia' and 'Trevithian'. These have large flowers but still require no digging in her garden: 'Ice Follies', 'Peeping Tom', 'Binkie', 'Audubon', 'Honeybird', 'Stratosphere' and 'Broomhill'. The best of the lot, she thinks, is 'Ice Follies', with its creamy petals and large, flat soft yellow cup.

Anderson plants new bulbs, or begins watering the established but dormant clumps, in November, never earlier, after the soil has cooled. She plants them in individual holes, or in trenches six inches deep, and she adds soil amendment to the dirt that goes back in the hole. She usually sprinkles ordinary granular fertilizer on the bulb areas in November and again just as the bulbs make buds in spring, then waters it into the soil with the sprinklers. If the soil dries between winter and spring rains, she waters. In late spring, she stops watering and tries to mulch the bulb areas with pine needles, if she can find enough. She never cuts the old foliage off until it is completely brown.

In the Santa Monica Mountains, Sherwood has clumps of daffodils scattered all over his property. He says they are "absolutely hassle-free." He planted the first eight years ago, and they have been "blooming furiously" ever since. Some of his best are 'Cheerfulness', 'Professor Einstein', 'Ice Follies' and 'Geranium'. Even some of the large-flowered kinds such as 'Carlton' reliably return. In fact, he manages to get the 'King Alfred' types to return. But it's important to note that Topanga Canyon gets quite cold in winter, cold enough to freeze citrus and colder than the 800-foot elevation would suggest.

Grier grows hundreds in her low-elevation Yorba Linda garden, but only a few come back year after year with little care and no digging. What she has found is that you can't go wrong with any daffodils from the Daffodil Society's Division VII or VIII. These are the groups that include all the jonquil and tazetta-type narcissus. All have smaller flowers, but clusters of them, and the flowers are fragrant or downright pungent. Some consider these the prettiest of all daffodils. Their ancestry is in the Mediterranean, a climate much like our own.

'Geranium', 'Grand Soleil d'Or', 'Minnow', 'Trevithian', Chinese sacred lilies and paper whites are commonly available narcissus from these groups. All could be called surefire in any garden, if they are not kept too moist in summer. If you insist on growing large-flowered daffodils, Grier can suggest several, including 'Arctic Gold', 'Gold Court', 'King's Court', 'Ice Follies', 'Falstaff' and 'Galloway'; don't expect any other big daffodils, including the 'King Alfred' types, to last in low-elevation gardens.

Grier gardens in a heavy adobe and she adds amendments whenever she turns the soil. She never plants before November, which is also when she begins to irrigate established clumps if it hasn't already rained. Her rule of thumb is to plant the bulbs in a hole twice as deep as the bulb is tall. Every three or four years in winter she fertilizes by raking in a bulb fertilizer and lets the rains carry it to the roots. She stops watering when the bulb foliage is half-brown. When it is completely brown, she pulls it off. The bulbs lie dormant and bake in the warm soil all summer, and in the fall, after the first rains, they return.

PLANTING SPRING COLOR

WEEK
44

For spring color, the trick is to choose only a few things from all those boxes full of bulbs and benches packed with bedding plants at the nursery. At no other time are there so many ingredients for making a flower garden. To help narrow the field I asked several experts for ideas, for individual standout plants and combinations you can plant now for a spectacular spring show.

Tulips top many people's list of traditional

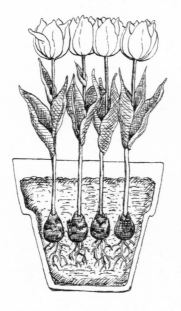

fall-planted flowers, even though they were bred for colder climates. But they can be grown here—even in the extremely mild coastal climate of Corona del Mar—if they are treated as annuals and given an artificial winter in the fridge. Cristin Fusano, horticulturist at Roger's Gardens and former color specialist at nearby Sherman Gardens in Corona del Mar, has a short list of tulips that do especially well here, in the ground and in containers. Her favorite (and she is not alone in this opinion) is the tall, slender white tulip 'Maureen', which is absolutely elegant in a pot. She also finds reliable: 'Asta Nielsen', 'Blue Jay', 'Cocktail', 'Elizabeth Arden', 'Halcro', 'Menton', 'Redwood', 'Renown' and 'West Point'.

Containers for tulips should be at least 16 inches deep. Plant bulbs so they almost touch, and cover with four inches of soil.

Tulips are best used in pots, or clumped here and there in the garden, because they bloom for a short time and then must be tossed out. Buy bulbs right away, but keep them in the refrigerator for six to eight weeks. This means you can plant them out around the holidays, and they will bloom in early spring. Fusano plants other things in the garden earlier in fall, but saves places for clumps of tulips by marking spots with Popsicle sticks. On each stick she writes how many to plant, typically 7, 9 or 11, nice naturally odd numbers. When the time comes, she spaces the bulbs three to four inches apart and *covers* them with four to five inches of soil. When the tulips finish blooming, she quickly digs them out and replaces them with the 'Bloomingdale' strain of ranunculus already in flower.

In containers, Fusano places the bulbs so they almost touch and covers them with four inches of soil, being careful to leave an additional two inches between the top of the soil and the rim of the pot. This little bit of space helps the tulips stand up nice and straight. Obviously, she uses large containers at least 16 inches deep.

In the garden, one of her favorite mixtures uses apricot-pink 'Menton' tulips with peach-colored ranunculus (planted from tubers in the fall), lavender 'Trysomic' stock in front and then 'Imperial Antique Shades' pansies. A recent rediscovery is the old-fashioned 'Giant Imperial Giant' stock, tall enough to go behind the tulips. "You start with little, teeny plants," she says, "and watch in wonder as they grow and branch to about two-and-a-half feet tall. They're so fragrant, and there are always enough to cut and bring in the house." She has similar admiration for the old-fashioned 'Rocket' snapdragons that grow to about the same height. "Plant lots," she says of both.

The trend continues for combining lots of different bedding plants instead of massing just one kind. Lillian Greenup, of Sperling Nursery in Calabasas, has several ideas along this line, good in containers or in the ground.

She's particularly fond of a new pansy called 'Imperial Frosty Rose' that combines white with rose purple. Planted with 'Cherry Blossom Harmony' stock and lavender 'Liberty' snapdragons, it makes a cool combination. If you want to warm it up a bit, speckle the bed with orange calendulas. Greenup also uses the dainty *Linaria maroccana* as a filler between plants. 'Fairy Lights' is a softer version of this linaria. She can't say enough about the new 'Harmony' stock, a sturdy, more floriferous midsize stock, growing to about 14 inches.

Another decidedly cool combination mixes purple ornamental kale with the new purple and white 'Princess' viola, with an edging of 'Easter Bonnet' alyssum. You could also add 'Harmony' stock and 'Coronet' snaps. The latter are about the same height as the stock, at 18 inches tall, and "they weather well in the west San Fernando Valley," Greenup says, taking unseasonable spells of heat and cold.

Though cool colors look best under the often overcast spring sky, you can plant things that are a little warmer. Along this line, Greenup likes orange and yellow 'Liberty' or 'Tahiti' snaps with 'Sunset Orange' or other orange ranunculus planted as tubers. She would also add some brightly colored nemesia and blue violas.

She even has an idea for that shady part of the garden. Use white cyclamen with the apricot obconica primrose, and mix in some perennial 'Silver Dragon' liriope, then edge with baby's tears.

Here are a few more from Greenup. These are not the double row of calendulas up each side of the front path that grandma used to plant!

🌿 A mix of 'Midget' stock and *Linaria reticulata* with the 'Imperial Antique Shades' strain of pansies in front: The 'Midget' series comes in shades of lavender, violet and rose and grows only eight to 10 inches tall so it needs no staking; *Linaria reticulata* is just as short, and the flowers are fuchsia and orange. A lot of people are raving about the new 'Imperial Antique Shades' strain of pansies, described as "autumnal" colors, with maple-leaf orange and reds blending with maroon and violet.

🌿 'Liberty' snapdragons, 'Wonderland' Iceland poppies and

'Carnival' nemesia with blue violas: The new 'Liberty' snaps are of medium height (18 to 22 inches) and are very sturdy. 'Wonderland' is a new shorter Iceland poppy that is equally sturdy, as is the compact 'Carnival' strain of nemesia.

    ✿ Linaria 'Fairy Bouquet' with 'Midget' stock, light yellow pansies and 'Easter Bonnet' alyssum: The 'Easter Bonnet' mix of sweet alyssum has much richer shades of purple, rose and lavender than the standard alyssum, and the linaria is an underutilized annual with masses of dainty pastel flowers.

    Greenup singles out linaria and the new pansies as annuals that are not used enough in gardens. Linarias are easy (even from seed), and planted close to other vertical flowers such as stock or snapdragons, they are great fillers. They bloom for a long time in spring.

    Annual bedding plants are not only for garden beds. They are also one of the best choices for containers. Toni Parsons, in charge of the colorful containers at Roger's Gardens, has some simple schemes for big pots. All use pansies.

    ✿ Iceland poppies and nemesia in the center of the pot, surrounded with 'Imperial Antique Shades' pansies and white sweet alyssum.

    ✿ White 'Midget' stock with 'Monarch' pansies and English daisies. 'Monarch' is another pastel series.

    ✿ Parsley and one of the faceless pansies, such as 'Crystal Bowl', 'Gold Crown' or 'Azure Blue'. If there's room, add annual phlox or dianthus.

Plant from six-packs at this time of the year. Quart, or four-inch, pots are best for last-minute planting in spring.

    All of these annual flowers bloom in spring and must be planted in fall because they grow and flower during the cooler times of the year. This confuses a lot of new gardeners who haven't discovered what one nurseryman calls our "two springs." He says a lot of customers come in during the fall months and ask, "Don't you have any more marigolds?" Everyone knows you can plant marigolds, petunias and other annual flowers in the spring, but they don't always realize that fall is another sort of spring, when you can plant all those things that grow in cooler weather, then bloom in March and April.

Most nursery people suggest planting small plants from packs, even though they carry plants in larger containers. Small plants have time to grow a good root system before blooming, so they make more flowers and last longer.

Prepare the soil before planting by mixing in bags of soil amendment, and do your mixing well. A two-inch layer turned into the soil will do the trick, though you must add more in heavy clay soils. Greenup adds Osmocote, a slow-release fertilizer, to the soil so plants have fertilizer available during the entire season. If you don't, be prepared to fertilize on a regular basis, once a month or even every other week. You will have to water these spring-blooming annuals, but not nearly as much as you might think. Because the sun is low and the weather cool, they do not dry out very quickly, so they are a lot easier to grow, and a lot thriftier with water, than summer annuals. And, if it's one of those lucky years, winter rains will do some of the watering for you.

Success With Iceland Poppies

I finally figured out how to grow Iceland poppies, those brilliantly colored annuals with the crinkled petals that seem to be made of tissue or crepe. Most are shades of orange or yellow, or are white, and their thin petals glow like stained glass when they are lit from behind by the sun. You may find some labeled "pink," and while these might be coral colored, calling them pink is stretching it a bit.

Iceland poppies are not considered difficult to grow, and they are quite common at nurseries, but some, including me, find them difficult to grow *well*. People like me have poppies that lean this way and that, with only a scattering of flowers. Others manage to make it look very easy. Their poppies all stand stiffly upright and the plants are covered with flowers.

You can plant Iceland poppies now or as late as February and still get lots of flowers. The problem that plagued Iceland poppies in the recent past—misshapen buds that did not open properly, or at all—seems to have pretty much gone away.

Some of the prettiest Iceland poppies I've ever seen grow in the tiny but flower-packed Sherman Gardens in Corona del Mar, so I asked director Wade Roberts the secret. His advice: "Fertilize and water consistently. It doesn't matter what you feed them as long as you are consistent." So that's what I tried.

I fertilized every other week with one of those soluble fertilizers that come as sticky granules that you mix with water (Miracle-Gro and Peters are two brands). I totally disregarded the old adage to fertilize with something low in nitrogen. I gave them lots of nitrogen, even when they were in flower. The formula I used had 20 percent nitrogen (it says 20-20-20 on the label; the first 20 stands for the percent of nitrogen). These soluble fertilizers work very well during the cooler times of the year because many fertilizers, including most of the organic types, need a warm soil to work in. Soluble fertilizers tend to have a lot of nitrogen in the nitrate form, which goes right to work regardless of the weather. Since it is soluble, it is also quickly washed from the soil by rain or irrigation, the reason one must fertilize fairly often—to replace what is being lost. Fertilizing every other week with all that nitrogen made for big, healthy plants, and those plants sent up hundreds of flower heads.

Rain tends to flatten Iceland poppies, but if you are quick to cut off the bent and broken flowers, they bounce right back.

I also made sure they never lacked water, and planted them where they got a full day of sun. I watered them from below, by flooding the beds so the flowers would not get wet. This is an important point. The weight of water bends the delicate stems and the droplets damage the petals. Rain tends to flatten Iceland poppies, but if you are quick to cut off the bent and broken flowers, they bounce right back. Individual flowers last only a couple of days.

I followed one other piece of advice from Roberts: Dead-head. I made it an after-work routine, with a flashlight if I had to. Every other evening I snipped off the stems just below the tops of the leaves with a little pair of scissors. If the plants are allowed to keep their developing seed heads, they stop flowering. I suspect that my diligent dead-heading made a big difference.

I should also add that they were growing in the best of soils, laboriously prepared in advance by adding several bags of organic soil amendment. I did not get this last piece of advice from Sherman Gardens because it probably never occurred to them to mention—after years of working it, they already have the best of soils.

I had no pest problems. Opossums ate all the snails in our garden a few years back—those with snails had better bait new plantings—and the squirrel did not discover them. I have heard from others that squirrels eat the buds as if they were crunchy nuts. We keep our lazy squirrel well-supplied with real, wholesome nuts, which may account for her disinterest in the poppies.

Because the seed is incredibly tiny, it's best to buy young plants in small packs at nurseries. Avoid the larger plants sold in four-inch or quart pots. The larger plants will not do as well in the garden—they won't grow as big or produce as many flowers, though they are a good choice to grow in containers or for real quick, if short-lived, color. Buy a bag or two of soil amendment while you're at it.

Space the plants about a foot apart and then: 1) Water often and from below, with drip or soaker hose or by flooding. 2) Fertilize every other week. 3) Diligently dead-head.

It's that simple.

November

NATIVE PLANTS FOR THE AVERAGE GARDEN

ONLY A FEW OF OUR LOVELY NATIVE CALIFORnia plants are suited to the typical backyard, but planting even a handful can bring a little of the hills into your garden. In the wild, most garden-worthy natives grow on sloping ground and are accustomed to fast-draining, porous soils, and those gardeners who live in the hills can grow just about any native. But in the gardens of the rest of us, with their characteristically heavy clay soil, most natives are doomed. They may fool you by growing, even thriving, for a few years, but one day they will suddenly up and die from root rots caused by too much moisture in the soil. Ask anyone who has tried growing the glorious fremontodendron, with its big golden flowers.

Natives are most susceptible to root rots if they get watered in summer, which is one reason they're best planted in fall. If you plant in spring, which is when most are in bloom and looking their best at nurseries, you have to water often in summer to keep them alive. Plant in late fall and they will have plenty of time to get their roots out into the surrounding soil. By summer they will be well established. You'll still have to water them once in a while that first summer, maybe twice a month, but it will be a lot less risky. In future summers, you may not have to water them at all.

Some natives are less finicky about occasional summer water or clay soils. Here are a few recommended for average backyards by Tree of Life Nursery, a large grower in San Juan Capistrano, and the Theodore Payne Foundation, which maintains a natives-only nursery in Sun Valley, in the eastern part of the San Fernando Valley.

Natives for mass plantings or ground covers:

~ Any of the low-growing manzanitas, or *Arctostaphylos*, will stand garden watering, as will some of the bushier kinds ('Howard McMinn' is one of the toughest shrubby manzanitas, growing to about four feet or more around). Be aware that the low kinds spread a lot wider than they grow tall, to at least six feet. The clusters of urn-shaped white flowers in spring are very pretty, and the reddish bark on many is spectacular. Sun or part shade.

~ Few of the beautiful California lilacs will tolerate garden water in summer, but Mike Evans, of Tree of Life, swears these two will. *Ceanothus griseus* 'Louis Edmunds', which grows to six feet tall by 10 feet across with sea-blue flowers, and *Ceanothus* 'Mount Vision', which makes a dense mat about four feet across with light blue flowers. Melanie Baer-Keeley, formerly with the Theodore Payne Foundation, suggests 'Yankee Point'. Sun.

~ Catalina perfume (*Ribes viburnifolium*) starts off slow but makes a tall, dense ground cover about three feet tall by six feet across. Handsome, delightfully fragrant foliage with insignificant flowers. This is one for shade or part shade.

Native perennials for the flower border or mixed with low shrubs:

~ *Aquilegia formosa* is our native red columbine. About two feet tall. Very pretty in partial shade.

~ The native coral bells (*Heuchera maxima*) and several related hybrids are excellent garden plants. They are generally bigger and more robust than the common coral bells, with clumps of foliage a foot or more tall and delicate flower spikes to three feet. Flowers may be pink, some shade of red or cream. Part shade or shade.

~ Bush monkey flowers (*Mimulus*, formerly *Diplacus*) come in many colors, from yellow through purple and red. They get about three feet tall and flower for months. Sun.

~ The matilija poppy (*Romneya coulteri*), with its gray leaves and big fried-egg flowers, may become *too* at home in your garden. One of the most beautiful of all natives, it grows to eight feet tall but may aggressively spread. Cut nearly to the ground in late fall. Full sun.

~ California fuchsias (*Zauschneria*, also sold as *Epilobium*) are

The matilija poppy, with its gray leaves and big fried-egg flowers, may become *too* at home in your garden.

fuchsia-like only in flower form—the flowers are bright orange red and dangle like a fuchsia's. Otherwise, this plant, with grayish leaves, likes heat. It slowly spreads to form arching clumps and flowers at a welcome time in the garden, in fall. Cut it nearly to the ground after flowering, and it will start fresh in spring. Full sun.

Native shrubs:

&. The bush snapdragons (*Galvezia*) make three-foot or larger shrubs with plenty of red flowers that are adored by hummingbirds. Sun or part shade.

&. Mahonias, in general, like garden water because they naturally grow in canyon bottoms or moist parts of the state. *Mahonia* 'Golden Abundance' grows six to eight feet tall and makes a nearly vertical screen or background in the garden. It has glossy, holly-like leaves and an abundance of golden flowers in spring. Sun or part shade.

&. The slow-spreading *Mahonia repens* makes a two-foot-tall thicket of similar appearance, though without the profusion of flowers. Tolerates shade.

&. Coffeeberry (*Rhamnus californica*) is a very handsome shrub, five to 10 feet tall and 10 feet across. 'Eve Case' is a compact form (about half as big), and 'Little Sur' is even smaller, making a three-foot ball. Takes sun but does best with some shade.

&. In the chaparral lemonade berry (*Rhus integrifolia*) is a common dark green shrub; in the garden it makes a good background plant, or even a tight hedge with trimming. It's also valued on slopes for erosion control. Best near the coast, it grows three to 12 feet. Sun.

&. Sugar bush (*Rhus ovata*) is a close relative of the lemonade berry, similar in appearance and slightly smaller, but better suited to hot inland gardens. Sun.

Native trees:

&. Did you know we have a native birch? The red birch or river birch (*Betula fontinalis*, or *Betula occidentalis*) is a small tree native to the eastern Sierra, growing about 10 to 20 feet tall. It is deciduous and has unusually pretty reddish bark. Those who have grown it say the leaf tips get less salt burn than does the common European white birch. It even grows in one very mild San Clemente garden, quite near the coast. Sun or part shade.

&. The western redbud (*Cercis occidentalis*) is a small deciduous tree with pretty pink flowers and a delicate form. It grows about 10 to 12 feet. Sun or part shade.

&. Pacific wax myrtle (*Myrica californica*) is a big handsome bush

Plant natives so the
crown, or base, of the
plant is about one inch
above ground. Don't
dig holes deeper than
the rootball. And on
hillsides cut into the
slope above the plant to
make a watering basin.

or small tree growing easily 10 or more feet around. Sun or part shade.

> Coast live oak (*Quercus agrifolia*) may seem like an unlikely candidate for this list because wild ones must be kept quite dry in summer. But if you plant one and it grows up being watered, it will tolerate quite a bit. Few trees make such a statement in the landscape, and they are home for hundreds of creatures. They easily grow to 40 feet tall. Full sun.

> Redwoods and sycamores are also fine garden trees though too big for most gardens.

Evans and others suggest planting natives in natural, unamended soil. However, where building pads have been carved from a hillside, there is no proper topsoil ("It's all at the bottom of the hill," says Evans), only subsoils (what he calls "the bowels of the hill"). Since plants have never grown in these soils, the soils need improving.

He suggests adding organic amendments such as composted forest products (the kind sold by the bag). Dig the hole only as deep as the rootball of the plant, set the plant in the hole, and then put a mix of one part amendment and two parts soil back in the hole. Be sure to thoroughly mix the two and pulverize the soil. Any extra can be used to make a watering basin.

In established gardens, or on flat land, you can amend the entire bed to be planted, and if it's going to get any garden water this is probably a good idea. Till or spade in a two- to three-inch-thick layer of amendments. Or try pulverizing the soil and planting without amendments. "Whatever has worked in your garden with ordinary garden plants will work with natives," says Evans. "Just use less of everything."

Except mulch. He recommends a two- to three-inch-thick mulch around plants. The same amendment used in the planting hole will work fine. Even better are the shreddings from a tree trimming service, if you can get it. Don't let mulch mound up against the very base of the plant. That can encourage crown diseases.

Another important point: Plant so the top inch of the rootball is above the soil. This guarantees that it will not settle or become covered. Either event could kill the plant because the crown is a very sensitive area and needs to "breathe."

NOTHING'S SWEETER THAN SAGE

Would you like to grow any of the plants that make Southern California's hills so fragrant, such as the various artemisias and salvias? Though they are notoriously difficult to grow in the typical flat backyard with its clay soil, I'm assured by the experts that there are a few that will survive and bring the scent of the chaparral into your backyard. All, of course, will thrive in hillside gardens if not overwatered.

Bart O'Brien, director of horticulture at the Rancho Santa Ana Botanic Garden in Claremont, says that of the relatives of *Salvia clevelandii*, the most fragrant salvia in the chaparral, 'Pozo Blue', 'Allen Chickering' and 'Aromas' smell the sweetest and "persist the best." Expect them to grow four to six feet when the tall spikes of bluish flowers are in bloom, spreading as wide. After they flower, cut them down by one-half to two-thirds so they do not become too woody.

'Mrs. Beard', with a slightly mustier scent and sky-blue flowers, is one that O'Brien thinks does very well in the average backyard, though it may be nearly impossible to find for sale. It grows four feet tall and about five feet wide.

Hummingbird sage (*Salvia spathacea*), with big grayish leaves and lax spikes of deep burgundy flowers, grows in the open shade around live oaks in Topanga State Park and is probably the next most fragrant salvia that will survive in a garden. Carol Bornstein, director of horticulture at Santa Barbara Botanic Garden, says it is "pretty reliable" in the slightly shaded garden, blooming at about two to three feet tall and spreading several feet on rhizomes.

Bornstein and O'Brien say the pungent white sage (*Salvia apiana*) makes a reliable garden plant, though they caution that as many people love the medicinal fragrance as detest it. Fans bind and dry the nearly white leaves and burn them as incense. It will grow three to five

The pungent white sage makes a reliable garden plant, though as many people love the medicinal fragrance as detest it.

feet tall and nearly as wide. Forms of the purple sage (*Salvia leucophylla*), with its equally white foliage, are also candidates for the average garden, especially 'Pt. Sal Spreader', which grows only three to four feet tall but six to eight feet wide. 'Figueroa Mt.' is a slightly smaller version at three feet tall by five feet wide.

Two forms of the native sagebrush (*Artemisia californica*) have a chance in the garden. These are the plants with the silvery, finely cut leaves that smell so good on hikes in the coastal sage community. Run your hands over the redolent foliage and cup them to your face, and see if you don't agree that this is a defining California scent. 'Montara' grows to about two feet tall and four feet across. 'Canyon Gray' can spread to eight or more feet.

With the exception of the hummingbird sage, all of these need full sun, and all should be watered once a week at the very most, though they live longest with only monthly irrigations, at least once they're established. With the coming of cool days and winter storms on the horizon, now is the perfect time to plant any California native.

These will be difficult to find at most nurseries, so try one of the native specialists: Tree of Life Nursery in San Juan Capistrano *(949) 728-0685*; Matilija Nursery in Moorpark *(805) 523-2298*, or the Theodore Payne Foundation in Sun Valley *(818) 768-1802*.

COMPOST HAPPENS

Compost, dug in as a soil amendment or used as a mulch, adds texture and nutrients to the soil, and a good soil is essential for a great garden. There are many other good reasons to make your own compost, and it needn't be much of a chore. Fall is the perfect time to begin, what with the falling leaves and all the necessary tidying up. Everything you rake up, cut back or pull up can go in the compost pile. What comes out is something you just can't buy, especially at that stage when the process has not gone too far, when compost is coarse enough to use as a mulch.

WEEK 46

If you live in an area that doesn't require separate garbage cans for yard waste, composting your own will keep it out of canyon landfills. Even if your garden clippings do go in a separate container, which is then composted by the city, you are throwing away the very stuff that could make your garden glorious.

Though there are dozens of gadgets and additives, and whole books devoted to the subject, composting is no complicated thing. All you need is leaves and clippings from the garden. You can also add kitchen scraps (but no fleshy vegetables, fats or meat, or you'll draw flies), even newspapers, but garden clippings work best, smell best and make piles that are the easiest to manage.

The simplest form of composting is a pile simply left in a corner to rot. It may take a year or more in our dry climate, but eventually everything will break down into usable compost. You can speed up the process by keeping the pile moist—like a sponge that's just been squeezed—in the shade and on soil, not concrete.

> ### TIPS FOR QUICK COMPOST
> ❧ Use half-brown and half-green material.
> ❧ Keep it damp.
> ❧ Turn it frequently.

A tidier way is to put everything in a bin. The best bin is one that you can build yourself. It looks like three horse stalls, three open-ended boxes made of sturdy slats nailed to four-by-four-inch posts. You start the compost in one section and when it's full, turn it into the next and a few weeks later, turn it into the last. If you keep it moist and thoroughly loosen and toss the materials each time you move them into the next compartment, you have compost in a month.

You can do the same thing, and in the same time, with a store-bought bin, sold by some city refuse agencies at bargain prices, and at nurseries. I particularly like one plastic bin with three bottomless sections stacked on top of one another. You fill the bin, keep the contents moist, and after a week or two, take off the top section, set it next to the pile and start transferring material from the pile into this section. As you work you remove the other sections until they've been restacked and the pile turned upside down and mixed.

Simpler still, but much slower, are the kinds of bins where you do no turning (even a wire cage works well). You simply add clippings to the top, and in about six months you can pull out finished compost from an opening at the base.

Turning the compost so it stays loose and aerated, though, dramatically speeds things up. Use a manure fork, spading fork or heavy garden gloves to fluff and turn the pile so the upper layers end up on the bottom.

Chopping up garden debris first helps too. Just stand over the compost pile and cut everything you've pulled or cut from the garden

into pieces about four to six inches long. Believe it or not, I chop up materials on a huge timber block with a machete. Or invest in a compost grinder or shredder, though unless you're willing to spend a lot of money (around $1,000), you'll find that most are hardly worth the expense and effort, at least in the average backyard. If you're clearing brush in Topanga, that might be a different story.

This compost creature is the larva of the iridescent fig beetle, a scarab relative, harmless to you and your garden, though the adults do nibble on fruit.

If you do get an expensive heavy-duty grinder, you can grind up branches and other woody materials and make a great ground-covering mulch for your garden, thick and permanent enough for paths. But it's much cheaper to buy shredded bark for paths and put those large limbs and branches in that trash container provided by the city for garden refuse, after first cutting off all the small branches and leaves and adding those to your compost pile.

Always try for a balance between green and brown materials. The ideal pile is 50 percent dry, brown carbon-rich materials, such as fallen leaves, and 50 percent wet, green nitrogen-rich materials, such as fresh grass clippings. This carbon/nitrogen ratio makes for rapid and hot decomposition. With such a mix, the pile will actually get hot, even steamy, which kills many weed seeds. It is still a good idea not to put weeds that have gone to seed in a compost pile because you may end up spreading that weed all over your garden. If you can't come up with this 50/50 mix, the pile will still decompose, though at a slower and colder rate.

In a cold pile, you'll tend to find all sorts of creatures, from spooky centipedes to very large white grubs that look like they're wearing brown football helmets. None is harmful to you or your garden and all help break down compost. The large grub is the larva of a fig beetle, a big iridescent-green beetle related to the sacred Egyptian scarab. The adult beetle does nibble on figs and other fruit, but the larva is nothing to worry about.

Similar but smaller larvae are sometimes found, growing to become the bumbling June beetles that bang against screen doors in summer. This larva eats roots but does little harm. The small red worms found in compost piles are called manure worms, and though they won't help your garden's soil, they do digest compost.

The only real pests in compost piles are ants, which may make colonies in cold piles. Turn the pile often enough and keep it moist, and they'll move on.

Although grass clippings can be an important part of a compost pile, if you add too much they'll turn into a thick smelly mat that attracts flies. Try to mix lawn clippings into the pile with leaves and other garden debris. Or simply leave them on the lawn. If you mow often enough or use one of the new mulching mowers, the clippings will be small enough to fall beneath the blades of grass. Recent tests have shown that they greatly benefit the lawn (they do not cause "thatch"). The other thing you can do with clippings is spread them loosely around the garden as a mulch. They'll quickly brown and help a little. But they're better mixed into a compost pile or left on the lawn.

Only a few thick-bodied leaves, like avocado and magnolia, don't compost quickly. And tests have shown that even eucalyptus leaves make a good compost. Deciduous leaves like liquidambar are pure garden gold.

You can decide to use your compost as a soil amendment. If so, dig a two- to three-inch layer of finished compost into the soil each time you prepare an area for planting. I find, however, that I use far more compost as a mulch. In my opinion, many people let their compost go too far, so it ends up like fertilizer, which is something you can easily buy. But you can't buy a good mulch for the flower or vegetable garden. A good mulch should look natural, contain some nutrients that will work their way into the soil and should be made up of pieces large enough and heavy enough to stay put. If the mulch happens to be a nice, rich, earthy, dark brown color, all the better. Compost looks just like this before it goes too far—when you can still see some of the leaves and other ingredients but after everything has turned a moist brown. At that point spread it around the flower garden, around roses, even vegetables. Don't worry if it contains the worms and other compost critters too. Pile the compost on an inch or two thick and see what a difference it makes.

THE SIMPLEST COMPOST BIN

A basic, no-nonsense, no-frills compost bin couldn't be easier to build, and you couldn't begin at a better time of the year than right now. Fallen leaves are too valuable a garden resource to set out on the curb. They make the best compost—for improving soil, adding to potting mixes and mulching—and a bin speeds the decomposition. It also keeps things neat and tidy, and—this should be the clincher—putting leaves in a bin is a lot easier than

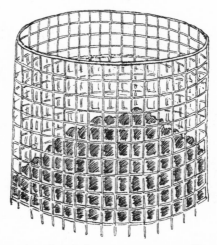

A 12-foot length of a three-foot-wide roll of concrete reinforcing wire with one-by-two-inch openings makes a simple compost bin.

trying to stuff them in plastic bags or even a tall trash can.

A basic bin can be made from welded wire mesh, the kind used to reinforce concrete or stucco, which is available at building supply stores. Ask for the kind with the one-by-two-inch mesh openings, which are small enough to keep leaves in. A three-foot-wide roll makes for the right height. A 12-foot length from the roll will make a circular bin about four feet across.

Since the wire comes off a roll, it will naturally form a cylinder. All you have to do is overlap the ends by about six inches and then fasten them together with wire. Or buy the nifty fasteners called cage clips. A special tool (it and the clips are usually found at large pet or feed stores) clamps the clips around the wire. You'll find other uses for these clever clips, such as making tomato cages, bean trellises and the like.

Find a place for the bin in the shade away from the house and then start filling it. Keep the compost moist. Or simply wait. As the leaves decompose, the pile will settle down in the bin making room for still more. When it is done, in about six months to a year, simply lift up the wire cage and dig in.

THE MOST USEFUL HERBS

H ow about adding some hardworking herbs to the garden this fall? It's a good time to plant and they're easy enough to grow. The only trick is choosing a few truly useful herbs from the daunting number crowding nursery benches. From anise to zingiber (the edible ginger), there are a lot of things called herbs out there. About 650 different kinds grow in Glenn Walker's Long Beach backyard, where, as president of the Long Beach Herb Society, he's building a botanic garden of herbs (of interest to balcony and patio gardeners, all are growing in containers).

An herb, according to Walker, is "any plant used for flavor, fragrance or medicine"—so not all herbs are edible. Shirley Kerins, who heads the Huntington Botanical Garden's large herb collection, is quick to warn that some herbs are quite poisonous if ingested, especially those with medicinal backgrounds, such as foxglove and hellebore. To help sort out the arcane (and maybe dangerous) from the useful, I asked several Southern California herb experts to list their favorites—the ones they use and like most. "These are the herbs I'd want on that desert isle," as Kerins puts it.

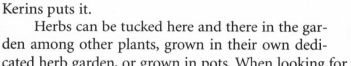

WEEK

47

Herbs can be tucked here and there in the garden among other plants, grown in their own dedicated herb garden, or grown in pots. When looking for a spot, keep in mind that most herbs like a very sunny location and taste best if not watered too often. Traditional Mediterranean herbs, such as rosemary and thyme, should be kept lean and on the dry side so the essential oils are not diluted. Some herbs, such as basil and dill, are annuals that you start anew every year in their season, while others are perennials, shrubs or even trees that become fairly permanent parts of the landscape.

Norma Jean Lathrop, herbalist and author of "Herbs: How to Select, Grow and Enjoy" (H.P. Books, Los Angeles), begins her essential list with rosemary and lemon thyme. "Everyone should grow rosemary, if for no other reason than to amaze visitors from the east," where it is difficult to grow (she gardens in the San Gabriel Valley). Rosemary comes in all sorts of garden forms, from low-spreading ground huggers to stately upright shrubs such as 'Tuscan Blue'. She uses it and the bushy little lemon thyme in all sorts of dishes, but especially with chicken.

Chives are another that Lathrop thinks everyone should be growing, for their fresh leaves, used for flavoring, and pretty lavender-pink flowers, which she uses as a garnish. Chives may take a year or two to become established but, once they are, they flower heavily and are quite stunning. English lavender she uses in potpourri and sachets as well as in cooking. Borage, prized for its pretty blue flowers, is another favorite. An attractive three-foot-tall annual, it self-sows every year (probably more than you'd like, but seedlings are easy to pull out). Her book shows how to candy the edible flowers.

Without even thinking, Cristin Fusano, who teaches the Potager classes at Roger's Gardens in Corona del Mar, names basil as her favorite fresh herb, and especially lemon and cinnamon basil. Both are annuals that can be started from plants or seeds in April and kept going for months "if you keep picking off the flowers." She's "fanatical" about pinching the plants back, right from the start, to keep them bushy and full of leaves. Fusano uses the cinnamon basil in surprising ways, in shortbread-like cookies and in a delicious basil and lavender bread. She says lemon basil is best in pesto and for flavoring chicken, fish and barbecue.

Next on her list are salad burnet and lovage, both of which she says are easy plants to grow all year. She strips the little leaflets off salad burnet and uses them in chicken salad and others salads and sandwiches, for its "mild cucumber and nuts taste." Lovage tastes more like celery, and she uses it in salads, soups and sandwiches, preferring the smaller leaves that come in fall and winter. Asked for just one more, she chooses lemon verbena, with its almost overwhelming lemon fragrance. She uses it in several kinds of teas and puts the tips of young leaves in salads. If not pruned regularly to keep it small and tidy, lemon verbena (*Aloysia triphylla*) makes a scraggly six-foot shrub.

Carole Saville, who wrote "Exotic Herbs" (Henry Holt, New York) and has a large herb garden off Mulholland atop the Santa Monica Mountains, has a few less common herbs on her essential list. Perhaps her favorite is the true sweet marjoram (*Origanum majorana*)—not what is commonly called hardy or Greek marjoram (*Origanum x majoricum*), or so-called pot marjoram. The true sweet marjoram, growing a little over a foot tall with grayish, felty leaves, is "literally sweet," with one of the freshest fragrances in the garden. She uses it in salad dressings and with chicken.

She uses Mexican tarragon (*Tagetes lucida*) just like French tarragon, only in smaller quantities since it has a stronger anise taste. "The Mexican tarragon is in the garden long after the ephemeral French is gone," she adds. This wild marigold relative, growing to four feet tall, has pretty, golden marigold-like flowers in late fall. In flower, it's a very ornamental plant. When it finishes, she cuts it to the ground for a fresh start.

In pasta sauces or with beans and chicken, Saville likes both traditional Greek oregano and Mexican oregano (*Lippia graveolens*), with its hint of lemon flavor. Greek oregano grows about two feet tall, while she must constantly prune the Mexican to keep it at about four feet tall and as wide.

FAVORITE HERBS

NORMA JEAN LATHROP'S BASIC LIST	A SELECT FEW FROM CAROLE SAVILLE	HERBS SHIRLEY KERINS CAN'T LIVE WITHOUT
Borage	Berggarten sage	Basil
Chives	Greek and Mexican	Bay
English lavender	oregano	Chervil
Lemon thyme	Mexican tarragon	Chives
Rosemary	Mint 'The Best'	English lavender
	Sorrel	Garlic chives
CRISTIN FUSANO'S FAVORITES	Sweet marjoram	Lemon thyme
	(*Origanum*	Lemon verbena
Cinnamon and	*majorana*)	Parsley
lemon basil		Rosemary
Lemon verbena		Saffron
Lovage		
Salad burnet		

Berggarten sage, one of the culinary sages (*Salvia officinalis*), is a handsome mounding plant with large, soft leaves. Try sage with pork. Saville says she always grows two kinds of the leafy sorrel—"My children liked sorrel soup better than Campbell's," she says—the tall garden sorrel and the shorter French sorrel (*Rumex scutatus*), with its "clear, tart flavor." Since mints are wont to spread, she keeps a mint sold as 'The Best' in a pot. This "really pungent" variety is perfect in fruit juices and iced tea.

Though she oversees hundreds of herbs at the Huntington's herb garden in San Marino, landscape architect Shirley Kerins has definite favorites for her Pasadena garden. Rosemary, lemon thyme and chives, with their "one million uses," top her list. When you need some chives, she cautions, pick entire leaves: "Don't just snip off the tops, or you'll have a messy-looking plant." She also grows garlic chives for those times when she wants just a slight garlic taste without the hassle of peeling cloves. Garlic chives grow a little taller and have white flowers with slightly wider, grayish leaves. They quickly make a thick clump. Lemon verbena is also on her list because, she confesses, "it's the only herbal tea I really like." Her recipe: Put three leaves in a cup and pour in boiling water.

Kerins likes lavender, but not in cooking. She dries the blooms in June, ties several together and uses them in the linen closet. "Try leaving some in the car," she adds, for a fragrance far better than that of a pine air freshener. Use only the true English lavender (*Lavandula*

"The Mexican tarragon is in the garden long after the ephemeral French is gone," says Carole Saville.

angustifolia) or one of the *Lavandula intermedia* hybrids, such as 'Grosso' or 'Provence', two commercial perfume varieties from France.

She grows basil is summer and annual chervil is winter. Chervil looks like a delicate parsley and has a milder flavor. It grows one to two feet tall and can be planted now. An essential ingredient in *fines herbes*, "you can't dry this one," she says. "It must be used fresh from the garden." Try it in omelets.

She grows her own saffron from bulbs that are available now at nurseries (use the orange-red styles when they flower), and she always keeps parsley handy.

Bay is one herb that grows to tree proportions, if you let it. "But it's the original 'whatever' plant," Kerins says. "You can grow it in the ground or in a container, leave it alone or clip it like a hedge, water it or not, good soil or bad, sun or shade—whatever." She uses it in stews and likes being able to give sprigs as gifts, a good thing to keep in mind at this time of year.

Kerins suggests ordering by mail from Mountain Valley growers [*38325 Pepperweed Road, Squaw Valley, CA 93675 (559) 338-2775; www.mountainvalleygrowers.com.*]

REAL WILDFLOWERS TO SOW NOW

D on't be misled: Growing wildflowers is work, though many would call it the most rewarding kind. "It's hard work if you're thinking of throwing seed on a vacant lot," says Kevin Connelly, who has fought weeds for years so that wildflowers could grow on Wildflower Hill at the Theodore Payne Foundation in the San Fernando Valley. "On the other hand, they're no harder than any other flower you might start from seed, if you're gardening in clean [weed-free] soil and planting during the cool season."

Although many people wait until spring, the time to plant wildflowers is from late fall through early winter, according to Carol Bornstein, who oversees the annually planted wildflower meadow at the Santa Barbara Botanic Garden. Wildflowers germinate with winter's rains, bloom in spring's cool sun, shrivel and set seed in summer, then die.

Be aware that there are many wildflower wannabes, those annual flowers sold as wildflowers but native to places other than California. Red flax, red European field poppies, blue bachelor's buttons, bright yellow coreopsis and similar annual flowers make up the bulk of the wildflower mixes found in many catalogues and sold by the can at some nurseries. They may be pretty garden plants on the same winter-spring cycle, but they're not California wildflowers.

The real wildflowers are dainty little things. What they lack in size, though, they make up for in numbers of flowers when they blanket our hills and high desert in spring. With a lot of work, you can grow a meadow of your own, or, with much less work, tuck them here and there in the garden. Even in my crowded city garden, I find room for wild-flowers, usually sowing some clarkias and  nemophilas among the pansies and tall bearded iris. The small nemophilas foam between the fuller pansies, and the clarkias fill that inevitable empty space between iris rhizomes.

If you have bigger plans and want to try growing a miniature meadow, here are some nearly surefire choices suggested by Bornstein, Connelly and Bart O'Brien, of Rancho Santa Ana Botanic Garden in Claremont, beginning with the first to bloom in late winter and ending with the farewell-to-spring.

Baby blue eyes (*Nemophila menziesii*): Short and truly blue.

Lupinus nanus: Also short and blue, and bountiful at the bottom of the Grapevine.

Meadow foam (*Limnanthes douglasii*): Short and spreading with yellow flowers. A vernal pool plant, it needs a little extra irrigation.

California poppy (*Eschscholzia californica*): Eighteen inches tall and nearly the definition of orange.

Clarkia unguiculata: Two feet tall with spidery orchid flowers. Particularly long lasting and tough.

Phacelia tanacetifolia: Two to three feet tall with lavender-blue flowers.

California bluebell (*Phacelia campanularia*): Superb inland, about a foot tall, with gentian-blue flowers.

Globe gilia (*Gilia capitata*): A foot tall with round blue flower heads.

Tidytips (*Layia platyglossa*): A foot tall with yellow flowers inside a white edging.

Chia (*Salvia columbariae*): Also a foot tall with deep, deep purple flowers.

Arroyo lupine (*Lupinus succulentus*): Two feet tall, purplish blue and commonly seen on road cuts.

Spider lupine (*Lupinus benthamii*): Also two feet tall but more delicate and bluer.

Mountain phlox (*Linanthus grandiflorus*): Eight inches tall, white or pale pink.

Farewell-to-spring (*Clarkia amoena*): A foot-and-a-half tall, soft lilac or pink. So called because it is the last to flower, often blooming in the wild among already-golden grasses.

Many more genuine wildflowers are growable, and most are described in Connelly's "Gardener's Guide to California Wildflowers," published by and available at the Theodore Payne Foundation. For information, call *(818) 768-1802*. The foundation also sells seeds and several ready-made mixes for special situations (including shade); its descriptive seed list is available for $1.50. Another source of true wildflowers, used by the Santa Barbara Botanic Garden, is Larner Seeds [*P.O. Box 407, Bolinas, CA 94924 (415) 868-9407*]. Its catalogue contains valuable growing tips.

In his book, Connelly suggests mixes that work best in certain locales (such as the beach), beginning with the most basic California meadow mix, good anywhere, of yellow, orange and blue—tidytips, poppy and lupine—that will make your garden look like a California plein-air painting. If you want to learn about the wildflower wannabes, "How to Grow the Wildflowers," by Eric Johnson and Scott Millard (Ironwood Press, Tucson), lists and illustrates many true wildflowers that grow from California to Texas, plus the pretenders.

So seed is not buried too deep, roughen soil with a garden rake, scatter seed, and then simply tamp down the soil.

To grow any plant called a wildflower, you must be prepared to battle weeds, which can overwhelm most kinds, and birds, which relish the seeds and seedlings. The easiest place is in a relatively weed-free garden bed. Elsewhere, wait until weeds sprout after the first rains, gently hoe them out, disturbing the soil as little as possible so as not to expose more weed seeds, and then sow the wildflowers.

O'Brien suggests not preparing the soil too much. Barely cover the seed and protect from birds and snails. At Rancho Santa Ana Botanic Garden the seeded areas are surrounded with low chicken wire and kept covered with bird netting until seedlings are well established. Or do what Bornstein suggests: "Sow more than you think you'll need" and consider the extra seed expensive bird feed.

If we have a rainy fall and winter, that may be all the water the plants require to germinate and grow; otherwise, keep seeds moist until they sprout, then water whenever the soil dries.

MAKING HOUSE AND GARDEN FIRE-SAFE

Fire is natural and inevitable in the highly flammable brush communities that Southern Californians seem to insist on living near. Every fall, when dry Santa Ana winds begin to blow, those living at the edge of the chaparral face losing their houses and gardens to fire. Though making the house fire-safe is most important, the way you landscape can help protect your property.

In a brush fire, the majority of houses catch fire from firebrands or flying embers, which can easily travel as much as half a mile from the actual fire. When they land, there should be nothing for them to ignite and no place to lodge. To that end, a fire-resistant house is clean and tight, "buttoned up," as one fire researcher puts it. No detail is unimportant—natural fiber doormats have spread fire to houses. Homeowners with houses that actually abut wildlands, or are surrounded by them, at what is called the wildland/urban interface, must be prepared for a frontal assault, and landscaping becomes important as a buffer.

It's hard to believe that any shingle or shake roofs still exist in fire areas, but they do. Roofs must be noncombustible with no gaps or places for embers to lodge. Curved Spanish tiles must have open ends plugged. In one brush fire, a house burned because the garage door wouldn't close all the way. Roll-down metal doors close tightly.

After the Oakland fire a few years ago, all vents under overhangs or eaves were banned in that city. Vents should be on rooftops (such as ridge vents) or in gables. Roof and foundation vents should be screened with a quarter-inch galvanized mesh. Even better, they should be closable, with panels or shutters, or automatic fire dampers. It's best to have no eaves, and no wood fasciae. Boxed eaves are next best, the underside covered with fire-resistant material. Fires race up hillsides, so houses on flat pads should be as far back from the slope as possible, with nothing overhanging the hill. Avoid single, high-walled construction; step tall buildings back from the slope. In areas that abut wildlands, use noncombustible stucco or stucco over cement building panels. Research is proving that double-glazed windows are much less likely to burst if confronted with fire, and little radiant heat can pass through. Behind conventional windows, consider drapes of fireproof fabrics.

In the landscape, avoid wood decks, even at ground level or with

In one brush fire, a house burned because the garage door wouldn't close all the way.

59

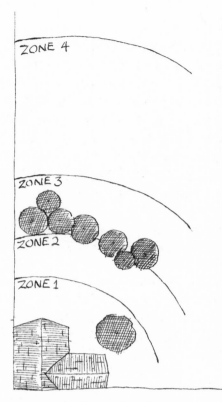

Zone 4:
Selectively saved
native vegetation
kept cleaned up.
Zone 3:
Knee-high native or non-
native plants or native
plantings that have been
pruned
and tidied up.
Zone 2:
A living firebreak of fire-
retardant plantings, such
as iceplant or myoporum.
Zone 1:
Irrigated garden of low-
growing plants with no
tall plants within 10 feet
of house.

their bases completely enclosed. Decks of concrete or other fireproof materials are okay. Be sure the support beams and columns are also protected. The jury is out on patio overheads; if they are open (so firebrands can pass through), made of heavy timbers and do not touch the house, they may catch fire, but it is much less likely. Wood fences act like fuses, leading fire to the house. Masonry walls, on the other hand, even low ones, can actually deflect heat and flames (and keep rattlesnakes out).

If you have a pool, provide access for the fire department (so they can pump from it), and consider getting your own gas- or diesel-powered pump, plus hose, for ember dousing. Leave access and turn-around space for firemen and fire trucks—as approved by the fire department—to get to the back and sides of the house. In remote areas this is extremely critical.

A fire-resistant landscape is more problematic than a fire-safe house, because of the number of clashing agendas—plants are asked to resist catching fire, hold the soil together with their roots, not use too much water, provide shade and energy-saving cooling and not threaten the natural environment with their exoticness. No plant is really fireproof—even iceplant can spread fire when there is an accumulation of dead leaves and stems underneath—but many plants are fire resistant if they are kept cleaned up.

The most important rule in landscaping, many experts say, is that no tree or tall shrub should grow within 10 feet of the house (fire departments prefer 30 feet). This alone can reduce the heat at the house walls by a factor of four. An expert warns: "Some trees next to the house or overhanging vegetation can be more flammable than the native vegetation." Also, avoid pyrophytes, plants that are almost explosive, especially when dry. Junipers, one of the worst, are disastrous when planted under eaves. Do not plant any conifers, including pines and cedars, dense eucalyptus, peppers, bamboo, pampas grass or tall palms near a home.

Try to create a "defensible space" for 100 to 200 feet around the house. Wind-driven flames can easily extend 100 feet on a slope and reach temperatures of 2000°.

One of the more interesting new ideas is that plantings of native live oaks make a good greenbelt around properties or subdivisions (the new Getty Museum, off the San Diego Freeway, is surrounded by newly planted oaks). Slow to catch fire, yet drought resistant, they have hill-holding root systems and provide habitat for a wide variety of wildlife. They may be the near-perfect buffer for the chaparral/urban interface.

Zoning is one way of designing, or redoing, a landscape in fire-prone areas: Divide the property into zones of increasing safety as plants approach the house, decreasing the height and volume the closer they are. Santa Barbara designer Owen Dell, who is on the Firewise Landscape Task Force, says, "It's not the plants themselves so much as the arrangement of plants," the idea being to eliminate "fire ladders" to the house. Always use a mix of low- and medium-height plants.

Call the area within 30 feet of the house zone 1. It should be an irrigated garden of mostly low-growing plants and lawn with, again, no plants under eaves and no tall plants closer than 10 feet from the house. If this area is irrigated regularly and there are fire-resistant plantings farther from the house, you can grow just about anything here, even a few small trees. If zone 1 is going to be drought resistant, though, stick with ground covers and low-growing plants and keep them tidied up.

Zone 2 (30 to 60 feet from the house) should be a greenbelt, or living firebreak, of the most fire-resistant or fire-retardant plantings, such as the rosea iceplants (*Drosanthemum floribundum* and *Drosanthemum hispidum*), cape weed, snow-in-summer, ivy geranium, yarrow, dwarf rosemary, *Myoporum parvifolium,* the native *Ceanothus griseus horizontalis* or *C. prostratus occidentalis.* Several handsome fire-resistant trees are live oak, western redbud, strawberry tree, toyon, mountain mahogany and carob.

Between zones 2 and 3 is a good place to try and block fire with deep plantings of particularly fire-resistant plants, such as citrus, oleanders or native live oaks (but not scrub oak). Some experts believe these three have actually stopped fires in their tracks.

There's some debate about what you should grow in zone 3 (60 to 100 feet from the house)—topography and the relative fire-safeness of the house influence the choices. Some recommend only "knee-high" native and non-native plants that contain little fuel, such as low ceanothus, native monkey flower, bush morning glory, fuchsia-flowering gooseberry, dwarf strawberry tree, white rockrose, photinia, dwarf California coffeeberry, mixed with any of the low-growing ground covers. Try for drought tolerance because you really don't want to water all this with the price of water what it is. Others feel that zone 3 should be like 4, and as much native vegetation should be preserved as possible.

> Quite a few experts now think that managing the existing chaparral is a better idea than trying to replace it with exotic, non-native plants.

In zone 4 (100 to 200 feet from the house, up to 400 feet on steep north or east slopes), you should selectively save native vegetation, removing the most combustible. In a remarkable turnaround from just a few years ago, quite a few experts—researchers and fire department personnel alike—now think that managing the existing chaparral or other plant communities is a better idea than trying to replace them with exotic, non-native plants. "Nothing's better adapted to this climate and these soils," one says.

Try to preserve a continuous canopy of foliage (to prevent erosion), but remove all dead material from inside the plants (what one fire official called "fine, dead, aerial fuel"), and remove branches from the bottom third of the plants. Get rid of all "soft" chaparral, especially chamise, buckwheat and sage, or cut it back severely and keep it as low, mounding, knee-high shrubs.

On steep hillsides, it's best to consult with an engineer or landscape architect, or serious erosion can occur. Since properties are seldom large enough, this might have to be a community effort. Any weeds or plants that grow back between plantings should be cut to three inches tall when they turn brown. Once a year (June is a good month), cut back annual grasses and prune and clean up dead wood that accumulates in and under plantings. You cannot walk away and forget fire-resistant landscapes, or they will soon grow to become woody and dangerous again.

WINTER

THOUGH FOR A GARDENER THE DAYS ARE impossibly short, I like whatever winter we get in Southern California. Indeed, I look forward to the season and savor every minute. Not all do. Many moved here to leave winter behind, and television weather personalities always seem to moan about the cold or the wet. But gardeners should love winter, for every drop of rain, for every degree of cold and for the peace and quiet that descends like a blanket of snow on even the Southern California garden. The crisp, clear mornings are precious times when the sounds of distant freeways are muted by the cold and the garden is so still it seems asleep. But in California it's only dozing—and not for long. While the cold slows growth and stops flowering, winter rains keep plants growing and incredibly green, and spring comes quickly, often by the middle of February.

I have heard that small amounts of nitrogen are present in every raindrop and that this accounts for gardens being so green during the rainy season. More likely, it is the way rain falls, and the purity of the water. Unlike irrigations, rain thoroughly soaks the ground, making it the one time of year when you are assured that everything has been watered properly.

Those who wisely sowed their Bermuda lawns with annual ryegrass in fall are now enjoying what must be the greenest carpet possible. But the green of other plants is nearly as luminous now, especially that of fall-planted perennials and annuals, which are slowly growing through winter in preparation for spring. They look doubly green because the soil is moist and dark in winter, which provides a better background for the plants. The soil is not bleached, cracked and hardened by the summer sun, though the occasional spell of Santa Ana winds may also have this effect in winter.

I even like weeding in winter. The weeds are not the persistent perennial types one battles all summer, but annuals for the most part, with shallow roots that are easy to pull out of the soft, moist soil. Weeding allows you to sit quietly and look at the garden without seeming too odd for doing so, discovering things like mushrooms popping up from under the litter of leaves, a plant you had forgotten or walnuts carefully hidden by the squirrels.

Weeding allows you to sit quietly and look at the garden without seeming too odd for doing so.

I also like winter simply because it is a change. When I step out the back door on a frosty morning, the garden looks and feels different. The low light is dramatic, and the warmth of the sun is more welcome on my back. On those sunny days between storms I'm more likely to say, "What a wonderful day" than I am in summer after months of sunny weather.

The gardener's craft is more apparent in winter after a good cutting back and tidying up, when more of the soil and the structure of plants show. Though the roses are mere sticks, they are neatly pruned and waiting. The perennials are trim clumps of new leaves, bulbs are pushing up—often in unexpected, forgotten spots—and the annuals just planted are still tidy tufts of leaves. The fallen leaves of autumn are in the compost pile, and the ground is weeded, raked, mulched and orderly.

When the soil dries a little following a rain, it is perfect for digging, and the weather is not too hot for this strenuous work. Do not go to work too quickly though, because working in a wet soil can physically harm it. Loosen a fistful and squeeze it first. If it crumbles when you loosen your grip it is just right, but if it stays in a tight ball it is still too wet.

You can consider December to be part of fall and plant just about anything, though most plants would have been happier planted earlier when the weather was warmer. Plant any flowers found at nurseries and they will bloom in spring, as well as any of the cool-season vegetables (see the chart in Autumn). Then, beginning right after the holidays, there is the opportunity to plant things sold bare root— roses and fruit trees, grapes and berries, strawberries and some vegetables—and this is the best time to plant any of these. It is also the best time to plant the camellias that begin blooming in winter. Camellias, and azaleas, are best planted while in bloom, which is helpful because you can see what colors you are adding to your garden. You can keep quite busy planting between whatever rains we get.

Too much of winter would not be a good thing either, but it will soon be over. The sun will climb higher and these short days will lengthen. And then it will be spring, which is another nice season.

December

FERTILIZING IN FALL AND WINTER

T HE DOOR DOESN'T EXACTLY SLAM SHUT ON fall planting, but it does begin closing about now. The weather cools rapidly from now on, days grow ever shorter, shadows longer, and plant growth comes to a near halt until sometime in late February. You can continue the fall planting of bulbs and annuals, vegetables, trees, shrubs and native plants right on into mid-December, but then it's really time to start doing other things in the garden, such as fertilizing the bedding plants and annual flowers you just put in the ground.

The rule is to begin fertilizing about two weeks after planting. Perennials, most bulbs, shrubs and trees can probably wait until early spring since they are mostly growing roots right now, but for the rapidly growing annual flowers, fertilizing now will make quite a difference in spring.

Fertilizing in fall and winter is best done with fast-acting soluble fertilizers because they can more easily be used by plants. I'm told that in cool weather many of the soil organisms that help convert a regular fertilizer into something that can be taken in by the roots are inactive. Fast-acting fertilizers are formulated to bypass the soil organisms.

The kind of fertilizer I am talking usually contains 3 to 6 percent of a form of nitrogen called nitrate, or nitric, nitrogen. It is available as a ready-mixed liquid but is more often sold as little crystals that you then dissolve in water. Peters Professional (20-20-20) and Miracle-Gro (15-30-15) are examples. All fertilizer labels spell out their contents with three numbers: In 15-30-15, for example, 15 is the percentage of actual nitrogen, 30 is the percentage of phosphorus and 15 the percentage of potassium. Nitrogen is by far the most important part since it is directly responsible for growth and is most lacking in California soils. It is also easily washed out of the soil, especially the soluble, fast-acting nitrate form, so it must be reapplied, or more must be converted from the other forms of nitrogen by the soil bacteria. Look at the back of the fertilizer label and you'll find the percentage of nitrogen subdivided further into the various forms—the fast-acting nitrate, the slower ammoniacal and organic or other forms that only slowly become available to plants.

When I was a child, my grandfather had me water the pansies and primroses with a watering wand.

Fast-acting soluble fertilizer is the only kind used all year at Sherman Gardens in Corona del Mar to produce what many consider the prettiest public flower plantings in the southern half of the state. The secret, according to director Wade Roberts, is "consistent watering and fertilizing." And the techniques used by this small public garden to water and fertilize work well in home gardens. The keyword is *consistent*—they never let a few weeks slip by.

And the plants are watered only at their roots using a long, hand-held watering wand. These wands have baffles at the ends that break the force of the water—some are shaped like big shower heads; one has a series of flat plates. Watering by hand this way, the ground gets thoroughly soaked, but the foliage and flowers do not get wet (wet foliage contributes to disease and may topple some plants such as annual stock and Iceland poppies).

This is not a new way to water bedding plants. When I was a child, my grandfather, an accomplished gardener, had me water the pansies and primroses in winter and the marigolds and zinnias in summer with a watering wand. It was, and is, slow work, because you must let the water run at the base of each little plant for several minutes, but it is also sure. At the time I was too young and impatient to realize how restful this activity was, but I now find it one of the more peaceful jobs in the garden.

At Sherman Gardens, they begin fertilizing two weeks after planting and, like clockwork, they continue every other week until the flowers are taken out. They use a 10-10-5 fast-acting liquid fertilizer, applied with a watering wand and a device called a hose-end siphon. Hose-end siphons are little brass valves that go between the hose and the spigot or faucet. A small rubber tube runs from a bucket filled with water and fertilizer up to this siphoning valve. Hozon is one brand, and Hyponex makes another. "Anyone who fertilizes any other way is working too hard," says Roberts.

The fertilizer in the bucket must be more concentrated than usual, since the siphoning device dilutes it further—the instructions on the hose-end siphon will tell you how strong. For instance, the directions that come with the Hyponex recommend "16 times"—so if the fertilizer label says to add a tablespoon of fertilizer to a gallon of water, you now add 16 tablespoons to every gallon in the bucket.

If you prefer watering with sprinklers, or have sprinklers installed for your flower beds, you can water each plant with a watering can filled with water and fast-acting fertilizer. After fertilizing, run the sprinklers for a few minutes to move it down to the plants' roots. Still another option is to use a hose-end sprayer and spray the whole bed with fertilizer, then run the sprinklers for a minute or two.

Those who garden in containers may want to fertilize all the time with these fast-acting soluble fertilizers. But remember, because they are soluble, they get washed out of the pots quickly, which is why many who are expert at growing things in pots fertilize regularly, at least once a month and probably every other week.

THE TRUTH ABOUT BIRDHOUSES

I f you've been wondering when birds are going to move into those cute birdhouses you put out in the garden, the truth is, according to one wildlife biologist, "most birds wouldn't be caught dead in a birdhouse." In most cases, birdhouses work best only as garden ornaments. Whether they sit on a post, hang on a wall or fence, from the eaves or up in a tree, there are literally hundreds of styles being made these days, most with a distinct old-time look. Some even look quite cozy. But looks can be deceiving when it comes to attracting birds. "No matter how cute or elegant," says Audubon Society environmental education specialist Dan Kahane, "you're going to attract only a few species in the Los Angeles area."

If you live near a wild area, you might lure a handful of native bird species. But in town, you will most probably attract what Kahane calls "junk birds," those non-native species that nest in traffic lights or street signs—"the same ones that hang out at McDonald's," he says.

The two most likely tenants are the greedy House, or English, Sparrow (males are small and brown, with black chests and white stripes on their wings) and the garrulous Starling, or Blackbird (glossy black in summer; brown and mottled in winter). Both originated in Europe, and both will eat insects and seed, including that annual ryegrass you just sowed.

Both are also cavity nesters. This is an important point, according to natural resource specialist Tom Scott at UC Riverside. Only cavity nesters—birds that normally build nests in hollow trees or in buildings—will even bother being birdhouse looky-loos. Most birds aren't cavity nesters, but instead build nests in trees or shrubs or on the ground. And many birds you see in the garden are just passing through, with no intention of staying.

The best birdhouses seek to imitate the most common natural cavity—vacated woodpecker homes.

The best birdhouses seek to imitate the most common natural cavity—vacated woodpecker homes—so they have narrow entry holes and smallish interiors. Small holes keep out some common predators, including other birds. Starlings, in particular, are aggressive birds that will kill the occupants of a birdhouse to gain its use (a one-and-a-half-inch hole will exclude them). The tight quarters help conserve heat. Scott points out that baby birds must stay very warm—he's measured nest temperatures of 101° to 103°. However, the best place for a birdhouse is probably in the shade, at least for most of the day, so the box doesn't get too hot. Face the openings south or east, out of approaching weather systems.

It's very important that birdhouses stay dry inside. They also must be cleaned out once a year—if not, birds will stop using them. So look for functional designs that can be taken apart to be cleaned. Good ones have the bottom or one side attached with screws.

Kahane says that birdhouses should be built of old, seasoned wood if they are to attract birds, which don't like the smell of sawdust and new wood. One birdhouse seen for sale at a nursery is "made from 100 percent recycled material found in the Central Coast and southern areas of California." So while it is new, it's made from old materials.

The accompanying chart lists the cavity nesters in Southern California, and the size hole and interior dimensions they are believed to prefer. Use it to help choose a functional birdhouse, or to build your own. The ornamentation doesn't matter. Most birds won't nest where you can see them, near eye level, but prefer to be very high off the ground, up to 80 feet in the case of the tiny Mountain Chickadee. You

BIRDHOUSE SPEC SHEET

These are some important dimensions for birdhouses designed for native cavity nesters (those that naturally live in holes and hollows). Wildlife biologist Tom Scott and the Audubon Society's Dan Kahane gathered the information from various records of nests found in the wild and from inhabited birdhouses.

Type of Bird	Locality	Height of Nest Above Ground	Size of Entrance Hole	Cavity Area (use for interior diameter of birdhouse)
Screech Owl	Found in many wild areas	10'-30'	2"-4"	7"-18"
Northern Flicker	Any woodland	2'-60'	2"-4"	7"-20"
Ash-throated Flycatcher	Oak and riparian woodland	10'-50'	Variable; try 1 7/8"	Variable, but nest is about 2" wide by 2" deep; try 5" by 5"
Western Bluebird	Oak and riparian woodland	5'-10'	1 3/8"- 1 7/8"	5" by 5"
Mountain Chickadee	Conifer woodland	2'-80' (15' is typical)	1 1/4"- 1 1/2"	Variable; birds often use small woodpecker cavities
Plain Titmouse	Oak and riparian woodland	3'-32'	1 1/4"-4"	Variable, but nest size is typically 2"-3" wide
White-breasted Nuthatch	Mountain or riparian woodland	15'-50'	Variable	Variable 6"-8"
House Wren	Chaparral, oak and riparian woodland	0'-10'	Variable	Variable, but nest is typically 2" wide by 2" deep
Bewick's Wren	Chaparral, oak and riparian woodland	0'-10'	Variable	Variable, but nest is typically 2" wide by 2" deep

would need a very tall pole indeed!

Unfortunately, few of the birds listed are found inside the city. You are most likely to attract them if they are already living nearby, in canyon bottoms, mountain forests, oak woodlands or chaparral. Bird-watcher Doug Martin has had spectacular luck at Omelveny Park in Granada Hills, but the park is surrounded on three sides by wildland. He's had Western Bluebirds, House Wrens, Ash-throated Flycatchers and one Plain Titmouse family nesting in 25 birdhouses, placed about eight feet off the ground. Holes are one-and-nine-sixteenths inch across, six inches above the floor. Interiors measure five by five inches and are a foot tall, with sloping roofs and drainage holes in the bottom. One side comes off for cleaning.

There's no harm trying to lure birds into the backyard. Birds know no rules and may nest in surprising places. The cute little long-billed Bewick's Wren has even been found nesting in the drainage hole of a one-gallon nursery can. But don't set your hopes too high. Most birdhouses are really better as ornament than abode. That's why biologists are so adamant about saving natural habitats. Man-made just won't do for wild birds, the ones that most help a gardener with pest control.

COMPANIONS FOR YOUR ROSES

L ike dogs and cats, roses and other plants don't always get along. That's why so many people plant roses, period, in a garden bed. But there are the exceptions—cats that don't hiss at dogs and dogs that don't chase cats—and adventuresome gardeners have discovered that there are plants that go and grow with roses, that will lie down peaceably in the same bed.

Rose aficionados are usually reluctant to plant anything under or too near a rosebush because of the plants' competition for food and water and the gardener's occasional need to clean up underneath.

Several diseases work their way from the ground up, rust in particular, so rosarians recommend raking up all fallen leaves and other debris on a regular schedule. They don't even like to use chunky mulches, such as bark or volcanic rock, because these can't be cleaned to their satisfaction.

Sandy Kennedy, of Kennedy Landscape Design Associates in Los Angeles, who has planted many

WEEK 50

rose gardens, finds annuals the most congenial companions for roses. She uses alyssum, lobelia and pansies, "scalloping" these plantings around and in front of the roses (though not directly under), where the annuals help hide the bushes' often bare bases.

In his El Cajon garden, Richard Streeper, consulting rosarian and a director of the American Rose Society, plants alyssum and forget-me-nots with his roses, and they "won't hold the roses back a lick," he says. He plants them from seed packets, and when they poop out he pulls them out and they come back in about three weeks from the seed left behind.

He gets about four crops of these annuals into each year (the blue of the forget-me-nots is especially nice with the roses). And because they are routinely pulled out of the rose beds, he can do a complete cleanup several times a year.

Other annuals would probably work as well, but Streeper cautions against growing two popular annuals—calendulas and marigolds—anywhere near roses because they are hosts for thrips and spider mites, two difficult-to-control rose pests.

Behind his roses he plants his favorite annuals—delphiniums, the tall 'Giant Pacific' types, which are actually perennials, though most people replant them each fall or winter because they do not do as well after the first year. He plants them behind the roses because they are so tall (four to six feet) and because he likes the way the blue and purple flowers complement the colors of the roses, which include just about every color but blue (despite what some rose catalogues claim).

Gardeners who are willing to give up a few blooms on their rosebushes, or sacrifice a little size, can plant a great many flowers among them.

Gardeners who are willing to give up a few blooms on their rosebushes, or sacrifice a little size, can plant a great many flowers among them, perennials in particular, if the experts we consulted are correct. "The trick," says Tom Carruth, horticulturist and hybridizer at Weeks Roses in Upland, "is to find plants that can put up with the water, fertilizer and sun that roses need in great quantities."

In the First Lady's Garden at the Richard Nixon Library and Birthplace in Yorba Linda, Lew Whitney, of Roger's Gardens in Corona del Mar, planted many flowers that live in harmony with roses. This is an especially colorful rose garden, planted entirely to the shorter but more floriferous floribunda roses, including 'Angel Face', 'Showbiz', 'Sun Flare', 'Celebrity', 'French Lace' and 'Amber Queen'. In back, between and in front of these bushy roses grow a few annuals and a lot of perennials. In spring it is a blaze of color, worth a visit, and the perennials and roses continue to bloom off and on through summer and into fall. Blue, lavender and purple flowers seem to be

A simple,
satisfying setting
for roses, with
Geranium
'Biokovo' and
lamb's ears
hiding the base
of the rosebush.

the favorite colors to plant with roses because they go with pink and red, or yellow and orange, the most common rose colors.

Prominent perennial players include campanulas, coral bells, *Dianthus deltoides*, lamb's ears, lavenders, *Linaria purpurea*, penstemon, *Salvia chamaedryoides*, *Scabiosa columbaria* and two true geraniums, *Geranium incanum* and *Geranium sanguineum*. Lamb's ears, with its downy gray leaves, was a favorite with nearly all the experts I talked to. Whitney went so far as to call it "the number-one rose companion" because it is the right size (less than a foot) and the perfect color. All of these perennials seem to thoroughly enjoy the water and fertilizer given the roses. And their colors are complementary: "They turn a rose garden into a flower garden," says Whitney.

Other gardeners' lists of rose companions include those on Whitney's list but contain a few one might not expect. Barry Campion, a Venice landscape designer and accomplished plantswoman, has found that both the silver and the green santolinas grow well with roses, though they must be cut back regularly to keep them neat. She also likes the blue-flowered, ground-covering morning glory (*Convolvulus mauritanicus*), *Verbena bipinnatifida* and the striking *Euphorbia rigida*. What's a bit surprising is that these plants are considered drought tolerant, which makes them curious companions for the somewhat thirsty roses. Campion's other favorites include a small lavender named 'Atlas', nierembergias and catmint. In England, catmint (*Nepeta faassenii*) is a stylish rose companion with its show of blue flower spikes and gray-green foliage. Here, it gets mixed reviews from gardeners and needs frequent cutting back to remain neat.

Sandy Kennedy also uses santolina and the ground morning glory in rose beds. Some of her other favorites include big-leafed bergenia, candytuft and *Saxifraga stolonifera*, often called strawberry

TOP 40 PERENNIALS TO PLANT WITH ROSES

Alstroemeria	*Geranium* 'Claridge	Penstemon
Aster	Druce'	*Platycodon*
Bearded iris	G. *incanum*	*grandiflorus*
Bergenia	G. *sanguineum*	Rehmannia
Brachycome multifida	Heliotrope	Trailing rosemary
Campanula	Isotoma (*Laurentia*)	*Salvia*
Candytuft	Lamb's ears	*chamaedryoides*
Catmint	Lavender 'Atlas'	S. *farinacea*
Columbine	*Linaria purpurea*	Santolina
Coral bells	*Lychnis coronaria*	*Saxifraga stolonifera*
Daylily	(white)	*Scabiosa columbaria*
Dianthus deltoides	New Zealand flax	*Thymus vulgaris*
Dusty miller	(dwarf kinds)	'Argenteus'
Euphorbia rigida	Nierembergia	*Verbena bipinnatifida*
	Pelargonium fragrans	V. *bonariensis*

geranium. Underneath roses she plants isotoma and Australian violets (*Viola hederacea*), they are so low growing.

In his own Altadena garden, which, naturally, is full of roses, Tom Carruth has tried many potential companions. "It's a Darwinian garden," he says, "where only the fit survive." His favorite survivors are repeat-blooming iris and daylilies, which bloom more than once in the gardener's year. And he has successfully tried several bulbs, including daffodils, Dutch iris and a strain of oxalis named 'Grand Duchess'. There are white, pink and lavender kinds of this oxalis grown from bulbs, and they grow and flower in the dead of winter when the roses are dormant, or nearly so. They do spread quickly but grow only inches tall. Most gardeners find them easy to pull out of unwanted places.

Successful perennials in Carruth's rose garden include several herbs (including trailing rosemary and sage), dwarf New Zealand flax, *Verbena bonariensis* (which stands up tall between the roses) and rehmannia. All of these can take the sometimes frequent watering (in summer, he irrigates about every three days), even though a few, like the rosemary and verbena, are considered drought tolerant.

Los Angeles garden designer Christine Rosmini likes the gray foliage of the white-flowered form of *Lychnis coronaria*, silver thyme and lamb's ears. She also likes the small-leafed pelargoniums, such as the nutmeg-scented "geranium" (*Pelargonium fragrans*) and the low, spreading true geraniums, such as 'Claridge Druce'—many feel that the true geraniums are the perfect rose companions. All of her choices are low, spreading or slightly mounding, and quite refined.

Sharon Van Enoo, who gardens in Torrance, can add a few more rose companions to the list, including heliotrope, blue bedding salvia (*Salvia farinacea*), dusty miller (*Senecio cineraria*), asters, balloon flower (*Platycodon grandiflorus*), veronicas, columbine, alstroemeria and brachycome.

Add up all these expert gardeners' suggestions, and you get more than 40 spiffy plants, grown either for their flowers or foliage, that can be planted along with roses. With the rose-planting season ready to begin (typically just after Christmas), this might be a good time to find a few things to plant with them. For those who want to liven up an existing bed of roses, the one opportunity to get between the prickly roses is also near, when the roses get their annual pruning in January or early February.

CUTTING BACK AND TIDYING UP

With winter arriving, it's time to tidy up the garden—clean out that patch of lamb's ears and cut back that coreopsis or Mexican sage. In a garden filled with perennials such as these, including all the drought-resistant kinds, there's lots of cutting back to do. Cutting back is gardening jargon for the pruning of perennial plants. Many perennials more or less die back each winter, sprouting anew in the spring. True "herbaceous" perennials die completely to the ground. Others simply look pathetic until spring weather perks them up.

WEEK 51

In our mild climate, many herbaceous perennials may not die back completely. They look only half-dead, the leaves worn out and ragged, the old flower spikes brown and stiff. If you did not cut them back, they would simply make new leaves and flowers above the old come spring, or maybe sprout anew from the base, but pruning them back tidies the garden and gives the plants a fresh start.

You need to be a little careful: Some plants sold as perennials do not like being cut back. Coral bells, those handsome perennials with the roundish leaves and the delicate stalks of tiny flowers, are an example. You can cut off the old flower spikes and old brown leaves, but never cut the main stems. On the other hand, Japanese anemones—perennials with leaves like a maple's and tall stalks of airy flowers that thrive in partial shade—look pretty ratty by this time. A lot of people wait until the new spring growth covers the old, but I hack them right to the ground after they finish flowering. Within weeks, the plants look brand-new. This ritual keeps them neat and not as tall as they might get (over six feet).

My choice of weapons for cutting back is a Corona No. 5 pair of shears (now sold as their GS 6750). They are made for edging the lawn but are sturdy enough to slice through a whole handful of stems. They don't even have to be terribly sharp. I grab a bunch of stems or flower spikes and cut as close to the ground as I can, though with some perennials you must leave several inches of stubble.

And I don't rake up the mess. Instead, as I cut off each handful of stems, I continue cutting them into pieces about three to four inches long. These I scatter around the plants as a mulch, which helps me cut down on weeding and watering. The more-or-less green foliage and brown stems look a little messy for a few days, but then they turn all brown and look like the natural leaf litter found on a forest floor. To my eyes at least, this natural mulch looks a whole lot better than parched earth, or plastic sheeting, or chunks of bark. If nothing else, make sure you have a compost pile standing by when you're cutting back.

You can do this cutting back at any time in winter, but I've found right about now is the perfect time for most perennials. In general, don't cut back anything unless it definitely looks as if it needs it.

Here are a few that need some kind of cutting back. (You can also tidy up agapanthus, bearded iris, daylilies and kniphofia by removing brown leaves and faded flower spikes. But don't cut them back.)

Alstroemeria: Pull off flowering stems with a yank as soon as the last flower on each falls off. Otherwise, they're likely to set seed, which readily sprouts. As nonflowering winter stems yellow, pull them off as well. If you have kept on top of this, clumps shouldn't need much attention now, but if the plants have become too full of dead stems, you can start all over by cutting everything to the ground at this time of year.

Aster: Cut most kinds to the ground. On *Aster frikartii*, simply remove dead branches.

Balloon flower (*Platycodon grandiflorus*): Cut completely to the ground.

Buddleia: Though this is a big shrub in a small garden, cut it to within a foot or two of the ground. You'll get fresh growth and plenty of flowers next spring and control the size.

Columbine: Most benefit if you cut them to within a few inches of the ground, leaving only short stubs.

Coreopsis: You don't have to cut these back, but plants look messy if you don't. Look closely at the plant and you can see that what bloomed in summer is attached to a separate stem, which you can cut off, leaving just the new growth that hasn't flowered yet. You can also cut it to the ground, or dig and divide old clumps.

Gayfeather: Cut this prairie plant completely to the ground, unless you want to leave some stubs to mark its place in the garden.

Geranium: Several kinds of the true geraniums (not pelargoniums) need cutting back including *Geranium sanguineum*. Just tidy up the other kinds.

Geum: Cut dead stems back. Every few years, dig and divide it, amending the soil in the process.

Helenium: Cut completely to the ground.

Japanese anemone: Though it doesn't look as if it needs it, cut it to the ground now. It pops right back.

Lamb's ears: Patches of this plant tend to die out. Gently pull the dead matter out of the clump, and mulch the bare ground with a mix of shavings and sand, or dig up healthy plants from the main clump and fill the voids. Eventually, you'll have to replace the clump with fresh plants as they are short-lived.

Lion's tail: Trim or cut to within a foot of the ground if you want to control its size.

Matilija poppy: Cut completely to the ground.

Mexican evening primrose: Cut completely to the ground.

Mexican sage: This will bloom twice a year if you cut off the dead flowers in summer, and then cut the plant to within a foot of the ground about now.

Ornamental grasses: Some, such as miscanthus and Japanese blood grass, go completely dormant, but before cutting a grass to the ground wait to make sure it is turning brown. Some, such as *Carex buchananii*, resent cutting back. Remove dead leaves by combing the clump with your fingers.

Penstemon: Cut off spent blooms, making cuts as low on the plant as you can just above new sprouts, then completely cut out old, thick woody growth.

***Phlomis russeliana*:** Same as lamb's ears.

Physostegia: Cut completely to the ground.

Rehmannia: Cut out old flowering stems to the basal clump of foliage.

Rudbeckia: Cut to within a foot of the ground.

Salvia: Cut back some shrubby kinds, such as *Salvia greggii*, by about half, others to the ground. There are so many kinds, many of them new, that you'll have to observe the plant to see what it needs.

Santa Barbara daisy: To tidy up this nonstop bloomer, clip it into an 18-inch ball with shears. It will quickly resume a natural shape.

Shasta daisies: Cut flowering stems completely to the ground.

Verbena rigida and the taller ***Verbena bonariensis*:** Cut completely to the ground.

Veronica: On upright, perennial kinds, cut the stems that have already flowered to the ground.

Yarrow: Cut out parts that have flowered, or for a fresh start cut completely to the ground.

Zauschneria: Cut completely to the ground, or leave stubs to mark its place in the garden.

SHORT-LIVED PLANTS

A lot of very nice plants being used in new gardens are short-lived, which surprises some gardeners. Some of these are called subshrubs in botanical texts, a quizzical classification if there ever was one, or shrubby perennials, even though they do not die down for the winter. A few are called shrubs although they are quite small; others are simply called herbs, a real catchall.

The point is, they are not your typical, long-lived, cast-iron shrubs—rhaphiolepsis, for instance—nor are they soft perennials that nearly disappear every winter, like coreopsis. They are something in between, sort of like semipermanent ink. The various artemisias, helichrysums, lavenders, senecios and santolinas are good examples. These are all great plants with handsome foliage or flowers. Several are a stunning, silvery gray, which brings sparkle and light to drab, all-green gardens. They also happen to be drought tolerant, which hasn't hurt their popularity. All stay relatively low and dense, at least at first, though they may spread quite wide.

But, after a few years, the centers fall apart and the plants flop open like dropped bags of cement. They begin to get twiggy, and a few years later they die or look so shabby they must be removed. Some people see

They are not your typical, long-lived, cast-iron shrubs. They are something in between, sort of like semi-permanent ink.

this collapse as a sign that the plants need water. But these are all Mediterranean-climate plants, quite accustomed to doing without much water. Try to perk them up with watering, and they die of root rots. In short, you're not doing anything wrong, they are just short-lived.

"Why should plants be permanent?" asks Los Angeles landscape designer Christine Rosmini. She uses all of these in-between plants in her designs because there is nothing else quite as good, or as fast to fill in—all of these plants are quick growers. A tiny lavender plant can make it to three feet across in a year, a senecio can cover four feet, and some artemisias will sprint to six feet around in a season. But, as is often the case with plants, speedy growth makes for a short life. Every few years when they begin to look a little peaked, she replaces them.

With heavy shears, lightly trim lavender and santolina into tidy rounded shapes to keep them from collapsing with age.

Can you simply cut them back after this fall from grace and let them start over? No, these not-quite-shrubs resent it. They do not recover when cut hard, cut back into old wood. "They're very much like a marguerite," says Rosmini, another plant that grows quickly, then falls apart and finally collapses. But that doesn't stop people from growing daisies.

The late Robert M. Fletcher, a plantsman and noted landscape architect on the Westside, came up with a way to stave off the inevitable. He discovered that lightly trimming these plants often, sometimes three times a year, kept them dense and bushy. He found it was hard for his clients to trim a plant when it might be in full flower, but trimming made a tremendous difference.

He did his trimming in the late fall so the flowers would return in spring, or even in late winter. Lavenders and santolinas in particular quickly rebound. If the plant again looked leggy after flowering, or looked as if it would split apart, he'd trim it again in late spring and sometimes again in summer. He even followed this routine with rosemary, which is much more durable and shrub-like, but also has a tendency to get scraggly.

Trimming means cutting off only a few inches, nothing drastic. You can even use hedge shears. Just go lightly and stay out of that old wood. Keep after the plants to prevent them from getting top heavy and collapsing. If you observe this behavior in other plants, try these techniques on them too. The plants will need replacing "about every five years," Fletcher figured, of the artemisias, lavenders and santolinas, though not the long-lived rosemary.

Favorite artemesias are *Artemesia arborescens*, which has large lacy leaves and can grow to six feet around, and the cultivar 'Powis Castle', which is smaller in all its parts and grows only to about three feet wide.

Senecio vira-vira, also sold as *Senecio leucostachys*, is the senecio best liked by designers. It makes a fluffy, silver two-foot-tall-by-three-foot-wide mound. Other senecios, usually sold as dusty miller, are more common at nurseries.

There are many lavenders—a favorite is the new *Lavandula pinnata buchii*, more commonly sold as *Lavandula multifida* or *Lavandula canariensis* (it's from the Canary Islands), with its bright, branched flowers spikes. Fletcher's favorite lavenders were the kinds used commercially in France for their long, fragrant flower spikes, one named 'Grosso' in particular.

A good time to plant any of these is right now, well before the heat of summer arrives. By that time they will have grown a lot and be sparkling in the summer sun.

The various *Helichrysum petiolare* are a similar story, though they don't like being pruned. The glowing chartreuse 'Limelight' spreads fast to six or more feet. Let long branches trail and mix with other plants. It can really liven up a garden, but it will also overrun it if not given enough room. You can try to manage the size by cutting out some branches and shortening others, making all cuts just above another branch so there are no stubs, to preserve its soft, spreading look. Working carefully, you can easily reduce the plant by about half without it looking any less lovely. But a wise gardener allows at least six to eight feet for a single helichrysum, and plans on replacing each with a new nursery plant every few years.

A FEW GOOD SHRUBS

Those in search of a few good shrubs to plant should seriously consider their eventual size. Even those called compact or dwarf may soon block the view out of a window or spread to garden-gobbling widths. For instance, *Pittosporum tobira* 'Wheeler's Dwarf', which looks small enough in a nursery container, can sprint to six feet tall and about 10 feet across. Though it won't grow

WEEK
52

much higher, it continues to spread, eating up more and more of the garden. *Prunus caroliniana* 'Compacta', a handsome glossy-leafed shrub, will get to the lowest wires strung between utility poles in no time, making a small tree, albeit a nice one.

This may appeal to some, but if you want more than a couple of shrubs in your garden, you must be selective about what you choose, so that there is still enough sunlight and space for flowers and vegetables or even a lawn. I can attest to how big the above-mentioned shrubs get because I've had to laboriously take them out of my own garden. But I can also vouch for a few very manageable shrubs that, a dozen years after planting, are still in my garden because they didn't get too big.

The best behaved is the incredibly plain Texas privet, *Ligustrum japonicum* 'Texanum'. The "Sunset Western Garden Book" brushes it off in two lines, ending with, "Useful as windbreak." But this common plant is probably the most useful shrub in my garden. Its very plainness makes it the perfect background for the perennial flowers in front of it, which seem to glow against the deep green foliage. In spring it briefly comes out of the shadows and shines on it own with spikes of creamy-white flowers. Twelve years old, it has grown only two feet taller than the fence behind it, to about eight feet—the perfect height for a background or property-line shrub. It casts a short shadow, staying amazingly compact at just six feet wide, with dense foliage easily pruned, even into a tidy hedge.

The sweet olive (*Osmanthus fragrans*) grows to the same controlled height. While it does not become as dense a shrub as Texas privet, it does make an airy screen (I suspect it would make a lousy hedge). It is a similar, though lighter, green, more graceful, and the ever-present tiny flowers are extremely fragrant to some noses (some people can barely smell them). One next to my front door has remained an eight-foot-tall shrub for years, while barely growing to a width of six feet. When an errant branch does stray in front of the door or over the path, it is amenable to pruning.

Both these shrubs keep their foliage right to the ground so they don't become bare underneath. And they seem to take sun or shade, doing fine in those tricky spots shaded part of the year but in blazing sun at other times. Sasanqua camellias, those with the smaller flowers, are also rather good at this sun-shade transformation in my garden, where some are proportioned like the privet and sweet olive, while others grow low and spreading.

If you want something that will stay under a window in height, I

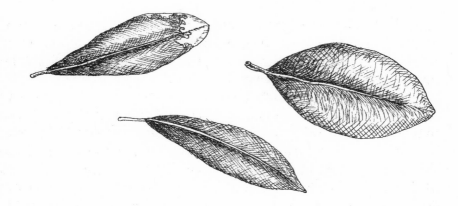

can suggest several that, in my experience, have. While *Pittosporum tobira* 'Variegata' didn't (by a long shot!), another cream and green variety of that plant has. It's named 'Cream de Mint', and though I don't know its eventual size, after several years in my garden it is barely two feet tall and only a little wider. Near the coast here, it takes sun or shade and grows under a lemon tree, against a wall. It's dense and very tidy, like its deep green sibling 'Wheeler's Dwarf', which also stays under a window but gets too wide for my garden. There is also a variegated version of 'Wheeler's Dwarf', but I have no personal experience with it.

For sunny spots, I'd suggest another pittosporum, *Pittosporum crassifolium* 'Compactum', which does stay low and compact, making a dense, slightly flattened, gray-green ball about four feet tall by six feet wide after many years. Like all of these shrubs, it's very tough and drought resistant.

My favorite small shrubs are the Australian fuchsias, though they are a little too architectural to serve as mere backgrounds in the garden. In particular, I like *Correa* 'Ivory Bells', which grows to about four feet tall and spreads to maybe six—but in an unusual fashion, sending out branches near the ground that then curve up so the plant appears to grow as a clump of very attractive upright stems. Little ivory bellflowers bloom at various times in the year. It is the foliage, though, that really stands out, green above, downy gray underneath, stems flocked with a light rust-colored fuzz—the whole effect is quite striking. Mine grow next to more rounded, deeper green shrubs, in a reasonably well drained soil with almost no irrigation. A warning: I understand they are not so happy in heavy soils or with frequent watering; the "Sunset Western Garden Book" calls them "easy to kill with kindness."

The cast-iron rosemary provides one of the deeper greens in my

Three trustworthy shrubs—'Cream de Mint' pittosporum, sweet olive and Texas privet.

garden. I have grown several kinds but have singled out the cultivar 'Tuscan Blue' as the best because it grows up rather than out and has made a very handsome six-foot shrub that remains but five feet across. A pair of these looks very elegant flanking a path or guarding a gate or entry, where their fragrance can be enjoyed when the foliage is brushed against. They even look great against the house as foundation plants.

The westringias from Australia have a similar appearance but are clothed in light green leaves that are quite gray underneath. *Westringia fruticosa* grows tight and dense to about six feet tall by eight feet across in time. It has white flowers, while the looser and larger 'Wynyabbie Gem' has light lavender blooms.

Myrtle, *Myrtus communis,* one of the oldest hedge plants (having been grown for at least 2,000 years), looks a lot like boxwood but with sweetly aromatic foliage and scented flowers. Though the "Sunset Western Garden Book" calls the various forms "some of the most useful, basic evergreen shrubs for California," it is not often planted nowadays and is more likely to be found in older gardens. 'Compacta' is the cultivar most often used as a hedge, but the ordinary myrtle can be pruned to almost any size. Left alone it is a handsome shrub, growing to about five feet tall by four feet across, just about right for fitting under a window.

One of the most elegant of all shrubs is the strawberry tree (*Arbutus unedo*). Though it grows slowly to tree proportions (it can make 25 feet), it is typically seen as an eight- to 10-foot shrub. 'Compacta', however, stays shrub-sized at about six feet around, and 'Elfin King' is a true miniature growing only several feet tall; it is very handsome in a large container. The bark is unusually attractive—reddish and similar to our native arbutus, the handsome madrone that grows in northern California. The deep glossy green leaves are toothed, and the bumpy red fruit is decorative and edible, though not very. The word *unedo* means "eat one," not several.

TOPSOIL

S o, whom do you call when you need good dirt? Maybe you are sick to death of your garden and the fact that nothing will grow and suspect better dirt might be the solution. Most people look under "Topsoil" in the classified pages of the phone book. But *topsoil* is a much-abused word that can mean just about anything: some horrible soil that someone else wanted to get rid of, or the heavy clay excavated for a swimming pool or (the best-case scenario) a wonderful weed-free, sandy loam that is a joy to dig in.

Soil amendments, such as peat moss, ground bark or shavings, are also called topsoil by some, though they are anything but. More often than not, what you really want is not topsoil but soil amendments.

"The first thing I ask anyone who calls is, 'Do you need to raise the level of the soil?'" says Jeff Van Ess, of Lewis Topsoil in Los Angeles. "The only time you really need topsoil is when you have to make a part of the garden higher, to fill low ground, or to fill planter boxes or raised beds. The rest of the time, what the caller really wants is a soil amendment."

Topsoil **is a much-abused word that can mean just about anything.**

What's the difference? It's really very simple: *Topsoil* is just that—dirt scooped from the ground; *soil amendments* are some organic or chemical product that improves dirt, makes it softer or helps it hold water. There is no difference price-wise if you are buying good topsoil or amendments. Both cost about $30 a cubic yard, plus a delivery charge. A reputable topsoil company will provide topsoil that is a weed- and rock-free sandy loam that has been ground up by machine so there are no chunks.

Precisely what kind of amendment you want is determined by your soil, situation and the plants you intend to use. "We always ask what the customer's soil is like and what they are going to plant," says Bernie White, of White Topsoil in Culver City. Something woodsy, like azaleas or ferns, needs lots of soil amendments because these plants like a porous soil full of organic matter, like the leaf litter found on a forest floor. Sandy soils need lots because organic amendments help hold water and fertilizer that otherwise would wash right through. In an average clay soil you may want to add sand to keep the surface from caking, and you certainly want to add organic amendments and gypsum. Gypsum is a powdery white mineral that helps keep a clay soil from getting too heavy and dense. It chemically separates the soil particles so they don't cling together.

Truly, there are lots of ways to go. "We have over 500 different mixes," says White. "From super-lightweight mixes that can go in planters on rooftops or balconies, to special azalea mixes." They even have a special soil mix for cactus and succulents, which will quickly rot in a normal clay soil.

But what about the average garden? "If you have a typical clay soil, do not need to raise the level of the garden and are just growing

ordinary garden flowers and shrubs," says Van Ess, "we would probably recommend adding a two-inch layer of redwood and fir shavings,
which have been nitrolized, plus some gypsum. If you needed to add
a two-inch layer over 1,000 square feet, you would need six yards of
amendment, which is about one truckload."

Why nitrolized shavings? Wood byproducts such as sawdust and
shavings that have not been thoroughly composted will rob the soil of
nitrogen, that all-important fertilizer element. To prevent this, topsoil
companies can add nitrogen, so it is readily available to aid decomposition. Be sure to ask whether the amendments have been
nitrolized, or have had nitrogen added.

Of course, you don't just spread amendments on top and plant.
You must mix them into the existing soil with a power rotary tiller,
which can be rented, or spade and mix it in by hand. That even goes
for topsoil. It too must be tilled in so there is no abrupt line between
new soil and old, which would repel water and roots.

So, if you want to *improve* your soil, you need amendments. You
want topsoil only if you want to change the soil level. Organic amendments can also be bought by the bag at nurseries, or you can bag it
yourself at building or garden supply stores. But getting a truckload
costs about half what it does by the bag.

Be sure you have a wheelbarrow to cart it around back (if that's
where it's destined) and a place to store it until you use it up. A truckload makes a very big pile.

Of course, you don't just spread amendments on top and plant. You must mix them in.

January

TIME TO PLANT ROSES

WHY WOULD ANYONE PLANT SOMETHING that looks like a bundle of sticks set out on trash day? Because with a little care, the leafless roses sold at this time of year (for the uninitiated, they're called bare-root roses) will be bursting with blooms in fewer than four months. Not only that—these thorny, lifeless-looking plants are a lot less expensive than roses sold in nursery containers later in the year. Roses that cost $17 in a container in spring or summer cost $7 right now, if they are the older, nonpatented varieties. Patented roses, including this year's newest, cost between $10 and $15. Discount chains sell them for less, but they usually stock a lower grade of smaller plants. It's a special once-a-year opportunity and, for a gardener, better than the after-Christmas sales at department stores.

WEEK 1

Also nurseries carry their largest selection of roses now. One year, one had more than 3,000 roses, of 100 different varieties, ready for the big planting rush. At any other time, you're lucky to find a few dozen. You'll have to act quickly, though. By mid-February, nurseries will look a bit picked over and the roses will have begun to leaf out.

So this week and for the next few, gardeners throughout Southern California will be bracing themselves against the cold, hands gloved, planting roses (though just as likely they'll be in T-shirts, since January's weather can be warm and dry).

Many believe that planting roses bare root is the best way because the roots can be positioned naturally in the soil, so they can continue to grow outward. One problem with planting anything from a container is that the restricted roots are growing in an unnatural fashion—circling around inside instead of growing outward (although once in the ground they may outgrow this condition).

A few nurseries still sell their bare-root roses the old-fashioned way, from bins or boxes filled with damp sawdust. It's a good way to buy because you can see the condition of the roots. Before you take the rose home, the nursery will carefully wrap it in paper and tie a neat string around the package.

Most nurseries, however, sell only prepackaged bare-root roses—where the roots and moist packing material are already wrapped up in a plastic bag. Because you can't see the roots you are gambling that they are alive and healthy, not dry, or (more likely) rotted. Dry roots can be soaked overnight and plumped up. Roses with rotted roots will not succeed and should be returned. Rotted roots feel squishy, and if cut, the inside is not white, but off-color.

You are also betting that there are enough roots. Many are lost when plants are dug from the field, but there should still be lots, a balance of thread-thin and heavier roots. If there aren't, consider taking the rose back to the nursery for another.

Some nurseries now are even potting up their bare-root roses. The reasoning: If you plant right away, you need only shake off the soil from the roots and plant it bare root; if you can't get around to planting or wait too late in the bare-root season, the rose will still be able to root into the potting mix in the container and then be planted like any other container-grown rose. A warning: If a rose comes in a container made of cardboard-like wood pulp, do not plant it still in this container, even though that's the idea behind pulp pots. In our climate and soils, it won't quickly decompose and will hamper the roots for years.

Plant bare-root roses from bins or bags as soon as possible. Cut any restraining ties and unwrap. To ensure that the roots are not dry, soak them overnight in a pail of water. If you buy a rose that already has whitish, elongated sprouts longer than an inch or so, snap them off before planting.

For each rose, dig a shallow (about 18 inches deep) but wide hole. Floribundas and the smaller shrub and English (or Austin) roses need holes about two feet wide, with plants spaced about the same distance apart. Hybrid teas and large shrub and English roses do best in holes

POLYMERS FOR THIRSTY ROSES

Roses are very thirsty plants. Water-storing polymers are one way to make more water available to roses, especially if they are planted with less thirsty things. Each tiny grain swells to ice-cube size when wet, and the water stored inside is easily tapped by roots. One brand is Broadleaf P4.

Add polymers when you plant. First add water to a tablespoon of granules, let them swell, then scatter about half a cup of the inflated polymers in the bottom of each hole. Mix them into the soil where the roots will be, adding a little fertilizer while you're at it.

On existing plants, auger holes around the bush and pour in a mix of soil and saturated polymers. If done at this time of year, any damaged roots will quickly regrow and tap into the polymers.

about two-and-a-half feet wide, with plants spaced three feet apart. (Don't work in a wet soil, or you'll turn it into something similar to concrete. Wait three to four days after a rain for it to dry out a little.)

A wheelbarrow is helpful at this point. Put the soil from each hole into it, or into a pile, and mix in organic soil amendments until the dirt, when squeezed in your fist, does not make a hard ball. Give it a firm push, and it should crumble apart. You may need as much as a one-cubic-foot bag for each hole, but probably half that. Some gardeners also mix in fertilizer. Use a slow-release form or an organic, so the fertilizer doesn't go to work too quickly. Follow label directions.

Now comes the fun part. Remember mud pies? Take some of the amended soil, put it back in the hole, and pat it into a tall cone shape. Evenly spread the roots over this cone, and fill the hole with more

Spread roots over a cone of soil in the bottom of the planting hole. Use a stick to set the rose at the the proper level, and temporarily cover canes with sawdust or ground bark.

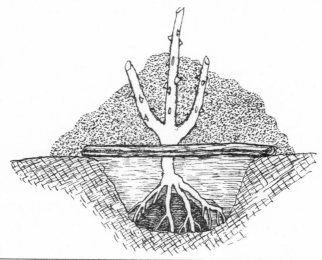

amended soil. Gently push it between the roots and firm it with your hands. When the hole is full, push the soil down with your foot, gently compacting it, so it doesn't drain, or dry out, too fast after watering.

There is a little debate on how deep to plant roses. Most gardeners plant so that the bud union is just above ground. Roses that are to be mulched should be planted with the bud union about two inches above ground. (A stick lying across the hole helps in judging the proper level.) The bud union is that enlarged area where the top of the plant was budded to the rootstock. Planting a little high lets you quickly identify suckers, which sprout from the rootstock. These you want to snap (not cut) off because they are a different, usually uninteresting, kind of rose.

Roses grown on their own roots have no bud union. Plant these at the same level they were growing in the field, usually detectable by a change of color on the bark near the base.

Mound up the leftover soil to make a donut-shaped watering basin around the edge of each hole. This will help funnel rain and irrigation water directly to the roots. Give the roses one thorough soaking, filling this basin at least twice.

Some gardeners pile pure amendment over each newly planted and watered rose, the idea being that the organic matter protects the canes from the sun and drying Santa Ana winds. Or mix the wood chips from the rose package with the amendments. Leave the mound in place until the rose begins to leaf out, usually within a week or so. Then remove the mound by washing it away with a gentle stream of water, and it becomes mulch.

For a month after planting, don't give the roses any additional fertilizer. If we get no rain, water them, but be careful not to overdo it. At this time of year the soil dries slowly and roses don't need much water. New growth will sprout quickly. Expect your first glorious blossoms during the first weeks of April (and keep in mind what a bargain you got).

THE BEST ROSES

With the rose buying and planting season in full swing, how do you choose only a few from the hundred or so roses available at some nurseries? I asked respected rosarians for a list of excellent roses they know do well in Southern California.

I polled Santa Barbara rose judge and consulting rosarian Daniel

ROSES FOR THE COAST

Here is a list, by type and color group, of roses that have received high marks from the South Coast Rose Society for their performance in cool, moist coastal areas where roses can get mildew. Some are no longer commonly available.

HYBRID TEAS AND GRANDIFLORAS

RED and RED BLENDS

'Alec's Red'
'Double Delight'
'Granada'
'Mister Lincoln'
'Mon Chéri'
'Precious Platinum'
'Red Devil'

PINK and PINK BLENDS

'Color Magic'
'Duet'
'Peter Frankenfeld'
'Queen Elizabeth'

ORANGE and ORANGE BLENDS

'Futura'
'Marmalade'
'Olé'
'Sweepstakes'

APRICOT COLORED

'Brandy'
'Oldtimer'

YELLOW and YELLOW BLENDS

'Gold Medal'
'New Day'
'Young Quinn'

WHITE and WHITE BLENDS

'Honor'
'Pascali'
'Pristine'
'Sweet Afton'

LAVENDER and LAVENDER BLENDS

'Blue Nile'
'Paradise'

FLORIBUNDAS

RED and RED BLENDS

'Interama'
'Merci'

PINK and PINK BLENDS

'Cherish'
'Sea Pearl'
'Simplicity'
'Tiki'

ORANGE and ORANGE BLENDS

'Marina'

APRICOT COLORED

'Cathedral'

YELLOW and YELLOW BLENDS

'Katherine Loker'
'Redgold'
'Sun Flare'
'Sunsprite'

WHITE and WHITE BLENDS

'French Lace'
'Iceberg'

LAVENDER and LAVENDER BLENDS

'Angel Face'
'Deep Purple'

CLIMBERS

'Altissimo' (red)
'America' (orange-pink)
'Golden Showers' (yellow)
'Handel' (orange)
'Joseph's Coat' (orange)

Bifano; Northridge enthusiast James E. Sefton; Luis T. Desamero of Studio City, editor of the American Rose Society's Pacific SouthWest District Proof of the Pudding survey; Julia Sudol of Alhambra, and Mrs. Helen Thorne and her daughter Mrs. Lois Penney of Bonsall— all rose authorities.

Don't feel constrained by these recommendations. Part of the fun of growing anything is taking a chance—at the nursery, you might find that a rose not noted here is just what you want. For instance, not included are the newest roses, because most experts thought it too early to judge how they will perform in Southern California gardens. The ones here have stood the test of time.

Hybrid teas and grandifloras remain the most popular of roses because their flowers are the most shapely and are the largest, with bushes to suit. Most easily grow to five feet, and flowers usually come one to a stem, which are long enough for cutting. Favorite hybrid teas and grandifloras receiving three or more votes include (alphabetically):

'Color Magic': Pink blend—"a dramatic variegated pink." "One of my best." "A *must* for the rose garden."

'Double Delight': Creamy white and red flowers. A favorite in Southern California because the "sunshine brings out the perfection" of colors. "Outstanding." "Excellent for container growing." Spicy fragrance.

'Duet': Medium pink. "Many blooms, and excellent repeat bloom." "Excellent garden variety."

'Gold Medal': Deep yellow. "Missed being an All-America Rose Selections winner by one point!" "A rose for all seasons displaying masses of bloom all year long."

'Honor': White with "good foliage." "Queen of all the whites." "Always in bloom."

'Mister Lincoln': Dark red. "The most fragrant of all the reds." "Usually rated higher than brother seedling 'Oklahoma', and probably is better, but not to quibble," said a fancier of both dark red roses. Another cautioned that it is susceptible to rust and has at times "leggy growth."

'Olympiad': Medium red. "Now found in many gardens; becoming a great favorite," perhaps because "the brilliant color does not fade in the hot sun."

'Paradise': Mauve—"silvery lavender shading to ruby red at petal edges." "An irresistible hybrid tea for lovers of mauve roses." And fragrant to boot.

'Pristine': White with pink edges. "The picture-perfect rose."

'Queen Elizabeth': Pink. An "oldie but goodie." "Always in bloom." "Warrants its royal name."

'Touch of Class': Orange blend—"pink-shaded coral and cream." "Hailed as the 'Rose of the Decade' for its truly classical shape."

Floribunda roses typically grow to three or four feet and have clusters of smaller flowers. Those receiving three or more votes include:

MORE ROSES OF NOTE

The information in the first list comes from a variety of knowledgeable California gardeners. Mendocino Heirloom Roses (P.O. Box 904, Mendocino, CA 95470; www.heritageroses.com) compiled the list of unthirsty roses, observed growing in their area with little or no irrigation.

ROSES THAT TOLERATE A LITTLE SHADE

HYBRID TEAS and GRANDIFLORAS

'Brandy'
'Brigadoon'
'Double Delight'
'Gold Medal'
'Graceland'
'Ingrid Bergman'
'Voodoo'

FLORIBUNDAS

'French Lace'
'Iceberg'
'Sweet Vivien'

ENGLISH ROSES

'Abraham Darby'
'Belle Story'
'Bow Bells'
'Charmian'
'Cottage Rose'
'Country Living'
'Dapple Dawn'
'Dove'
'English Elegance'
'English Garden'
'Fair Bianca'
'Golden Celebration'
'Heritage'
'Hero'
'Lilian Austin'
'Mary Rose'
'Othello'

'Pretty Jessica'
'The Countryman'
'The Pilgrim'
'The Prince'
'Winchester
     Cathedral'

SHRUB and OLD ROSES

'Blanc Double de
     Coubert'
'Chapeau de
     Napoleon'
'Comte de
     Chambord'
'F.J. Grootendorst'
'Gruss an Aachen'
'Hansa'
'Honorine de
     Brabant'
'Jacques Cartier'
'La Reine Victoria'
'Louise Odier'
'Mme. Plantier'
'Old Blush'
'Reine des Violettes'
'The Fairy'

CLIMBERS

'American Pillar'
'Ballerina'
'Buff Beauty'
'Cécile Brunner'
'Constance Spry'
'Golden Showers'
'Climbing Iceberg'

Lady Banks'
'New Dawn'
'Penelope'

DROUGHT-RESISTANT ROSES

'Albertine'
'American Pillar'
'Belle of Portugal'
'Climbing Cécile
     Brunner'
'Complicata'
'Dorothy Perkins'
'Double Plum'
'Dr. W. Van Fleet'
'François Juranville'
'Gardenia'
'Homestead Hybrid
     China'
'Mme. Gabriel Luizet'
'Mme. Plantier'
'Navaroo Ridge
     Noisette'
'New Dawn'
'Paul Ricault'
'Paul's Double Musk'
'Rambling Rector'
Rosa banksiae 'Lutea'
R. harisonii
R. rubiginosa
R. rugosa
'Russelliana'
'Silver Moon'
'Veilchenblau'

'Angel Face': Mauve. The "color remains even and consistent," and "flowers hold well even in Valley heat." "It grows and grows," however, and "will get huge if permitted." (I've seen them five feet tall and eight feet across.)

'**Cherish**': Medium pink. "Massive sprays; ideal for landscaping."

'**French Lace**': White. "The perfection of the blooms will be admired by all." "The most perfect blooms."

'**Iceberg**': White, or more precisely, "ivory to blush apricot." "Very fragrant, vigorous." "A longtime favorite," especially with garden designers.

'**Sexy Rexy**': Medium pink. "The new floribunda on the block that everyone is mad about." "Huge clusters of flowers."

'**Showbiz**': Medium red. "Large clusters of blooms that last nearly a month."

'**Sun Flare**': Medium yellow. "Glossy foliage." "All perfect blooms, single or in clusters."

'**Sunsprite**': Deep yellow. "Fine, full foliage, many blooms." "One of the few yellow floribundas that performs well in Southern California."

PICKING THE PERFECT FRUIT TREE

Most of us have room for only a few fruit trees. My own choices for a small garden are a lemon and a juice orange, plus a peach and maybe an apple, even though apricots are my favorite fruit (they just don't grow well where I live). A good cook like my wife needs lemons almost daily—lemon trees oblige with a nearly constant crop. Oranges also bare over a very long period; apples bare slowly and keep well, and, while peaches don't, I can think of no other fruit that tastes so different from the store-bought types when ripe, which they never are in markets. In summer, some people drive all the way to California's Central Valley to pick their own, so why not plant one and simply walk out the back door?

A really ripe peach is so soft, sugary and juicy that you must eat it outside, or over the sink. Even then you must wash your hands and face when you're finished. It is so sweet that even children don't mind the fuzz. If you dislike the fuzz, plant a nectarine instead. To my palate, though, they are not as tasty, nor are they as easy to grow.

While it is definitely not the time to plant lemons or any other citrus or subtropical fruit, it is the time to buy and plant deciduous fruits such as apples, apricots, plums and peaches. Like roses, they are briefly sold bare root now, when they are a bargain and nurseries have lots to choose from. Deciduous fruit trees are those that go dormant in winter, losing all their leaves, which is why they can be sold *sans* container, with no soil around their roots.

Before deciding on a variety to plant, you must do your homework (the list below should help). Not all varieties do well in our mild Southern California climate. Peaches and other deciduous fruit trees including apples, apricots, nectarines and plums are not completely at home here, needing a little more cold to trigger blossoming or sprout leaves. This required chilling, defined as the number of hours below 45°, is called the chill factor. Coastal areas of Southern California may get as few as 100 hours of chilling, while cold canyon bottoms and higher elevations may get as many as 600. In general, trees that need more than 300 to 400 hours of chilling don't do well in low-elevation Southern California.

If you already have a peach or nectarine that isn't doing well, it is probably one of the high-chill varieties.

In general, peaches and plums need the least amount of chilling (about 400 hours for plums). But even with these one must be wary, since some varieties are much more adapted to Southern California than others. Most apricots need about 500, so are best in the colder interior valleys, such as the San Fernando. Apples are even more finicky, except there are a few remarkable varieties that need as few as 200 to 300 hours. 'Dorsett Golden' needs only 100! Pears and cherries, needing as many as 800 hours of chilling, are for much colder places.

You'll find this information conspicuously missing from nursery labels. Many nurseries—especially places that sell plants only as a sideline to hardware and lumber—unabashedly sell deciduous fruit trees that are very poor bets in Southern California. I have seen 'Elberta' peach trees for sale, yet this peach was bred for cold, cold weather and bears poorly, if at all, in Southern California. I'm sure it's a big seller in Spokane, but it shouldn't even be tried here. There are much more suitable candidates, many of which were developed here.

(If you already have a peach or nectarine that isn't doing well, or that reluctantly leafs out, it is probably one of the high-chill varieties. If you have a low-chill variety, very little can go wrong until the tree is quite old—20 years or so is the working life expectancy of most deciduous fruit trees.)

Once you are at the nursery, be careful not to get carried away by the bargain prices and buy too many fruit trees. Even those labeled "semidwarf" grow easily to 20 feet across. The "genetic dwarfs" do stay quite small, but, unfortunately, the fruit I've sampled has never tasted all that good. Some may, but I have no recommendations.

Planting a bare-root fruit tree is a satisfying weekend project that easily fits into these too short midwinter days. And it's a snap—even easier than bare-root roses. Simply spread out the roots in a large hole, over a cone of soil mounded up in the bottom, and fill it in. Just be careful to not bury the plant deeper than it was when in the growing field. Look carefully, and you'll find a color change in the bark that marks the old soil line. Make sure the bulging bud union stands above ground. Pulverize the soil that goes back in the hole so it is not lumpy—there is no need to amend it.

Radical pruning of newly planted trees is often suggested to compensate for the lost roots, but I just cut all the branches back by half. Many trees for sale are already pruned; just thin the branches so the remaining few will make a strong frame. Remove any branches that are too close together along the trunk, and try for three strong branches evenly dispersed around the trunk.

FRUIT TREE VARIETIES FOR MILD CLIMATES

The UC Cooperative Extension office in San Diego recommends these deciduous fruit tree varieties for the mild coastal areas of Southern California. For a complete list, including varieties that are not recommended and that will succeed in inland climates, send a stamped, self-addressed envelope to UC Cooperative Extension, Bldg. 4, 5555 Overland Ave., San Diego, CA 92123; ask for County Publication CP336.

APPLE	APRICOT	PEACH	PLUM
'Anna'	'April Gold'	'August Pride'	'Santa Rosa'
'Beverly Hills'	'Autumn Royal'	'Desertgold'	**POMEGRANATE**
'Ein Shemer'	'Floragold'	'MidPride'	'Wonderful'
'Golden	'Newcastle'	'Royal Gold'	
Delicious'	'Nugget'	'Shanghai'	** needs another
'Dorsett		'Springtime'	variety of the
Golden'	**NECTARINE**	'Tropi-berta'	same fruit tree
'Gravenstein'*	'Desert Dawn'	'Ventura'	in the area for
'Valmore'	'Gold Mine'		pollination*
'Winter		**PERSIMMON**	
Banana'		'Fuyu'	
'Winter		'Hachiya'	
Pearmain'*			

FRUIT TREE CARE

A nother reason not to plant too many fruit trees is that deciduous fruits need yearly pruning, also done at this time of year when they are leafless. Pruning fruit trees is one of the real gardening arts, not easily or quickly explained.

In general, though: Peaches need the most pruning (it will feel as though you have removed about a third of the tree) because they grow so fast, apples the least because they grow slowly and produce fruit on short little branches (called spurs) that last for years. Apricots and plums fall somewhere in between. On all, you are trying to maintain a balance between older growth (especially the spurs), which produces flowers and fruit, and new growth, which helps keep the tree growing and producing a few years down the road.

If you want to study pruning, order the authoritative and amply illustrated University of California "Pruning Fruit and Nut Trees"; to purchase, call *(800) 994-8849* and ask for publication #21171. Two other books are the old "How to Prune Fruit Trees," by R. Sanford Martin (self-published), and "Western Fruit, Berries and Nuts," by Lance Walheim and Robert L. Stebbins (H.P. Books, Los Angeles).

It's also important to spray fruit trees while they're completely dormant, before the buds begin to swell. Dormant sprays made of horticultural oils are not poisons but work by smothering insect pests that might be overwintering on the trees. Drench the bark, and wash off any spray that gets on nearby plants that still have leaves, since it can burn them, especially on hot days.

On peaches you need to prevent peach leaf curl, a common disease that deforms leaves, since there is no way to cure it. Spray trees with a dormant spray that also contains a simple fungicide such as lime or lime sulfur or fixed copper. Spray now, and in autumn after leaves fall, then again in January before buds swell.

RECIPE FOR PRUNING PAINT

Homemade pruning paint protects pruned fruit trees and roses against fungal infections. This one was developed by the UC Cooperative Extension. (Bordeaux powder is getting a little hard to find at nurseries, but it is still manufactured.)

- 1 1/2 ounces Bordeaux powder
- 1 pint linseed oil

Mix the two ingredients. Store in a container—it keeps for several years. Apply with a paintbrush on any cut over an inch in diameter. Reapply each year until wound heals.

APRICOT PROBLEMS

Many Southern California gardeners have trouble growing apricots, even though this fruit used to be a commercial crop here. I once asked UC pomologist James A. Beutel why, since it is my favorite fruit and I have failed several times, in several gardens. He pointed out that apricots were grown commercially only in the San Fernando Valley, upper Ojai and Hemet, all with colder winters. Those areas are now much warmer because of all the pavement and houses (as much as 10° warmer in winter).

There are the exceptions, of course. Some trees do bear well and some places seem to get enough cold, but, in general, apricots are difficult in Southern California, and they often lack flavor. In our sometimes warm winters, apricots will drop their flower buds, and may not set much fruit. In February, you can find flower buds all over the ground.

The variety 'Royal' (called 'Blenheim' by the canneries) is still frequently planted here, although it has always been a poor choice. It grew best in the Santa Clara Valley in Northern California, now better known as Silicon Valley, the ideal apricot climate.

There are reports that one new apricot, 'Katy', may need less winter cold and so may do well here. 'Gold Kist' is another new variety that one San Diego nursery says does well in that mild climate. Both these varieties apparently need only 300 hours of chilling each winter.

Newly planted trees tend not to bear for at least three years because it takes time for them to develop the little fruiting branches, called spurs, where most fruit forms. Apricots tend to be alternate bearers, which means they naturally fruit heavily one year, then barely at all the next. An old agricultural bulletin suggests trying to keep the leaves on later into the fall with good culture and adequate water.

ALL ABOUT BLACKBERRIES

Blackberries are as much a part of California as, say, Knott's Berry Farm. Native to this state, they grow so well here that that big conglomerate was able to become so much more than just a roadside berry stand.

I can't imagine kids growing up in California without blackberries to pick when they please during summer vacations, or berry-stained hands and faces. When I was a child, my grandfather thought-fully planted trellised blackberries right outside my bedroom window so I would know when they were ripe. Adults who do without are also missing out on one of the tastiest of fruits, and the opportunity to make blackberry cobbler.

Still, blackberries don't get planted in too many gardens here. Perhaps one reason is that, once they are put in the ground, it will probably take two full years for them to start bearing. Other than that, though, there is no reason why they shouldn't be. They certainly don't take up much space. Although wild blackberries may sprawl for 20 feet or more along a creek bank, in the garden they are easily trained on a trellis that needs to be long but can be very narrow, narrow enough to fit in places where little else can

WEEK

3

grow, such as along a driveway or against a fence. They can even get by on less than a full day of sun.

In the dead of winter, when they are available bare root, is the time to plant blackberries. Unfortunately, what you are going to find at many places selling bare-root plants right now are varieties not suited to Southern California at all, such as 'Ebony King', which is for cold climates. These don't even grow like the others, but have short stiff canes, and the fruit is not very sweet.

I suggest trying to find either one of two varieties: 'Boysen' (as in boysenberry) is a variety of blackberry, and so is 'Ollalie', though it too is often called an ollalieberry.

Another variety with a long-standing history in Southern California is 'Young', with very sweet fruit and very thorny canes. 'Cascade', 'Marion', 'Himalaya' and 'Thornless Evergreen' are other varieties often grown here.

If you can't find 'Boysen', 'Ollalie' or one of the other varieties suited to Southern California, keep looking. If you find a variety you haven't heard of, ask whether it will grow here, but if it was packaged

To support a single blackberry, build a trellis 16 feet long using four-by-four-inch posts with wire strung between. During first summer, let canes sprawl, then weave them over wires.

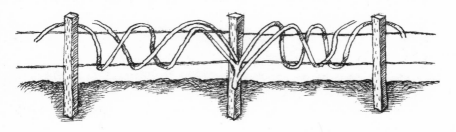

in the east, I'd be suspicious.

Although planting one or two blackberry plants (one seldom plants more) takes no time at all, building the support does. So berry planting turns into a tidy weekend project. You can put the building off, but I wouldn't recommend it. In no time the little sticks you plant will be growing furiously and you'll soon have a tangle of prickly stems to contend with—and blackberries are very prickly.

The support for blackberries should be sturdy. You can tie them to a fence or a wall of the house, or build a free-standing affair just in front, which is easier to tie to. To plant one blackberry, use a post-hole digger and bury three six-foot four-by-fours about 18 inches deep and eight feet apart. Attach two wires to the posts, one three feet above the ground, the other one-and-a-half feet above that. Or nail two-by-fours at these heights. Plant the blackberry in front of the center post. With that done, the hardest part of planting blackberries is over.

Blackberries like good soil but can survive just about anything. They do need lots of water, which is why they grow beside creeks, and some fertilizer in spring and early summer. If they do not grow by leaps and bounds in late spring and summer, water more often or more thoroughly.

Allow canes that grow the first year to sprawl under the trellis until they are about eight feet long. At that point cut the tips to stop growth and tie the canes to the trellis, weaving them around the two wires to take up less space. Keep an eye on those tips. When they sense the ground is nearby, they get fat and turn slightly red. Then they plunge into the ground and make lots of roots. In the blink of an eye, you have more berry vines.

The new canes will go semidormant next winter and the following summer will produce fruit, on little side branches that sprout from the main canes in the spring. In the meantime, a new batch of canes will grow next spring. Leave these on the ground while the others ripen fruit. Then (don't lose me now) in August cut the canes that have borne fruit to the ground and tie the new canes in their place.

In other words, blackberries make biennial canes—growing one year, fruiting on those canes the next, while growing more for yet another year. You get bushels of fruit every summer, but the canes require two years' growth. Remember to do the summer pruning, or your backyard may disappear under a mound of prickly blackberries. They do go wild in California.

Be very careful not to cover the crowns of strawberries when planting. A pine needle mulch helps keep fruit clean.

STRAWBERRY FIELDS

S trawberries are another one of winter's genuine bargains. One large building supply chain had my favorite variety, 'Sequoia', advertised one January weekend for $1.44 a dozen, or exactly 12 cents per plant. Strawberries sell for so little now because what you find in the nursery section aren't plants growing in little pots but bare-root plants packaged in plastic bags, like roses and fruit trees.

Strawberries are an important agricultural crop in California. Whenever you see a roadside field covered in plastic sheeting, you're looking at bare-root-planted strawberries. Also, they are planted in mounded rows and usually in sandy soil, two horticultural hints not to be ignored.

You can easily satisfy the demands of strawberries—for good drainage and ample water—in a container filled with a good potting soil. You would need a very large one, though, or several, to grow enough to harvest a decent crop.

Consider growing them in the ground if you have an available sunny spot. If you garden in a sandy soil, strawberries will be very easy to grow. You can't, however, grow them in a heavy clay soil on flat ground; you must improve clay soils. So while you're at the nursery, buy a couple bags of soil amendments (planting mix), which also might be on sale this weekend, and pick up a few two-by-six-inch boards. Three six-footers ought to do it, one of which you cut in half.

With all this, you are going to make a little raised bed. Spade up the soil and mix in the amendments until you have a fluffy, loose soil that will drain quickly. Since we're talking about a fairly small area, I'd get down on my knees and do the final mixing with my hands, partly because it's fun and partly because it guarantees that there are no dirt clods left. Crush any found with your hands. The soil should be prepared to a depth of about a foot.

Once you have added all this soil amendment, the level of the soil will be higher. Nail the two-by-six-inch boards together to make a crude frame that is three feet wide and six feet long, burying part of the boards about an inch or two deep, so the water won't run under them. Level off the soil and rake out any clods you may have missed.

Space 18 plants about a foot apart—the outermost plants will be only six inches from the sides of the raised bed. (But buy two dozen, so you can choose the best.) Planting strawberries too deep will kill them. Look at a plant and note the little crown from which the leaves sprout; with strawberries, it is actually shaped like a crown. This must be above the soil with just the base touching the dirt but no roots showing. Dig a hole, untangle the roots a little, and plant, firming down the soil. I usually end up planting a few several times, trying to get them at just the right level.

Now stand back to admire your handiwork. What you have is a little strawberry factory. Raised above the ground, it drains excess water quickly and allows air into the soil for the shallow strawberry roots.

When they get going, strawberries need lots of water, and, about once a month, a liquid fertilizer from a watering can. If you want to save water and simplify things greatly, lay drip irrigation tubing or tape along each row, and then cover the whole bed with plastic, cutting little holes for each plant. The drip system will use less water, and the plastic will help conserve it and cut down on weeds. If you're going to water by hand or with a sprinkler, mulch the berry plants with hay or pine needles (two I've tried) to keep the berries clean. A mulch keeps the berries off the ground so they don't rot and ensures that they don't get splattered with dirt.

Planted now, the berries will probably start bearing fruit in late March and will continue through June. While they're fruiting, drape protective bird netting (sold at nurseries) over the bed or birds will pick you clean.

In summer, each plant will make many little plantlets, called runners. Cut these off while the plant is still fruiting. After June, you can let these runners develop if you want to grow your own plants for next year. In August, once their rooted, sever them from the mother plants and pot them up. In winter you can pull out and toss dead plants and replace them. But, because you can buy new plants for as little as $1.44 a dozen, saving the runners just doesn't figure in my book.

TAKING THE FEAR OUT OF ROSE PRUNING

T his weekend, rain or shine, I prune my roses, though with a certain amount of trepidation. You thought you were the only one? Every time I prune a rose I worry that I am pruning off too much or too little, because there are so few rules to guide one and so many opinions on how to prune (not to mention so many branches). But roses turn out to be forgiving plants; if they were not, they wouldn't be so popular.

Most rose experts would agree that there are at least two rules of rose growth that can serve to guide you. First, roses flower only on new growth, so you need to encourage the rose to grow. Second, new growth cannot be any larger than the branch from which it sprouts, so that skinny growth makes for skimpy flowers.

WEEK 4

The fact that you are not likely to see huge flowers on skinny branches, or thick branches sprouting from thin branches, is why some rose growers prune so hard. They want thick, sturdy new growth so they can get big, exhibition-size flowers. I have on occasion pruned hard so that only a few thick branches, or more properly, canes, are left—and they only about 18 inches tall. I've done this to roses that have become old and woody with too many little branches and too much dead wood. Generally, though, this is not a good idea.

In Southern California, roses should not be cut back so hard. Even roses being grown for exhibition, or just for cutting, are pruned less, and roses being grown for their beauty in the garden much less than what is typically illustrated in books. Attempting to explain how to lightly prune roses with words, drawings or photographs is very difficult. The best way to learn is to attend one of the demonstrations held at public gardens, but here are the basics.

Begin by eliminating any dead canes, and any that rub or cross, saving the younger of the two. Then remove the ones with a heavy

HANDS-ON PRUNING WORKSHOPS
AND DEMONSTRATIONS

Every winter various Southern California public gardens encourage you to bring your own shears for some hands-on experience at pruning. Contact each for dates and times.

- The Arboretum of Los Angeles County, 301 N. Baldwin Ave., Arcadia; www.arboretum.org.
- Descanso Gardens, 1418 Descanso Drive, La Canada Flintridge (818) 952-4401; www.descanso.com.
- Orange County Rose Society, at the Westminster Civic Rose Garden, 8299 Westminster Blvd., Westminster (714) 895-2860.
- Pageant of Roses Garden, inside Gate 1 at Rose Hills Memorial Park, 3900 S. Workman Mill Road, Whittier, (562) 699-0921, extension 329.
- South Coast Botanic Garden, 26300 Crenshaw Blvd., Palos Verdes Pennisula (310) 544-1948
- Tournament of Roses Association Garden, 391 S. Orange Grove, Pasadena (626) 499-4100.

coat of bark that produce only small, twiggy growth. These are the culprits that make a rose grow old before its time. Using a small keyhole or compass saw, cut them back flush with the bud union, that bulging base of the plant. Pruning compound can be used to protect the cut, but it isn't necessary.

You may have to leave a few canes that are covered with heavy bark, or there will be nothing left. Leave only five, and cut these to about two or three feet. What you want to do here is encourage new canes to sprout from the base. If you are successful, you can remove more of the old bark-covered canes next winter, or the winter after; if no new canes sprout, it is probably time to start over with a new bush.

Younger bushes will have plenty of young canes that are still green or only lightly encrusted with bark. These will produce the best flowers and the most leaves. These younger canes should be preserved but shortened and tidied up.

If you are most interested in cut flowers, shorten canes of hybrid teas (by far the most common roses, with the biggest flowers) to about three feet. Floribunda roses are naturally shorter (and have smaller flowers); cut these to about two feet. If you want the rose to flower more profusely so it makes a better show in the garden, leave the canes even longer. The rule then is: Shorten the plants by a third—a six-foot hybrid tea would end up four feet tall.

Tidying up consists of removing all side branches thinner than a pencil, though on bushes grown for cut flowers you may want to remove most of the side branches to encourage long flowering stems. Make each cut close to a bud that faces out from the plant, which will encourage growth in that direction and allow light into the center of the plant for healthier growth. Buds are located all along the branches and are either at the base of a leaf cluster or are represented by a slight bulge that makes a ring around the branch.

When you are finished pruning, pull off all remaining leaves, rake up everything and send it to the dump so pests and diseases are not carried through the winter. As an added precaution, spray the pruned bushes with a dormant oil spray, a nonpoisonous spray available at nurseries that smothers pests that may be hiding in the bark. It is also available with lime sulfur or other fungicides added that will help prevent diseases such as rust. If the oil spray gets on other plants that still have leaves, wash it off.

Finally, sprinkle a little granular fertilizer (and maybe the Rose Cocktail mentioned here) around the base of the plant and lightly work it into the soil. While you are at it, pull out all weeds. The next rain will settle the soil and send the fertilizer to the roots, and the roses will be ready for a new round of growing and flowering.

One final piece of advice: I try to err on the side of pruning too little, rather than too much. You can always cut off a little more, but you can't glue any back on.

Tidying up consists of removing all side branches thinner than a pencil.

MIXING A ROSE COCKTAIL

This interesting recipe for healthier roses was originally developed by people who grow old heritage varieties. Says one devotee: "You can really see the difference."

Most of the ingredients are aimed at improving our alkaline soil, though Epsom salts reportedly helps make basal breaks—new growth from the base of the plant. (Makes enough for one rosebush.)

- 1 cup gypsum
- 1 tablespoon soil sulfur
- 1 tablespoon chelated iron
- 1 tablespoon magnesium sulfate (sold as Epsom salts at pharmacies)

Mix, then scatter around the base of the bush and rake into the soil. Rain and irrigation will do the rest. Try it right after pruning and a dormant oil spraying.

THE NEW "ROMANTIC ROSES"

For charm and fragrance, it's hard to beat the Austin, or English, roses, which are finally becoming more common at nurseries. These remarkable roses, developed in the last 30 years by David Austin in England, seek to combine the frilly elegance and soft colors of antique roses with the vigor, disease-resistance and repeat blooming characteristics of modern roses, on plants that have a naturally bushy shape—plants that many gardeners find more attractive than hybrid teas mixed with other flowers, perennials in particular.

Their lineage, though always complex, includes classic old roses, such as Gallica and Portland, and more modern hybrid teas or floribundas, such as 'Iceberg' and 'New Dawn'. Though David Austin classifies them as English roses, one aficionado, Sharon Van Enoo, thinks they should be called "romantic roses." Van Enoo may have a good idea—other, similar roses are on the way from France (such as 'Yves Piaget'), and the French are bound to take exception to calling them English! But nobody can argue that they are romantic, evoking an earlier era in gardens.

Other than their classification and a charming demeanor, the various English roses have very little in common with one another. They grow to a great variety of heights and widths, from a couple of feet to more than 10, at least in our climate. The shape of the flowers, even the way the flowers are held on the bush, can be antique or more modern in appearance. Some flowers nod on supple stems; others are quite upright. Some are many-petaled; some are seductively simple with few petals. Disease resistance varies greatly.

Most gardeners know that roses often grow quite differently on the coast than they do inland, where the summers are hotter and drier and the bushes get so much bigger. That's why I asked Clair Martin, curator of rose collections at the Huntington Botanical Gardens in San Marino, and Van Enoo, who gardens in Torrance's coastal climate, for their suggestions—between them, they have grown almost all of the English roses. Since these are shrubby or arching plants, most are as wide, or even wider, than they are tall, so don't try spacing them as closely as similarly sized modern roses. Also, don't expect them to be as easy to grow as the modern hybrid teas and floribundas—they are

---

SMALL AUSTIN ROSES

These English roses are small enough for the typical garden
(three to four feet tall).

'Ambridge Rose' (peach)
'Belle Story' (a lovely silvery pink)
'Bow Bells' (goblet-shaped pink
  blooms)
'English Garden' (apricot)
'Fair Bianca' (white)
'Francine Austin' (white)
'Hero' (pink)
'Pretty Jessica' (pink)

'Prospero' (deep crimson)
'Sharifa Asma' (pink with a hint
  of yellow)
'The Nun' (white)
'The Squire' (crimson red)
'Symphony' (yellow)
'Tamora' (apricot)
'Wise Portia' (dark purple-red)

---

a little more challenging—but those recommended here should behave themselves.

For her list of favorites, Van Enoo chooses the smaller bushes that grow to about three feet on the coast, staying away from any she observed getting mildew. Of the newer English roses, she likes 'Bow Bells', with its sprays of goblet-shaped pink blooms; 'Sharifa Asma', pink with a hint of yellow at the petal base; 'Tradescant', a decidedly old-fashioned rose that fades from a wine red to a sultry purple-red, and 'Symphony', with sprays of bright yellow rosettes—one of her favorites.

Of the older, easier-to-find Austins, she likes 'The Squire', a "great crimson red" with a powerful old-rose scent and consistent repeat bloom; 'Belle Story', a simple, delicate pink flushed with yellow; 'Pretty Jessica', a many-petaled "fluffy" pink; 'The Nun', which "looks like a white tulip"; 'Francine Austin', with masses of smaller, white pompon flowers, and 'Heritage', a pearl-pink classic that gets a little larger than the rest at four to five feet, maybe even six.

Clair Martin grows the English roses on a grand scale at the Huntington as well as at his own home. He suggests tall and short English roses.

The shorter kinds, at about three feet, are just about the right size for the average garden. He likes 'Tamora', with its strong fragrance (he put in a 65-plant hedge at the Huntington), even though its delicate apricot flowers are "kind of modern." He likes the similarly sized peachy 'Ambridge Rose', 'Prospero' (deep crimson flowers), 'Wise Portia' (dark purple-red), 'Fair Bianca' (white), 'English Garden' (apricot), 'Pretty Jessica' (pink), 'Hero' (pink) and 'Belle Story' (a lovely silvery pink).

The best of all English roses, even though it was one of the first,

The best of all English roses, even though it was one of the first, Clair Martin says, is 'Mary Rose'.

he says, is 'Mary Rose', a ruffled pink that grows to four or five feet inland. He also likes 'Symphony', which, inland, grows to three to five feet and tolerates extreme heat (the first year, the initial blossoms opened on a 100°-plus day in spring), and 'Charlotte', with soft yellow flowers, growing to five or six feet.

'Lilian Austin' is a more modern color, a sort of salmon pink, with more modern growth, but it is distinctly shrubby, growing about three feet tall but spreading to up to six feet. 'Emily', "a really sweet [soft] pink," is another favorite with complicated flowers composed of round petals on the outside and a dense whorl inside; it gets to about six feet. 'Charles Rennie Mackintosh' (a famous art nouveau architect and designer) is a grayish lilac-pink that blooms even when the heat has turned everything else off; it grows to about four or five feet. He also likes the new wine-red 'Tradescant', but says it grows to six or more feet inland. He's taken to training it on a small trellis.

Martin has developed a way to deal with the taller Austins that is a little like the old-fashioned technique of pegging. He ties the tall ones—such as 'Graham Thomas', which can tower to 10 feet—back onto themselves. That is, the tallest canes are bent into an arch, and then the tips are tied about halfway down the same canes with soft green plastic tape. (Martin cautions that this is a two-person job, one to bend and another to tie.) The plant responds by throwing lots of short flowering branches all along its length, much like a climber. He also cuts some of the canes at different heights so blooms come all along the plant. The result is spectacular.

A visit to the rose garden at the Huntington at this time of year, when plants are nearly leafless, will make it easier for you to see how this is done.

Martin's book "English Roses in Southern California," available at Hortus in Pasadena, describes most of the other English roses and suggests care. "David Austin's English Roses," by David Austin (Little, Brown and Company, Boston), contains glorious photographs of most English roses, though the advice and the eventual sizes given are based on Austin's experiences in England, not Southern California.

More nurseries are carrying at least a few English roses. Some mail-order catalogues offer them, but you'll find the greatest variety at the huge Arena Rose Company, P.O. Box 3570, Paso Robles, CA 93447, (888) 466-7434; www.arenaroses.com.

February

YOU'LL BE GLAD YOU PLANTED SUMMER BULBS EARLY

JUST WHEN YOU THOUGHT YOU'D PUT THE LAST BULB of the season in the ground (as they had better be), along come the gladiolus. Gladiolus have their own season: They are planted in winter and spring (not in fall), the earlier the better if you want to avoid a tiny critter called a thrips. Thrips are so small they are almost invisible, but their damage isn't. They thrive in warm weather, and the warmer the weather (when gladiolus bloom), the worse the damage. In spring, leaves may simply be stippled and striped; in early summer, flowers may be blotchy and freckled, and in late summer, flowers may not even open. There is, by the way, no such thing as a thrip, only thrips.

Plant gladiolus now between the rains, and you may never see a thrips, even with a hand lens. Should you run into trouble, you can spray, repeatedly, with Orthene or diazinon, but it is better to avoid them altogether.

This month, nurseries are well stocked with gladiolus. And you also have a once-a-year opportunity to buy bulbs at bargain prices: The Southern California Gladiolus Society holds its bulb sale at The Arboretum of Los Angeles County in Arcadia; call *(626) 821-3222* for the dates and times.

At nurseries, or at the sale, you will find several sizes of glads, some called miniatures. Let me warn you: No gladiolus is small, much less miniature. A so-called miniature glad grows three to four feet tall, while a regular glad grows to four or five feet. The first time I planted miniature glads, I put them up front in the flower bed because I thought they'd be short. They ended up rising over the flower bed like the Sears Tower over the Illinois prairie. *Miniature* refers to the size of the flowers, which are somewhat smaller—though still large by most flowers' standards.

Put some glads in now, some two weeks later and so on, and you'll spread out the harvest of flowers.

If you've had trouble keeping these large-flowered plants from falling over, you are not alone. As a solution, gladiolus growers suggest planting regular bulbs six inches deep and miniature bulbs three inches deep. This is deeper than gardening books recommend, but the flowers won't need staking. One of those bulb planters that look like an oversize cookie cutter is helpful here.

Space regular glads six inches apart and the smaller ones four inches apart. Adding fertilizer to the planting holes isn't necessary. I was surprised that even gladiolus enthusiasts—who regularly enter their flowers in shows—fertilize very lightly only after the plants are about a foot tall, and then again as the buds form. They do consider watering extremely important, however, suggesting an inch of water every week.

Unlike most bulbs, gladiolus bloom about two-and-a-half months after planting, no matter when you plant them. So make a succession of plantings. Put some glads in now, some two weeks later and so on, and you'll spread out the harvest of flowers. Just don't plant too late, or you run up against those thrips.

While browsing my local nursery one February, I realized that many other bulbs are for sale at this time. Called summer bulbs by some (because they flower in summer instead of spring), they are planted in winter or spring, rather than in fall. You will find boxes and bags filled with them at nurseries about now.

Some are so spectacular in flower that I have always suspected they must be impossible to grow, so I never tried. Not so, says Don E. Christensen, of the Davids & Royston Bulb Company, a grower and wholesaler. In his Pasadena garden, he finds that some of these summer bulbs will even naturalize—gardener's jargon for going wild in the garden—so easy are they.

Perhaps the most spectacular is the gloriosa lily, a vining plant that makes shocking red and yellow lily-like flowers. It is, in fact, a lily (in the *Liliaceae* family) native to India and Africa. It will climb whatever is nearby, or you can let it clamber up a stake. Growing about three feet tall, it won't overwhelm its host.

Tubers are shaped like a boomerang, and, according to Christensen, both ends are growth tips. Plant this one horizontally, not up and down, in a hole four inches deep, in good soil, in full sun. "One commercial grower in Pomona grows his where the temperatures reach 106°," says Christensen. "So it can obviously take the heat."

Expect the gloriosa lily to move a little each year. After each season new tubers form, and where there was one plant there will be two a little farther away (but not more than six inches). Yes, this spectacular flower will naturalize, dying down each winter, but coming back for summer.

Equally sensational, bordering on ostentatious, is the tiger flower, or tigridia, a true bulb native to Mexico (bulbs at nurseries are commercially grown in Northern California). Its big, four-inch flowers come in a startling variety of vivid colors, most speckled or marked in the throat. Although they last but a day, the plant, which grows to about two-and-a-half to three feet tall, "throws them continually," says Christensen.

Plant each bulb in a hole four inches deep, Christensen recommends, to help support the tall stems. Again, good soil and full sun suit tigridia. When it first sprouts, don't weed it out by mistake—the new foliage looks like a sprouting palm seed (a common weed in some gardens).

Tuberose, tigridia, and gloriosa lilies are three summer-blooming bulbs that look difficult but aren't.

To see tigridia in full flower, visit Descanso Gardens in La Cañada Flintridge in July or August. Former director George Lewis finds that if the first flowers are cut in July, more will form and bloom in August. Make the cuts about six inches down the stem at a leaf joint, or axil. He says also that planting low-growing flowers over the tigridia planting will provide color in between its flowering times.

Bulbs go completely dormant for the winter. And once planted, Lewis says, "they will be with you for a lifetime." How about that?

Another bulb I thought difficult that becomes quite at home in the garden.

Well, if those two are so easy, surely the powerfully fragrant tuberoses are more difficult. Nope, these too can naturalize. However, they may skip blooming for a year to build up strength for the next time, says Southern California bulb expert George Harmon Scott in his book "Bulbs: How to Select, Grow and Enjoy" (H.P. Books, Los Angeles).

There are two kinds of tuberoses, both white. 'Mexican Single' has simple, single flowers and looks a lot like stephanotis, though it is even more fragrant. 'The Pearl' is a double-flowered form. Bulbs are grown here commercially, though most bulbs come from Arkansas and Florida.

Plant these odd-looking, elongated bulbs in holes about six inches deep, in good soil and full sun. Christensen offers a secret to growing tuberoses: Don't let them dry out once the flower buds form. Expect them to bloom late in summer, in August. If you go on vacation, make sure someone waters while you're gone.

The Peruvian daffodil, or sea daffodil (*Hymenocallis*), is yet another summer bulb that naturalizes here. It does look somewhat like a daffodil, but one that has been working out at the gym (both are in the amaryllis family). The flowers are much bigger, fragrant and white, or yellow in the variety 'Sulphur Queen', and they are borne on sturdy stems about two feet tall. The leaves, however, can be a little floppy.

Plant each bulb in a hole about two inches deep with the very top of the neck just out of the ground. Again, full sun and good soil suit the Peruvian daffodil.

Give all of these summer bulbs regular waterings in summer—don't let them go dry. Some are native to an interesting area in Mexico with a climate the exact opposite of ours—it rains in summer and it's dry in winter. Keep this need for water in mind when planting, and make sure to plant them with other flowers that require summer water.

WATCH OUT FOR COLD WEATHER

In Southern California good gardeners learn to expect occasional frosts and have some kind of plan ready. Killing frosts usually occur right after a storm passes through. Though it might feel coldest during a wind, the real cold descends when the wind stops. That is why citrus growers use those big wind machines—if they keep the air moving it won't get as cold.

Cold air is much like water in that it seeks the lowest spot. In your own garden, look for the low parts that are open to the sky— with nothing overhead—and you have found the coldest spots. If you garden on a slope, the cold will roll to the very bottom, and if it encounters a fence or other obstruction, it will become impounded, just like water, and damage any plants there.

For this same reason, plants that are low to the ground are more likely to be damaged than those up off the ground. And plants just outside the eaves of the house are likely to be damaged from the cold air rolling off the roof. Under the eaves where they are protected is, in fact, a good place to put plants likely to suffer frost damage, especially on the south wall of the house where warmth from the day is likely to last into the night. A patio roof or even a tree overhead is usually enough to protect plants from light frosts, so this is where to move tender portable things like cactus, bromeliads and orchids on those very cold nights.

How do you know that the cold is coming? Weather forecasts often include agricultural frost warnings, so that is one place to look. Those who must know can buy a little weather radio—such as those sold at Radio Shack—which is permanently tuned to the National Weather Service stations that regularly broadcast frost warnings in winter.

The next best thing is to watch the weather pattern yourself: When it has been cold and suddenly also becomes very still, be prepared. Just before going to bed, check the thermometer to see whether it is getting colder than usual.

When a frost is expected, cover the larger frost-sensitive plants that cannot be moved. Old sheets are my preferred covering. Though plastic sheeting works fine, you must be sure to take it off the moment the sun comes up or it will act like a hot house and cook the plant. An old sheet can be left on longer with no ill effects. You don't have to

Cold air is much like water in that it seeks the lowest spot.

worry about the wind blowing these coverings off—if there is wind, there will not be hard frost.

If plants do get damaged, do nothing, for now. Do not prune them back. And don't attempt to revive them; be careful not to over-water, since they have little use for the stuff in their present state.

Most plants will probably survive, but you won't know for sure until spring. In late March or April, when they begin to resprout, prune off any damaged wood that shows no sign of growth. If you prune sooner, you will only encourage the plant to start growing again, and that new growth is particularly vulnerable to frost of any kind. If there is no sign of recovery by late April, you have lost the plant. Replace it at that time.

RAINED OUT?
WHAT TO DO WHEN IT POURS

What do gardeners do when their weekend ends up wet? I, for one, put on my rubber boots and head outside. Sometimes it seems that only small children and gardeners really appreciate rain—and this month we're bound to get some. Even in the driest years, rain is likely in February; it is historically our wettest month.

The rubber boots are no joke. I have a huge pair that I use for gardening on wet days, or on those muddy days that follow. They sit

right outside the back door so, like a fireman, I can jump into them at a moment's notice. Since we don't get all that much rain, I confess they aren't used very often, but they are fun to wear and do help put one in a wintry frame of mind.

Properly attired, I first make sure water is running down the downspouts. I don't want it pouring out of the gutters and washing away the soil around any plants underneath. Los Angeles designer Robert Cornell, who has lost calla lilies and azaleas during past record storms, suggests also that you drain any planted areas that have standing water, which can suffocate roots. Like the Army Corps of Engineers in miniature, dig little trenches so the water can flow away.

A wet stroll through the garden (staying out of the flower beds) can be very informative. Wherever there are puddles, there is a drainage problem. I make a mental note to do something about it in fairer weather, either by improving the soil so the water can sink in faster or by making it possible for the rainwater to move along in the direction of the street. One rainy year, for instance, I discovered that the entire center of one garden bed had become a puddle. I then realized that was why I had trouble growing things there. In drier weather, I added organic matter to the soil and mounded it up a little so it was no longer low ground. Things have been growing happily ever since.

Check to make sure that raindrops are not weighing down any flower spikes, like those of stock and tall snapdragons. If flowers are threatening to fall flat on their faces, quickly tie them to stakes. I always keep short bamboo stakes handy at this time of year.

Take out the indoor plants—if it is actually raining and not too blustery or too cold. In Southern California, tap water tends to be full of mineral salts. When these salts accumulate in potting soil from repeated watering, they can stunt growth or turn the leaf tips brown. A good soaking of rainwater washes them out the drainage hole. It also cleanses dust from the foliage.

An important rainy day rule: Stay out of the flower beds until they have had a little time to dry.

This is true for garden plants as well. Heavy rains push harmful mineral salts below plants' roots. But they can also wash away soluble fertilizers. So, if it has rained a lot—say, several inches in a few days—you may want to fertilize growing plants again after the soil dries a bit. Light rains, however, help move fertilizers down to the roots. Many gardeners fertilize just before a rain to take advantage of this.

I like to fill up all of my watering cans with rainwater from the downspout (first I let the rain wash all the dirt and pollutants off the roof). Stockpiling the salt-free rainwater to use later on sensitive plants, such as orchids, is almost as satisfying as stacking up firewood in the fall.

An important rainy day rule: Stay out of the flower beds until they have had a little time to dry—usually a few days, or in clay soils a week or more. If you go tramping through the beds, especially in big boots, you compact the soil, squeezing all the soil particles together, which will then exclude air and water once the soil dries. In other words, you'll undo whatever effort you have put into improving the porosity of the soil.

If you must step into a garden bed, say, to tie up a snapdragon, lay a board in there to stand on. It will help disperse the weight. For this purpose I keep a 12-by-12-inch square of plywood right next to my boots. Where I must step into the larger beds fairly often, I've put single, ornamental stepping stones. Nearly invisible buried under spreading plants, they are very handy on wet days, and after watering the garden.

Go ahead and buy your bare-root roses, if you haven't already. But wait to plant until your soil no longer sticks to the garden spade. In a sandy soil, drying out may take only a few days; in clay soils, perhaps a week or even two. Make sure the soil is crumbly, or you will be planting your new rose in a wet gumbo, "and the rose will not be able to breathe for the rest of its life," says Tom Carruth, horticulturist at Weeks Roses in Upland.

If you buy packaged roses, immediately take them out of their wrappings and put them in a bucket or five-gallon nursery can. Then cover the roots loosely with the sawdust they were packed with and keep moist (or leave the bucket out in the rain).

Carruth suggests a radical way of storing bare-root roses and fruit trees for long, rainy periods: Completely submerge dormant plants in water, in a trash can or some other deep container; if plants have already leafed out, submerge only the roots. They can stay this way, he says, for several weeks. After planting, pinch off the tips of any growth that has leafed out. If it is elongated or bleached from lack of light, snap it off at the base, and other buds will sprout.

On rainy days, be sure to allow time for soaking up the wet, dark vision of the garden. Although I may be doing so from under the eaves, snug and dry in my rubber boots, it gives me pleasure to see the plants enjoying the rain as much as I am.

IS IT SPRING ALREADY?

I f you step outside at this time of year and are very quiet, you can probably hear the first sigh of spring. In another week or two you will see the first signs as well, or perhaps you already have. It is definitely in the air. Deciduous magnolias and evergreen pears are blooming, and the Los Angeles city tree, the orange-red kaffirboom coral tree, is coming into full flower. Early azaleas, camellias and abutilons are in bloom, as are New Zealand tea trees. The ornamental oxalis 'Grand Duchess' is also in full flower, and freesias are ready to pop.

In typical California fashion, not everything is on the same timetable, of course. Fruit trees are completely dormant, some bulbs are just pushing out of the ground, and roses have just begun to leaf out. Most of the perennials are looking nice and plump but are still only growing—flowers are a ways off yet.

Much of this is the result of fall planting. But the opportunities to plant are still with us. Right now, for instance, is the perfect time to plant deciduous magnolias and New Zealand tea trees. In fact, this may be just about the only time of year nurseries carry a good selection, since they tend to stock them only when the plants are in flower.

The New Zealand tea tree (*Leptospermum scoparium*) is worthy of special note. Blooming heavily for several months in winter and early spring and sporadically at other times, the flowers look much like tiny fruit-tree blossoms, and, as with fruit trees, they carpet the ground after they fall. Plants are full and bushy but airy in appearance, with foliage a little like rosemary but more prickly. Though they easily grow to eight feet, you can keep them pruned to about six. The flowers come on new growth, so summer pruning actually encourages more flowers in winter. Do not hack away at them with hedge shears, however. Instead, prune out entire branches to reduce the whole without losing any of the graceful, airy look.

Yellow flax (*Reinwardtia indica*) is another remarkable plant, with delightful flowers blooming bright at this darkish time of year. The flowers, sunny trumpets of yellow, bloom the length of the stems. A low, shrubby perennial (to about three feet), yellow flax is a rare plant but easy to grow. At least one source has them on occasion: Hawthorne Nursery [*4519 W. El Segundo Blvd., Hawthorne (310) 676-8242*].

Two other excellent choices for planting now are primroses and pansies, both of which will flower into summer. Primroses—the multicolored English types, the fairy primrose and the stocky *Primula obconica*—are the perfect replacements for impatiens that didn't make it through the cold. All primroses do best in partial shade, just like the impatiens, and, here in Southern California, are best replanted every year, though they are technically perennials. Pansies are perfect for those bare spots out in full sun. No bare spots in the place? Both are also great in containers.

LIST OF LAST-MINUTE SPRING FLOWERS

It's not too late to plant these bedding flowers:

Anemone
'Bloomingdale'
  ranunculus
Delphinium
Foxglove
Iceland poppy
Nemesia
Pansy
Primrose
Stock
Sweet William, or any
  other annual dianthus

Some swear that Iceland poppies are best planted at this time of year, because the delicate flowers of the fall-planted poppies blooming now can be shattered by winter storms. Those planted now will skirt that problem. Start the gorgeous blue and purple cinerarias now, or wait until March, because even the hint of frost will blacken them.

Fertilize all spring flowers already in the ground again.

Prune fruit trees, if you didn't get around to it before—they can be pruned even in full flower. Put the trimmings in the house in a vase. If you haven't already pruned your roses, do so right away. Don't worry about pruning off some new sprouts in the process—the rose will produce more and do just fine.

A GOOD TIME TO PLANT DELPHINIUMS

Delphiniums are true garden aristocrats—strong vertical shapes that tower above everything else, in colors that are most regal, including that most precious of garden colors, true blue. No wonder some of the favorite strains have names like 'King Arthur', 'Guinevere' and 'Galahad'.

Delphiniums would probably be in every garden if it were not for their reputation as being difficult to grow. If you know but a few delphinium secrets, however, they are not. For instance, did you know  that delphiniums are not light-sensitive? Ken Dorwin, with Hi-Mark Nursery in Carpinteria, a wholesale grower, tells me this bit of information, which means they can be planted at any time, in the middle of summer or the dead of winter. The best flowers come on plants that do their early growing when it is fairly cool, but flowers will bloom in any weather, just on shorter spikes. Now is one of the most favored delphinium-planting seasons, because they will bloom in late April or May, in harmony with so many other flowers that also flower in late spring.

Did you know that there are full-sized delphiniums and compacts? Though there are many kinds, the two types most commonly available are the 'Giant Pacific' strain (more properly, the 'Pacific' strain) and the 'Fountains' strain. The 'Giant Pacific' strain lives up to its name by growing to five or six feet, even eight on occasion. Spikes

WEEK 8

are fat and full, or should be. The 'Fountains' strain (sometimes labeled 'Dwarf Fountains' or 'Blue Fountains') grows much shorter, from three to four feet tall, sometimes even less. These too should have fat, full spikes, but don't always.

The reason plants are not always as they should be is that they are now grown from seed that is open-pollinated in fields and so do not always come true to type. Many years ago, the 'Giant Pacific' plants were as uniform as corn in a field, but then they were hand-pollinated and carefully selected for their seed. Dorwin, who used to work with Frank Reinelt, the originator of the 'Pacific' strain, notes that flowers now are not always double so the spikes look less full; that the height is no longer uniform, and that often they aren't even the color they are supposed to be. Still, there are few flowers that make such a spectacle in the garden.

The 'Giant Pacific' strain is actually a group name for several individual strains, and each group is supposed to be the same color. For instance, plants labeled 'Galahad' are all supposed to be white; 'Black Knight', dark purple; 'Summer Skies', blue with white "bees" (centers), and 'Blue Bird' should be pure blue. But since these are strains, they will not be identical, just similar. You may find them simply identified as a mix, which means they could be any of these colors, and probably will be.

The 'Fountains' strain also has its faults. Seed growers are working to develop better strains, and in time a new dwarf strain should become available as bedding plants.

The variability of the 'Giant Pacific' strain may change for the better in the near future. Dorwin is busy trying to redo the 'Pacific' strain. He is also working with *Delphinium zalil*, a yellow species, and *Delphinium cardinale*, a red, in an effort to get a strain that includes red and yellow (the Swiss have already produced some small red and yellow strains, but they are not commercially available).

In California we grow delphiniums only from seed-started plants—seedlings—not from root divisions, as most are on the East Coast and in England. Despite the fact that delphiniums are perennials, and that some are native to California, garden types grow poorly as perennials here, so are best replanted every year—from plants begun from seed. This is important to know because you shouldn't waste time trying to keep the plants alive for more than a year (though some lucky gardeners have), and you must expect some variability among the plants you buy. You certainly do not want to throw money away on plants purchased from mail-order growers back east. They seldom thrive here.

Delphiniums like more water than most flowers. Here I can pass along a trick developed by nurserywoman Pamela Ingram, of Sassafras Nursery in Topanga: Add polymers to the soil that goes back in the planting hole. Looking a lot like coarse salt, polymers (the most commonly available is Broadleaf P4) increase the soil's water-holding capacity, soaking up water and storing it for the plant's use. In other words, you can provide the delphiniums with more water without watering them more often, and without drowning other plants in the vicinity.

You can probably guess from their size that delphiniums need lots of fertilizer, and they do—another secret of success. The easy way to provide it is with a slow-release fertilizer, Osmocote being the best known. As the package points out, this kind of fertilizer slowly releases the nutrients to the plants for as many as 120 days, so the delphiniums get nourished constantly. Be prepared for a little expense here—Osmocote and Broadleaf P4 are expensive, high-tech products, but in this case worth every cent.

At the nursery, find plants that have not yet made spikes. At this time of year, plants in four-inch pots are the best bet, plants from packs are better earlier in the year, and plants in gallon cans are only for those in a real hurry (the size of their spikes will disappoint you).

Here's how you might plant your delphiniums this year, using this new knowledge. A few hours before planting, soak the polymers in a can of water, so they have time to swell. Select a sunny spot with the best soil in the garden (or thoroughly prepare a garden bed by digging in organic amendments until a rich soil results). Working in moist, not wet, soil, dig one hole at a time about eight inches deep and across. (Dorwin tells me that delphiniums have fairly shallow roots, but a deep hole lets you add the fertilizer and polymers so they will be beneath the roots.) Put the soil you dig out of the hole in a big plastic bucket or basin. Add several handfuls of an organic amendment, such as Kellogg's Gromulch, and mix it in thoroughly, breaking up any clods as you go. Partially refill the hole with this amended soil until it is full enough to support the size plant you are working with.

Now add a handful of the already saturated polymers and a teaspoon of Osmocote, and mix these into the bottom of the hole. Lightly press this soil down with your hands, unpot the delphinium and plant, adding the rest of the soil and firming it around the plant.

Space 'Giant Pacific' plants 12 to 14 inches apart, 'Fountains' 10 to 12 inches apart. When all the plants are in, water thoroughly. Make

You can probably guess from their size that delphiniums need lots of fertilizer.

sure plants don't dry out even for a moment during the first few weeks—this gives them time to find those polymers. This all may sound complicated, but it isn't and work progresses quickly.

If you are growing 'Giant Pacific', there is one more thing to do, what the late George de Gennaro, who grew magnificent delphiniums, called "rule number one": Immediately after planting, put in sturdy six-foot-tall stakes to support the flowers. The delphiniums are going to need them as soon as they begin to shoot up (tie them to the stake as they grow), and you had best be prepared (and you do not want to damage roots or leaves by shoving in stakes later on).

When delphiniums finish blooming, cut the spikes back, leaving only two leaves at the base, and scatter a granular fertilizer over the bed. In a few weeks, they will make new sprouts and begin a second cycle of flowering, though this time the spikes will be smaller if more numerous. If you plant now, the first bloom will come in late spring and the second in summer.

I like to think of delphiniums as the church steeples in a village of other flowers.

I like to think of delphiniums as the church steeples in a village of other flowers, and it doesn't take many to make a statement. I plant them in small groups of five. Try them with lower, bushy flowers, such as Shasta daisies (which can be planted now and will bloom with the delphiniums), coreopsis or just about any other perennial. They are equally elegant behind annual bedding plants. You will not be disappointed, and you will probably never again consider planting flowers without the royal company of delphiniums.

SNAIL ATTACK ALERT

With everything beginning to grow furiously toward spring, it's time to be on the alert for snails, which become much more active as the weather warms. Watch new plants, especially seedlings, very closely.

Make a snail trap from a piece of one-by-12-inch board. Crush snails on the underside to lure others in.

In my own garden opossums seem to have won the war against snails, if not slugs. The cat's food on the back porch attracted them, but they stayed on to eat all the snails. At night I could hear their crunching, and, once I realized what it was, it became music to this gardener's ears.

If you're still fighting the war, try some of the latest defense technologies. Deploy copper strips, for example. "The snails and slugs receive a mild shock that deters them from proceeding when their skin comes into contact with copper," says one catalogue in describing the copper strips called Snail Barr, available from several sources including Peaceful Valley Farm Supply, P.O. Box 2209, Grass Valley, CA 95945, *(530) 272-4769*; www.groworganic.com. (The shock is delivered by natural ground currents–no batteries required.) Wrapped around the trunks of trees, the strips keep snails out of citrus and other trees, as long as no branch touches the ground, which would only give the snails a ladder to scale. Connect strips end to end, or buy 100-foot rolls to make a Maginot Line around tender seedlings.

Another strategy: Enlist mercenaries, such as the famed predator, or decollate, snails. It was once believed that these snails seek out ordinary garden snails and destroy them with single-mindedness. The latest word, though, is that they simply occupy the same niche in the garden, eating the competition or pushing them out. That is, they replace the garden snails, even slugs, in the local ecology. If they ate the same things, or as much, they would be no better than the garden snails. But because they are scavengers (they eat all sorts of things), they do much less damage to your plants, though they have been known to eat a tender seedling or two. Unfortunately, snail bait also works on decollate snails, so you have to stop baiting. One mail-order source is Buena Biosystems in Santa Paula; call *(805) 525-2525*.

You can also ambush snails with traps. The University of California favors this method of snail eradication, and Dr. Ted Fisher of UC Riverside gets the credit for inventing it. Build the trap from an ordinary one-by-12-inch board, about 15 inches long. At each end, nail on a one-by-two-inch piece of lumber, on edge. These hold the board just above the ground. Now comes the part difficult for the squeamish. Rub crushed snails on the trap's underside—the carnage attracts other snails. Place the trap in a shady, damp area near where snails are feeding. Every five or six days, pick up the trap to see what you have lured, and crush those snails, thoroughly, because maggots breed inside decaying snail shells.

Between the decollate snails, the copper defense works and the sneaky traps, you can vanquish the enemy. And by not using poisonous baits, you win the war while still abiding by the Geneva Convention.

THREE EASY WINTER-FLOWERING ORCHIDS

T hat so many orchids are in flower in the middle of winter always surprises me. But three easy-to-grow orchids do: cymbidiums, moth orchids and lady's slipper orchids. Cymbidiums, the most abundant at nurseries, are the easiest, growing best outside and taking considerable cold, even down to 28°. For the most flowers, at the nursery look for large, strong, well-rooted, even pot-bound plants.

Earl Ross, the orchid specialist at The Arboretum of Los Angeles County in Arcadia, provides the secret to growing them: Give them enough light in early winter, before they flower. This is a tall order, since cymbidiums that get enough light look as though they are getting too much. Their foliage should be yellowish—*not* a dark healthy-looking green—which in any other plant is a sign of trouble.

The ideal situation for cymbidiums is under shade cloth (the arboretum uses one that screens out 55% of the sunlight), because while they need bright light, they prefer it somewhat filtered. Under trees is not a good place—unless they are deciduous in winter and not too dark when leafed-out in summer. Many cymbidium growers, especially near the coast, grow them in full sun in winter (November to March) and then shade them somewhat in summer.

Fertilize cymbidiums, and any orchids in pots, every month with a complete liquid fertilizer, and keep them moist all the time. Do not be in a hurry to repot should they seem to outgrow their containers—that will most likely keep them from blooming for a couple of years.

Orchids can be tricky as indoor plants. Almost all orchids need good air movement (that is why you always see fans in orchid greenhouses) and humidity. Furnaces dry the air in winter, while air conditioners dry it even more in summer. Trays filled with pebbles and water, misting the foliage and other means of providing humidity really don't work.

The answer is to keep orchids only in the kitchen or the bathroom, the two most moisture-laden rooms in the house. That's one place you can grow the two other orchids blooming now, the moth

Cymbidium foliage should be yellowish—not a dark healthy-looking green—which in any other plant is a sign of trouble.

orchids (*Phalaenopsis*) and lady's slipper orchids (*Paphiopedilum*), both of which are among the best choices for indoor orchids.

Grow lady's slippers, or "paphs," as they are called by orchid people, on a north-facing windowsill, in the bath or kitchen. A greenhouse window that faces north in the bath or kitchen is the perfect spot. Most window-mounted greenhouses, however, seem to face the sun. Covering them with shade cloth—on the outside—makes them more habitable for orchids and other plants. The shade cloth should screen out about 70 percent of the sun.

Lady's slippers also do surprisingly well outdoors as well—to look at them you would think them impossible. Their flowers are most elaborate and appear to be made of fragile wax that might melt at any moment. But they are quite durable. Outdoors, lady's slipper orchids need shade—just look at their dark green foliage—and will grow with as little as 700 to 900 foot-candles of light, which is pretty dark and one reason they do well indoors.

A north-facing windowsill will work for the moth orchids, so-called because their flowers look like dainty moths hovering over the plant. These will not grow outdoors because they do not like it hotter than 95°, or colder than 65°. But since most people keep their homes within this temperature range, they do well indoors. In the right place in the house, moth orchids are one of the easiest to grow, but remember they too need humidity and bright light, but no direct sun.

Do-It-Yourself D.G.

Decomposed granite may be only a step above ordinary dirt, but this humblest of paving materials is seen in some very grand gardens—from the golden estates of the 1920s by designers such as Florence Yoch to the most contemporary gardens by designers such as Nancy Goslee Power (who plans to use decomposed granite paths around the new Walt Disney concert hall in downtown Los Angeles).

Landscape designers and contractors call it "d.g.," and it is an inexpensive, gritty, crumbly, over-the-hill mineral that tends to stick together when compressed. They love it because it looks so indigenous to the garden, and they use it for paths and patios, even driveways, anywhere the look of a country road or wilderness trail is desired. It's even

WEEK **9**

tough enough to be used for equestrian trails.

In the Los Angeles area, most d.g. is an earthy yellow ocher, the color of our hills. Nancy Boswell, of Mid City Granite in Los Angeles (a large supplier to contractors and building supply yards), tells me that their d.g. is dug right out of the Hollywood Hills—it's no wonder that the soft golden color looks right at home in our gardens. There are other colors: In the Central Valley, contractors use a gray d.g. from the Sierra, and a redder color comes from Arizona.

But can you do it yourself? The answer is: Nothing could be easier, according to contractors I talked to. A wheelbarrow, shovel, rake and a lawn roller are all you need (you can rent the lawn roller, sometimes even at a local nursery). Another plus: "It's considerably cheaper than concrete, or just about anything else," says Jerry Collins, a grading contractor in Tulare. Another contractor suggests that it is three to four times cheaper than concrete.

Nothing could be easier. A wheelbarrow, shovel, rake and a lawn roller are all you need.

Pacific Palisades contractor Joan Booke has used it in elegant Brentwood gardens, on terraces in Silver Lake and for driveways in Topanga (for driveways, it must be thicker). She likes it so much she used it in her own garden, brought in by the wheelbarrow load. The natural-looking paths wind their way through the garden giving her easy access to all the flowering perennials she grows.

You can plant right through d.g. (simply clear a little away), which really gives it that country lane look, with plants popping up in a path or the patio as they would in nature. Weeds, on the other hand, are slow to sprout in compacted d.g. If they do, simply hoe them out. Collins, who uses a lot of d.g., says, "Nothing will grow through three to four inches of d.g., except maybe Bermuda grass."

Booke has replaced many Bermuda-grass lawns with d.g. paths and patios. She doesn't even bother to kill the lawn first (though the very cautious might first kill Bermuda grass with the herbicide Roundup). Instead, she removes about four inches of soil and sod and replaces it with three inches of d.g. This usually brings the thatch-fattened soil profile back down to where it ought to be.

D.g. is best on flat, level ground, and where it doesn't get watered by sprinklers, which causes erosion. "It is not a permanent hardscape," says Booke. "It does require refurbishing every few years." To do so, you just add a little more. (The fact that it is not permanent can be seen as another plus: You can change your mind later on.) Rain and sprinklers cause most of the wear and tear. "Don't ever put a path under a downspout or where water can roll off the roof and down the path," Booke says. A hard downpour will make ruts.

Another reason not to put d.g. near sprinklers: Dry d.g. tends to stay put. When wet, though, grains stick to shoes (some kinds are worse than others because they contain more clay), but it does not get muddy. "You probably won't like d.g. if you have white carpets," says Booke. To keep it out of the house, end the d.g. paving before the house, at a patio, for instance, or a landing.

Contractors can make d.g. very firm with an organic soil binder called Stabilizer, but usually they don't. Booke used Stabilizer on the Topanga Canyon driveway because it wasn't level. A very few building supply yards sell Stabilizer by the bag, or sell d.g. already mixed with it; for more information, call the manufacturer at *(800) 336-2468*.

So how do you do it yourself? Simply remove about three inches of soil, lay down three inches of d.g., wet it, roll it with a lawn roller, wet it again and roll again. That's all there is to it, according to Booke. The rolling compacts the d.g. so it becomes almost like stone again. Contractor Collins, however, simply lays d.g. on top of the ground (he doesn't excavate) after first compacting the soil with a roller and raking it flat. He then likes to "crown" the paths so they're a little higher in the middle, better to shed rainfall. Use a lawn rake to tidy it up, or a wispy Japanese broom, as Booke does.

Paths and patios look best if the d.g. simply melds into the garden soil. Contrived edgings ruin the effect of a natural path through the garden, though some designers use similarly colored stones at the edges of paths.

You can buy d.g. by the bag (about $3), or the cubic yard (about $30). A cubic yard will cover 120 square feet three inches deep. A skip load (about 10 cubic feet) dumped into your pickup or delivered, covers about 40 square feet, three inches deep, and costs about $10. That will fill a large contractors' wheelbarrow at least two or three times and make a path four feet wide by 10 feet long, all for 10 bucks. For covering ground, there's not much you can buy that is as dirt-cheap.

GOOD OL' OXALIS, THE GARDENER'S CONSTANT COMPANION

The most persistent weed in California gardens must be oxalis. People look at me in disbelief when I tell them that, at various times, I have eliminated most weeds from my garden. But I have never vanquished oxalis. If you are unfamiliar with this weed, you simply don't know it by its proper name. Many call it clover because of the similar leaf. But this "clover" has little yellow flowers; true clover has bushy, bristly pink and lavender ones.

The observant gardener has probably noticed that there are at least three distinct kinds of oxalis. One is very pretty, sending up big, bright yellow, buttercup-like flowers. *Oxalis pes-caprae* grows from bulbs deep underground so nothing you do to the top will effect it for more than a season. It will be back unless you dig the deep bulbs out of the ground.

Much more common is *Oxalis corniculata*, which spreads on above-ground runners that root as they go. A variety of this, *Oxalis corniculata atropurpurea*, has leaves that are usually a purplish red. Leaves on the variety tend to be flat, while leaves on the other tend to flair back. Both have small yellow flowers.

These two are the ones you will never be rid of. They grow in sun or shade; taller in shade, low and flat in the sun. The variety *atropurpurea* comes up every time you water from what must be millions of seeds that persist in the garden for what must be generations. They are best done in with a hoe and will not usually come back from the roots, but the next watering will bring up a new crop. In my garden, plain old *Oxalis corniculata* is the worst because it spreads through all kinds of low-growing plants. It has probably caused more work in the garden than everything else combined. Give it a week or two, and it will so intertwine itself with small plants that you can get rid of it only by pulling out the plant it has invaded—by starting over.

Oxalis corniculata and O. c. atropurpurea— these two are the ones you will never be rid of.

To weed it out you must be diligent and eagle-eyed. When you spot the leaves, follow them back to the runner and follow that back to the main clump of roots, carefully uprooting as you go. This would be impossible were it not for the fact that the runners are often reddish so you can see them, if you look carefully, among the green of the plant it has invaded. But that's the only break this plant will give you.

It is constructed cleverly; the runners are very fragile near where they root. So pull too hard, and they break off leaving the roots and the rest of the plant in the ground and you holding but one of the many runners. Also, you must act before they set seed because simply touching the plant will cause the seed pods to explode, sending seed everywhere. At some times of the year you can hear them popping in the garden, scattering seed.

Oxalis, members of the *Oxalidaceae* family, are good at being weeds because they are native to just about everywhere in the world. *Oxalis pes-caprae* is native to South Africa, which has a climate very similar to ours, though this oxalis has the common name Bermuda buttercup because it is a weed of great stature there. Pesky *Oxalis corniculata* is native to Europe, though it has been a cosmopolitan weed for so long that no one knows quite where in Europe it originated. It goes under the common name of creeping oxalis.

Irish shamrock is an oxalis (*Oxalis acetosella*), though it is native to Japan and much of Asia as well. *Oxalis deppei*, native to Mexico, is called the good-luck plant, or the lucky clover, because it has four leaflets. Even the remote Falkland Islands are not safe from oxalis. Scurvy grass is the common name of *Oxalis enneaphylla*, which grows there and saved many a sailor on a trip around the Horn.

For generations, hikers have chewed on wood sorrel (*Oxalis oregana*), an oxalis native to California's woods. And I don't know how anyone could call something with clover-like leaves a grass, but children in Southern California call *Oxalis pes-caprae* sour grass and like to chew on the sweet-sour leaves, a practice that will do them no harm.

Convinced of the indomitability and universality of oxalis? Well, how about an oxalis that grows to six feet and is native to Chile, or a succulent oxalis (*Oxalis herrerae*) native to Peru? Oxalis grows on mountaintop and desert floor, forest and beach—and in the garden.

I wish I could tell you some easy, surefire way to get rid of oxalis, but I can't. *Oxalis pes-caprae* has bulbs so deep you need a shovel, not a trowel, to get them out; the other two must be pulled or hoed. In lawns you can use herbicides made to take oxalis and other broadleafed plants out of grasses (they are often sold mixed with fertilizer granules; ask at a nursery), but elsewhere it's hands-and-knees stuff.

SPRING

N O DOUBT ABOUT IT, SPRING HAS ARRIVED. Take a look outside. All over town, fruit trees are flowering, bulbs are up and out of the ground—some are already in full flower. Soon the whole garden will be in bloom. Spring can last a long time in Southern California, beginning early and often overlapping our rainy season, then lingering into summer. In a typical year, expect (and hope for) some rain in March with snow on the mountains, look forward to the clearest skies in April, and be prepared for weeks of overcast in May and June. Late spring can be gloomy, except that under those high clouds, spring's pink, lavender and other pastel flowers look their brightest and the fresh greens seem to glow in the soft, gray light.

You can be very busy in the garden, planting all sorts of things. And there's always a little maintenance to do—fertilizing, pruning and, of course, weeding. But if you've taken full advantage of the autumn months, and with the days getting longer, there is plenty of time to sit and enjoy the flowers of your labor (fruits come later).

If you're quick about it, you can still do some last-minute planting of spring bedding flowers. Try using the four-inch, or quart, pots that have spring flowers already in bloom. The problem with waiting this late is that flowers planted now bloom later, and that in turn postpones the spring planting of summer flowers, such as marigolds and zinnias, so they too end up planted too late. It quickly becomes a vicious cycle, with spring flowers delaying summer flowers and summer's delaying spring's so things never flower when they should.

My advice: Wait until late March or April and plant summer flowers at the right time.

Still another tack is to plant perennials, since they do exceptionally well planted now. They will flower later in spring and summer,

WHAT TO PLANT DURING THE WARM SEASON (APRIL TO JULY)

FLOWERS

These are annuals best started from seed:

Portulaca
Sweet alyssum
Zinnia

These are annuals and bedding plants best started from nursery packs:

Ageratum
Amaranthus
Aster (annual kind)
Balsam
Bedding begonia*
Candytuft
Celosia
Chrysanthemum paludosum
Coleus*
Cosmos
Bedding dahlia
Gloriosa daisy
Impatiens*
Lobelia
Marigold
Nasturtium
Petunia
Annual phlox
Verbena
Vinca rosea
  (*Catharanthus*)

Most perennials can be planted in early spring, but these are most likely to flower through summer, or in early fall:

Agapanthus
Chrysanthemum
Coreopsis
Daylily
Dusty miller
Gaillardia
Gayfeather (*Liatris*)
Gazania
Gerbera
Japanese anemone*
Nicotiana
Border penstemon
Bedding salvia
  (*Salvia farinacea*)
Tulbaghia
Yarrow (*Achillea*)

BULBS

Plant these in early spring for summer bloom:

Caladium*
Gladiolus
Gloriosa lily
Tigridia
Tuberose
Peruvian daffodil

VEGETABLES

Plant these now for summer harvests:

Basil
Snap and lima bean
Beet
Carrot
Chayote
Corn
Cucumber
Endive
Leaf lettuce
Melon
New Zealand spinach
Onion
Parsnip
Pepper
Pumpkin
Radish
Salsify
Summer and winter
  squash
Sunflower
Swiss chard
Tomato
Turnip
Watermelon

LAWNS

Spring is the best time to start lawns from seed; install sod at any time. Sow tall fescue and other cool-season grasses soon. Wait until the weather gets warmer in May or June to start Bermuda or other warm-season grass from seed.

LANDSCAPE PLANTS

You can plant just about anything now, though autumn is generally the better season. Late spring, in May or June, is the best time to put in those things that are frost-sensitive, such as hibiscus and bougainvillea, citrus and avocado.

* will grow in a fair amount of shade

and some even flower in fall. Or try marigolds and petunias, two summer flowers that seem to do best planted in early spring.

It's possible to undertake big landscaping projects, but any trees, shrubs or ground covers will need a lot of water this summer. Fall is really the better time. If you are up to the constant watering, however, or have everything under sprinklers, you can plant at almost any time.

Lawns are one permanent part of the garden that are best planted in spring—fescues and other cool-season grasses in early spring, and Bermuda and other warm-season grasses in late spring.

Fertilize everything in early spring, especially those things that are growing so furiously, and your spring flowers, even those in bloom. The best way is with a liquid fertilizer high in nitrogen.

Most gardeners prune now, finding it impossible to stop with just the roses, moving right on through the garden with the shears looking for more subjects—fuchsias, hibiscus, even azaleas and camellias in bloom (put the cut flowers and stems in a vase). Pruning now will least effect the present look of the plants, since most are just beginning to make the new year's growth.

Finally, spruce up the garden and get out all those little weeds that are vulnerable now. Spring is the time that the garden should look its neatest—moist, cultivated, fertilized, planted, pruned and weed-free—a proper setting for all the flowers blooming now.

March

AZALEAS AND CAMELLIAS

W E ARE RIGHT IN THE MIDDLE, ALMOST TO the day, of azalea and camellia season. The first began blooming back in December and the last will finish up in June. Unlike most plants, azaleas and camellias are perhaps best planted while in flower, or just before, because as soon as they stop flowering, they start growing.

Camellias seem happiest on the east side of a house, though they will also grow on the north, or in the shade of trees, or even in some sun. The Southern Indica azaleas like sun; the Belgian Indicas prefer shade. Even out in Azusa, the wholesale Monrovia Nursery Company grows the one in full sun on a hillside, the other under shade cloth. Kurume and Satsuki azaleas like some sun, even if it is only dappled through a tree.

WEEK **10**

Preparation of the soil before planting needs to be more thorough with azaleas than with camellias. Both prefer a soil that is similar to that found on a forest floor—neutral or slightly acidic and full of humus. Changing our naturally alkaline soils is not easy, but adding lots of organic amendments is a start. These amendments, sold by the bag at nurseries, are usually made from specially treated sawdust or finely ground bark. Some enthusiasts prefer peat moss, the most acidic amendment, but be careful—once it dries, it is hard to wet again.

For azaleas, add as much as 50 percent by volume of amendments to the soil. If you dig up the soil to a depth of 10 inches, add a five-inch layer of amendment on top, and then mix it together with the soil so one can't be distinguished from the other. That's a lot of amendment, but it is a conservative amount—some experts recommend adding two-thirds amendment to one-third soil. Camellias need less soil amendment; in a good soil they may need none, but most camellia fans add about one-third amendment to two-thirds soil. For either, if you want only to fix the soil in the planting hole, make the hole double the size of the plant's container.

When you're finished, the soil will be fluffed up and considerably higher than when you started. This is good. Azaleas and camellias so like a raised position in the garden that some gardeners grow them only in raised beds or on mounds. When you plant, make sure that the top of the rootball sticks out of the ground—so it is about an inch higher. Water them often in this fluffy soil, but don't overdo it. Tom Nuccio, of Nuccio's Nurseries in Altadena, one of the leading growers of azaleas and camellias, says that overwatering is the number-one killer of both plants. There is no hard-and-fast rule, but once plants are established let the soil partially dry between waterings.

In time, you will discover that the camellias need less and less attention. Camellias, in fact, become tough and treelike with great age. They are even somewhat drought tolerant, as camellias growing on their own in vacant lots demonstrate. Azaleas, however, may start to decline. Help them along by continuing to work on the alkaline soil. Always fertilize them with an acid-type fertilizer (usually labeled for azaleas and camellias), and keep a two-inch-thick mulch of organic matter on top of the soil (but be careful not to bury the trunk or base of the plant). A thick mulch is also recommended for camellias, though is not crucial.

In winter it is natural for most azaleas to lose leaves. Some, such as the common 'Fielder's White', lose a lot. The leaves first turn yellow then fall. If leaves turn yellow but the veins remain green, the plant probably needs iron, a more acid soil or more fertilizer. First try cultivating in iron sulfate or iron chelate (both at nurseries), or use a liquid form of iron and spray it on the foliage. Next try fertilizing.

If that doesn't work, consider digging them up, redoing the soil and then replanting—the benefits of the initial soil preparation have probably worn out. This sounds radical, but it has worked wonders for many azaleas. Should they be too big to lift, you may simply have to start over again. Nuccio suggests digging around and even under

When you plant azaleas and camellias, make sure that the top of the rootball sticks out of the ground— so it is about an inch higher.

them, improving this soil, then packing the soil back in.

Those long branches that shoot up from azaleas are typical. Simply cut them back to match the rest of the plant.

What about camellia buds or flowers that turn brown and sticky, or buds that dry out? Most gardeners blame these symptoms on camellia petal blight. But, according to Nuccio, the dropping of buds can be varietal (some kinds, such as 'Pink Perfection', do it, others don't), or it can be brought on by the weather—Santa Ana winds or rain. Some camellias will bull nose—the petals stick together, the bud looks wet and shiny and never opens. Overhead watering with sprinklers may be the cause, or it may just be the variety or the weather.

Dried brown buds can also be varietal, or cultural. It usually happens on plants that are not happy with their care or environment. Flowers that turn brown may just be old or getting too much sun. This often happens on plants that have outgrown their shady locations and now grow up in the sun.

If camellia flowers become heavy with water, turn to mush (test by rubbing the petals between your fingers) and the veins in the petals become darker than their surroundings, then you have camellia petal blight. According to Dr. Art McCain, a UC Cooperative Extension plant pathologist, there really are no sensible chemical controls, although some books recommend that PCNB be applied to the ground in winter, or that benomyl be sprayed on the flowers "nearly every day."

The only real control is cultural. The mushrooms that cause this disease sprout from fallen decaying blossoms. So pick up every blossom from the ground, rake up all leaves and mulch, and put it all in the green waste container on trash day. Even this is not surefire, because the mushroom spores can drift back in the wind, but give it a shot.

Incidentally, Sasanqua camellias, which bloom much earlier in the year, do not get petal blight. Though the flowers are smaller and the plants stiffer, some, such as the pinkish white 'Little Pearl', are a spectacle in full flower.

EUGENIA PSYLLIDS AND SUBS

G ood news: Eugenia plants and hedges may soon return to their normal healthy states. A control for the minuscule psyllids that curl and buckle eugenia foliage has been found in Australia and imported to California. An almost invisible wasp (don't worry, it doesn't sting humans)—less than 1.5mm long, so smaller than the psyllid—preys exclusively on this aphid-like creature, *Trioza eugeniae*.

If you have been spraying with the expensive Mavrik (the chemical name is fluvalinate)—found to do a better job of controlling the eugenia psyllid than the often-recommended Orthene (though it too does a good job)—this might be the time to stop, since the sprays kill the wasps as well. Sprays work for only about eight weeks, while the wasp will permanently keep the psyllids under control. They will never eliminate the pests, but they will so decimate them that their damage is barely noticeable. Reducing psyllid populations also lessens the black sooty mold that grows on the pest's sugary excretions.

One good thing that came out of the psyllid nightmare was the rediscovery of other suitable narrow hedges, substitutes, of a sort, for eugenias, although nothing grows as tall and stays as narrow, with or without the handsome reddish foliage. According to several nursery people, good old privet may be the best hedge choice if speed of growth is all important. The plain species of wax-leaf, or Japanese, privet (*Ligustrum japonicum*), and not one of the shorter cultivars (such as 'Texanum'), grows the tallest and remains the narrowest, though it requires regular shearing to even come close to a eugenia's skinny silhouette. It does tolerate some shade (as does eugenia); leaves are glossy dark green.

Other suggestions include the narrow, long-lived *Pittosporum eugenioides* with wavy medium green leaves, which works inland but is not recommended near the coast. *Prunus caroliniana*, which does best in coastal areas, also stays reasonably narrow (allow four to five feet) if regularly pruned. Foliage is a handsome glossy green, and it is fairly quick to grow to eight feet.

If speed of growth is not so important, consider what one nursery person calls the "prettiest plant for the property line," *Podocarpus macrophyllus*. Even better is the slower but denser and more upright variety *Podocarpus macrophyllus maki*. Shear both to keep them narrow.

> One good thing that came out of the psyllid nightmare was the rediscovery of other suitable narrow hedges.

INSTANT COLOR

It looks like April already at nurseries, thanks to what nursery people call quart color. Quart-sized containers, also called four-inch pots, are the preferred size for flowers that have grown enough to already have buds or blossoms. If you didn't get around to planting flowers in the fall for spring bloom, and the garden is looking a little bare of color, quart pots might save the day. They cost more than smaller plants in packs or flats, but the results are almost instant, guaranteeing a colorful spring. "For those getting a late start on spring, this is the way to catch up," says Lew Whitney, of Roger's Gardens in Corona del Mar, where many colorful beds are kept that way with quart color.

Flowers planted from quart pots will not last as long, grow as big or flower as much as the same plants do when started young, but they can come pretty close. Small plants started back in the autumn months have had the time to grow big, healthy root systems. To help the quart-sized contenders catch up, give them a better soil. "These plants have been pampered by the grower, with lots of fertilizer and a good potting soil," says Whitney. "The trick is to pamper them in the garden as well." He suggests spending a little extra time preparing the soil, so the plants will find their new garden soil as good as the soil they've become accustomed to.

WEEK

11

One way to do this is to fluff up the soil with organic soil amendment, or planting mix (not potting soil or mix), so it is nearly as porous and rich as potting soil. Armstrong Organic Planting Mix and Mulch, Bandini Soil Builder and Kellogg's Gromulch are such products. Spread a two-inch layer on top of the garden bed, and sprinkle on an all-purpose granular fertilizer. Thoroughly mix it into the top six inches of soil, making sure that there are no clods of dirt or clumps of amendment. In a heavy clay soil, you might want to add even more organic amendment and a dusting of gypsum, which helps break up California's clay soils.

Now you can plant. Some suggest *not* untangling any circling roots or root masses near the bottom of the containers, as you usually would. After the plants are in the ground, immediately water each one individually at its base with some kind of watering wand, thoroughly soaking the rootball, even if the surrounding soil already looks moist enough. "When those roots begin to grow, you want them to find happy sur-

BEST BETS TO PLANT NOW FROM QUART POTS

Anemone
'Bloomingdale' ranunculus
Delphinium
English primrose
Foxglove
Iceland poppy
Nemesia
Pansy
Stock
Sweet William and other annual dianthus

AFTER PLANTING: A FINAL CHECKLIST

Here is a checklist I use of things to do after planting anything, from a quart pot to a gallon can, before I turn on the sprinklers and get everything muddy. If I've made a mistake, I can still carefully dig up the plant and reposition it. Believe me, I've done that more than a few times.

🌿 *Did I leave enough room between plants?*
Often I don't leave nearly enough room. This question forces me to stand back and honestly appraise the situation. At this point I can dig them up and space them a little farther apart.

🌿 *Are the plants going to be growing in sun or shade?*
This is especially important at this time of year when the sun is still low. Some spots are going to become shady as the sun climbs in spring. Conversely, some spots in shade are going to get much hotter and sunnier.

🌿 *Do the plants have the same water requirements?*
I want to avoid planting things that need lots of water next to those that need little because one or the other is going to suffer.

🌿 *Do their colors go together?*
If not, I move them.

🌿 *Can they be easily watered?*
This reminds me to build basins around shrubs that are going to need deeper, more thorough irrigations (by hand, with a bubbler or watering wand) and prompts me to check sprinklers or drip emitters, or to make sure I have some method of watering.

---

roundings fast so they don't stop flowering or growing," says Whitney. To keep them going, he suggests, fertilize two weeks after planting and then every two weeks thereafter, and water on a regular basis.

When choosing quart pots at the nursery, Whitney says, "look for those that have only buds or flowers that are just beginning to open. These will last the longest. To make sure the plants have not become potbound, tap them out of their container and check to see if the roots have become too tangled or matted. Potbound annuals are not a good bet." It is easy to turn the plant sideways and let the root-ball slide out of the container to look, cradling the plant in your fingers, and just as easy to slide it back in.

You can plant almost anything that blooms in the spring—those things that are usually fall planted—but some do better than others started this late. Even ranunculus, usually planted as bulbs, are a possibility if you find the 'Bloomingdale' strain, developed just for quart pots. So it's not yet too late to plant spring's brightest flowers, from quart pots.

FERTILIZER FACTS

If you do nothing else in March, fertilize. You can actually see it take effect at this time of year. Lawns, for instance, turn greener overnight and seem to grow a couple of inches. Spring flowers seem to double in size and immediately burst into bloom. Shrubs get greener, grow taller and look happier. Fruit trees set an enormous amount of fruit and, in the case of citrus, lose that yellowish cast they had all winter.

To many, fertilizing is a great mystery, which is not too surprising if you compare it to feeding a baby or a cat. Except for plants growing in containers, plants are already being fed by the soil, so what you are really doing is supplementing their diet. In the average soil, they will grow fine without any fertilizer, but fertilizing (which is really the proper term, not feeding) makes them bigger and better.

Buying a fertilizer is confusing at best—so many kinds are sold on nursery shelves. According to an article in the April, 1984, issue of *Sunset* magazine, there were no fewer than 169 different kinds of fertilizers available on the West Coast back then. The article proved what some gardeners have suspected for a long time: Fertilizer is fertilizer, and a lot of what you see at nurseries is just packaging.

The label of a package of fertilizer, by law, must list what's in it—the percentage of nitrogen, phosphorous (phosphoric acid), potassium (potash) and perhaps some other elements (such as iron), called micronutrients, or trace elements. The percentages of the three major elements, however, are listed in big numbers, such as 20-10-10, on the front of the package.

From left to right, the numbers on a fertilizer package tell you the percentage of nitrogen, phosphorus and potassium.

An old gardeners' rule says that you must use a fertilizer high in nitrogen to encourage growth (such as a 20-5-5), then switch to one low in nitrogen but high in phosphorous and potassium to encourage flowers (such as 0-10-10). In fact, this simply isn't true. For the *Sunset* article, the University of California tested many kinds and found that, at least in California's soils, only nitrogen makes a difference in the size and quantity of flowers and fruit.

It turns out that it isn't really possible to add potassium or phosphorous to the alkaline soils of the west, at least from above ground. These elements simply can't move down to where the roots are. Only nitrogen moves easily through the soil, so easily that rain and watering quickly wash it out. This is why you have to fertilize in March, after the rains, and preferably several times during the growing season, if you want better than average growth, flowers or fruit.

The exact numbers on the label are not that important—there is not much difference between a 10-6-6 and a 12-4-2. What is important is the first number, how much nitrogen there is, which determines whether that fertilizer is a good buy or not. A fertilizer very high in nitrogen (such as ammonium sulfate at 21 percent) is the best buy, but it can be tricky to use because too much of it can chemically burn plants (just be sure to follow label directions carefully). I use ammonium sulfate on lawns and flowers.

The all-purpose fertilizers, with numbers such as 8-8-4, or 14-14-14, I use with some indiscretion because they're not as strong. I add these to the soil at planting time because that is the only way to get phosphorous and potassium near the roots. In this case, too, I buy the cheapest. My preference is a so-called organic, or natural, fertilizer such as cottonseed meal because it works slowly and is best when dug into the soil. At other times, I simply scatter an all-purpose chemical fertilizer around the plants and then thoroughly water to get the nitrogen down to the roots.

How about special fertilizers such as those for citrus, roses and acid-loving plants? In a nutshell, only a fertilizer for acid-loving plants offers any advantages over other fertilizers. However, citrus fertilizer probably contains more micronutrients than other fertilizers, which citrus often need, but these are not usually required on a regular basis. Interestingly, according to the *Sunset* article, the acid-type fertilizer turns out to be useful in that it helps potassium and phosphorous work their way down into the soil by making it less alkaline. Drilling holes in the ground and adding these two nutrients, or better yet, mixing them in at planting time, would appear to do the same thing.

Containers, however, are a different matter. Because there is often no natural soil in potting mix, plants are more dependent on fertilizer, which is why I fertilize pots once a month and why I use a soluble, high-nitrogen fertilizer that must be mixed with water. A number of these are available (Miracle-Gro and Peters are two), and almost all are very high in nitrogen with numbers such as 23-19-17, 23-15-18 or 20-20-20. Some also contain many micronutrients, essential for long-term container growing.

I also use these fertilizers in winter and at this time of year to give plants a quick boost. They tend to be high in nitrate nitrogen, which is the form that goes to work the fastest. Others forms such as ammoniacal and urea work slower but last longer. Soluble fertilizers are also expensive, and applying them is not as easy as simply scattering granules about.

There is one other type of fertilizer I use. Slow-release fertilizers, purchased as tabs, stakes or little pellets that look like cheap caviar, let a little fertilizer out at a time. They are useful in containers and under certain plants that I want to make sure never go hungry. For instance, I bury a little in the bottom of every planting hole I dig for delphiniums. Osmocote is one that is readily available.

If you're still confused, remember this sentence from the *Sunset* article: "We can say that since phosphorous, potassium and micronutrients don't need to be added to the soil frequently, the only element you should provide with regular fertilizing is nitrogen."

TIME TO PLANT PERENNIALS

On my calendar next to the month of March I have "Plant perennials" written in big red letters. This is because I have such great success planting them at this time of year. True, they can be planted in the fall, winter or spring, but in March they waste no time in becoming something. They grow fast and strong and seem to bloom almost instantly. Equally important: Perennials are in good supply at nurseries now, and that is not always the case.

They do not do this growing all on their own. I spend a great deal of time and effort preparing the soil, digging it up and mixing in organic amendments and handfuls of organic fertilizer. I water quite often for the first month. The peak of flowering comes in May—a glorious month for perennials—and continues into June. I make sure also to plant perennials that will bloom in summer and even in early fall.

Once established, they take little work; I fertilize every couple of months and water about once a week or less; farther inland, gardeners must water more often. Perennials tend to need less water than most annuals and certainly less than lawns, which is one reason I converted part of my lawn to an

WEEK

12

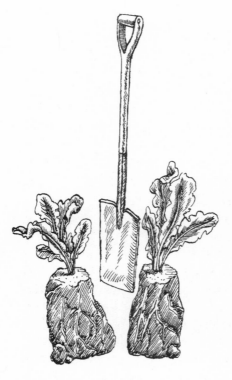

expanded perennial bed.

For the uninitiated, what are called perennials in California are plants that live longer—more or less—than annuals, but are not quite as sturdy or woody as shrubs. They are valued for the variety of shapes and colors they add with their flowers or their dramatic foliage. The true, or herbaceous, perennials are commonly grown in England and on the East Coast, where they die completely to the ground each winter. Here, we also grow many plants called perennials that are actually something else, most often small shrubs, or sub-shrubs. In addition, we grow some perennials as though they were annuals, planting them each year and pulling them out at the end of their season because they do better treated that way.

True herbaceous perennials grow as spreading clumps of stems and roots and can be divided into individual plants, by pulling or splitting

Most herbaceous perennials need to be cut back and, in time, divided. Phrases such as "when to cut back" and "how to divide" intimidate many gardeners. But you can learn these techniques by trial and error—most perennials are very forgiving. They come from climates where, to survive winter, they die to the ground. In the mild California garden, though, they may not, and we cut them back instead, much like we stick tulip bulbs in the refrigerator to simulate winter. The champion tool for cutting back perennials is actually made for edging the lawn—the Corona GS 6750 shear, formerly their No. 5—long and hefty enough to cut a bunch of stems at once.

Be aware that not all perennials sold as such should be cut back to the ground this way. Those that are not herbaceous perennials are usually just tidied up. If you're in doubt, leave the plant in question alone and see if it dies back or not, or if it needs partial cutting back because it gets ratty looking or overgrown, or nearly leafless as some of the salvias do.

Division is necessary for most herbaceous perennials because they grow as spreading clumps. Look closely at a herbaceous perennial, such as a veronica, and you will see that what appears to be one plant is actually a number of smaller plants growing together. As they grow ever wider, they so totally deplete the soil beneath them that the center of the clump declines. At this point, dig it up and then either pull the clump apart or slice it apart with a sharp spade, or even a big serrated kitchen knife. Most serious perennial gardeners keep a flat-bladed spade sharpened with a coarse bastard file just for this purpose. The old center of the clump is usually discarded and the younger outer growth divided into smaller pieces and replanted. Extra divisions can be given away—most gardeners get pretty good at swapping their extras with others who might have some perennial they covet. Most of this dividing (and the swapping) occurs during winter.

Because perennials use a soil so heavily, it is very important to thoroughly prepare it before planting. The idea is to make the soil as rich as possible by adding fertilizer and organic amendments (the kind sold by the bag at nurseries, usually a mix of specially treated barks and sawdusts) or, best of all, homemade compost. Mix these in with a spade, spading fork or a tiller. The result is a fluffy, rich soil that will sustain perennials for a number of years. When it is time to dig and divide, renew the soil with still more organic material and fertilizer before you replant.

A well-prepared soil is also a lot easier to dig in, so the perennials are easier to dig up and divide, or just move about. This is one advantage of using perennials. If you don't like how they look where they are, or if they get too tall, dig them up and move them somewhere else (save this job for winter). Most of the good gardeners I know do this regularly with perennials, as they hone the composition of their perennial borders.

How you mix perennials into some sort of scheme is a matter of taste, but I'll pass along a plan that works for me. In my perennial beds, I always include roses. I think they look better mixed with other flowers (so you can't see the bare, thorny lower branches), and they bloom so often that they help carry the show should most of the perennials be temporarily out of bloom.

The basic rules I follow are:
- Never plant fewer than three or five of anything.
- Let one part of the color spectrum predominate.
- Vary the heights.
- Buy a variety of plants that flower at different times of the year.
- Make sure the bed is deep (or wide) enough.

In one bed in my garden, I used three English roses to anchor the plantings, then planted three or five of each perennial. In most cases, there is no point buying just one—it will not make enough of an impact. A plant that appears at one end of the garden and reappears somewhere at the other end helps provide a sense of continuity, and the repetition adds to the impact. If you don't use roses as anchors, use some kind of permanent plant with a bushy shape, even a small shrub. For instance, in the shade, use azaleas, though you must be careful with azalea colors, since they often don't go with the typical perennial hues.

The colors in this border are all from the blue-red end of the spectrum—reds, pinks, blues, lavenders and purples. Another scheme is to use only yellows, oranges and purples. Many gardeners more expert than I think that there are only these two color groups and that one should not be mixed with the other, except as an accent. In this particular pastel bed, I did use a few soft yellow perennials as accents, which enliven the scheme. Don't forget foliage color: Many perennials have leaves as handsome as the flowers. Gray foliage in particular adds much to the look of a perennial garden.

Before shopping and planting, it might be helpful to use colored pencils to plan your perennial garden on paper. Let one inch equal one foot, then draw shapes of the approximate sizes, in the appropriate colors, and see how everything may look together.

In my beds, not all tall plants go in the back; a few choice ones (the delphiniums and a few alstroemerias in this case) move up front. This adds the feeling of depth, increasing the drama. In general, however, the plants get taller toward the back.

I did not try to fit all of this into a narrow little space. I had to dig up two feet of lawn to get the necessary six feet of width; another foot would have been even better. The wider the bed the more opportunity you have to stage the plants and the more variety you can fit in. It allows you to plant things that bloom at various times, one in front of the other.

This brings up one other rule I try to follow: Don't buy plants that are in full flower only in spring. If you do, you will end up with plants that flower all at the same time and then stop. To prolong the show, shop at other times of the year to see what's blooming. I also make sure to leave room for annuals and bulbs. And herbs add fragrance and look right at home.

There's no doubt in my mind that the real bargains at nurseries now are the perennials sold in four-inch pots, also called quart containers. These are the perfect size to start with, and, at about $2 each, there's no arguing about the price.

For what you might spend on a single large citrus or a couple of roses, you can buy an entire perennial border. Many of the perennials sold in four-inch pots are smallish, perfect for planting around roses, beside a path and even in paths or patios between the paving stones. A few are great shade plants, and all are just right for filling that empty hole in the garden.

I've probably planted hundreds of four-inch pots through the years, and just about every one has taken hold and grown quicker than any plant purchased in a gallon can (and you don't need to dig as big a hole). Because they are such a bargain, I sometimes get reckless and plant perennials I've never even heard of. If they don't work out (they're the wrong color, say, or grow too big or die), I just toss them out figuring I spent less than I did on that expensive bag of popcorn at the movies.

Here are a few of the perennials I've grown that would be foolish to buy in any container larger than a four-inch pot.

Achillea: All yarrows spread quickly from four-inch pots. Use them to add a little vertical color to the herb garden in spring and summer, or beside a path. Choose from those with silver or green foliage, or those with yellow, lavender or red flowers ('Paprika' is choice). They come in all heights—*Achillea tomentosa* is short enough to grow between stepping stones.

Adenophora: New to California gardens, these are relatives of the campanulas, with similar lilac-blue bells that seem to bloom all the time on stems two or more feet tall. Rapidly spreading to form colonies of low leaves, they can get a little rampant, but the foliage is only inches tall so not much of a problem.

Aegopodium: For the shade, this spreader grows only a foot tall with light green and cream leaves. It's great under roses and easy to pull out should it spread too far.

Armeria: Sea pinks make little cushions of narrow leaves, then send up spikes of globular pink flowers. Try them in front of roses or around paving.

Brachycome multifida: As dainty as a wildflower, this is the perennial version of the annual Swan River daisy with lilac flowers. A great foot-tall filler, it spreads to a foot across and blooms nearly all the time. Try it with roses and in paths.

Campanula: All the bellflowers are great from four-inch pots, whether they are the tall spire-like kinds or the creeping ground cov-

I've probably planted hundreds of four-inch pots, and just about every one has grown quicker than any plant purchased in a gallon can.

ers. Most have lavender or purple flowers, usually called "blue." Good around roses.

Candytuft: The perennial *Iberis* looks much like the annual—with low, dark green foliage and bright white flowers in spring and early summer. For the front row, and good with roses.

Centranthus: Also called valerian, this one is so tough it grows in vacant lots. Blue-green leaves make slowly spreading thickets three feet tall. White or rose flowers always seem in bloom. Looks sad in a four-inch pot but grows quickly.

Columbine (*Aquilegia*): Delicate, airy gray-green leaves and distinctive, usually spurred flowers. 'Grandmother's Garden' is decidedly old-fashioned, spurless and double. Most flower at two to three feet tall from a foot-tall clump of foliage. Despite the woodsy appearance, columbines need full sun. If plants look ragged by December, cut almost to the ground for a fresh start. Clumps cannot be divided, but last about three years.

Convolvulus mauritanicus: Small, lavender morning-glory-like flowers on a plant that stays under a foot tall but densely covers several feet of ground. Great around roses.

Coreopsis: Tough golden-yellow daisies bloom in late spring and summer. 'Sunray' has fully double flowers. Needs cutting back every winter and dividing in time.

Cotula: Very low growing with gray leaves and yellow button flowers, this spreads quickly to cover a square yard or more. *Cotula* 'Silver Mound' gets a foot across with feathery foliage.

Dianthus: Dainty carnation-like flowers on plants with gray foliage bloom mostly in spring. Plants are short-lived so buying them any larger is a waste of money. Some are extremely fragrant. Great around roses.

Diascia: These low-sprawling plants with spikes of coral or pink flowers ('Elliot's Variety' is the best pink I've grown) are great around roses. Technically a perennial, but I start with new plants every fall or early spring.

Erigeron karvinskianus: Santa Barbara daisies have small white flowers with a pink or lavender blush. The improved form, 'Moerheimii', has larger flowers. To keep tidy, shear into a ball every now and then.

Erodium and **Geranium:** True geraniums and the smaller erodiums are the best rose companions. Most go semidormant in winter and need tidying up then. A few go completely dormant.

Francoa ramosa: Makes clumps of fairly large leaves about two feet across in shade, with white flowers on graceful two to three foot stems in summer.

Heuchera: All the coral bells, with their tall, delicate flower spikes (mostly pinks and reds) and low clumps of foliage, do well around roses, or in some shade. 'Palace Purple' has handsome purplish foliage.

Lamium maculatum: A spreading mat of gray-green and white leaves sends up short spikes of pure pink flowers. Best in moist shade.

Liatris: Plant gayfeather now, and it will make tall spikes of orchid flowers by late summer or fall. Goes completely dormant in winter, so whack it back.

Nepeta: Though they never look as neat in California as they do in England, all the catmints are classic rose companions with floppy bluish flower spikes.

Origanum: Several ornamental oreganos stay low and flop about but have pretty sprays of lilac flowers all summer.

Physostegia: The plain purple species is so strong it can get out of hand, spreading underground (though it is easy to dig out), making mats of low leaves and flower spikes two to three feet tall in late summer.

NURSERIES SPECIALIZING IN PERENNIALS

- Sierra Azul Nursery, 2660 East Lake Ave., Watsonville, CA *(831) 763-0939*
- Turk Hessellund Nursery, 1255 Coast Village Road, Montecito, CA *(805) 969-5871*
- Sperling Nursery, 24660 Calabasas Rd., Calabasas, CA *(818) 591-9111*
- The Outdoor Room, 17311 Sunset Blvd., Pacific Palisades, CA *(310) 454-5252*
- Burkard Nurseries, 690 N. Orange Grove Blvd., Pasadena, CA *(626) 796-4355*
- San Gabriel Nursery, 632 S. San Gabriel Blvd., San Gabriel, CA *(626) 286-3782*
- Marina del Rey Garden Center, 13198 Mindanao Way, Marina del Rey, CA *(310) 823-5956*
- The Garden, 845 N. Garey Ave., Pomona, CA *(909) 629-2062*
- Brita's Old Town Gardens, 225 Main St., Seal Beach, CA *(562) 430-5019*
- Roger's Gardens, 2301 San Joaquin Hills Road., Corona del Mar, CA *(714) 640-5800*
- Laguna Hills Nursery, 25290 Jeronimo Road, Lake Forest, CA *(949) 830-5653*
- Buena Creek Gardens, 418 Buena Creek Road, San Marcos, CA *(760) 744-2810*
- Perennial Adventure, 10548 Anaheim Dr., La Mesa, CA *(619) 660-9631*

Prunella: Low, slowly spreading plants with handsome leaves and short spikes of purple or pink flowers. Good next to a path or around roses.

Purple coneflower (*Echinacea*): Perennial cousins of the gloriosa daisies, these grow three to four feet tall, though only half as wide, and carry purple flowers all summer and fall. 'White Swan' is a white-flowered form.

Rehmannia elata (also sold as ***Rehmannia angulata***): Rose-purple foxglove-like flowers on stems two to three feet tall, spring through summer. Forms two-foot clumps in time, spreading slowly underground. A good choice for shady spots.

Scabiosa: Several kinds are tall and good with roses and also good for cutting. I especially like the form with the creamy, slightly green flowers that go so well with everything, though one named 'Butterfly Blue' has the best flowers and blooms the longest. *Scabiosa farinosa* 'Crete' is different, making a dense, shiny two- or three-foot-wide mound of dark green foliage. It's good beside a path, though the flowers are less than exciting.

Shasta daisy: Clean white daisies on plants that can be as tall or as short as you like and bloom in June with agapanthus (a nice mix). 'Snow Lady' is a seed-grown strain only a foot tall. Others can get to three or four feet. Some, such as 'Marconi' and 'Esther Read', have frilly double flowers. All spread and form clumps that are best dug up and replanted every few years.

Stachys: The only way to plant lamb's ears—a wonderful low and spreading foreground for roses—is from four-inch pots. Needs to be dug up and restarted every few years.

Thalictrum: Meadow rues are tall lacy plants for the shade. Flowers are small and usually white.

Verbena rigida and ***Verbena bonariensis*:** Two useful, even exciting, spring and summer bloomers with vivid purple flowers. The former is short, does great in and along paths, and spreads but is easy to pull out. The latter flowers on very tall, skinny stems—a real eye-catcher. Both seed about but, in my garden, always come up in the right places.

Many other perennials are not sold, or are seldom sold, in four-inch pots, and probably wouldn't do well started that way. Examples are the floriferous alstroemerias, which no garden should be without, and *Veronica spicata*. And don't forget some of the most tried-and-true perennials—those that have been part of California gardens for so long that we hardly think of them as such: agapanthus, bergenia, bearded iris, calla lilies and daylilies, to mention just a few. Agapanthus, hard to grow anywhere outside of California, are a must because they absolutely astound any visiting English or eastern gardeners—an opportunity not to be missed.

DOES THE LAWN
NEED RENOVATING?

F all-planted flowers are coming into full bloom, deciduous trees are leafing out, shrubs are flowering, and the garden is beginning to look its best. Except for the lawn. The annual rye you tossed on top in the fall is fading fast, and all that is left are weeds—dandelions, clover, coarse grasses. The Bermuda grass and the Kikuyu—Southern California's two most common grasses—are present but struggling. Or perhaps this better describes your lawn: You have a thick stand of Bermuda or Kikuyu, so thick it is like a mattress, but each time you mow, all you have left is brown stubble.

Both conditions beg for renovation, which generally means revitalizing an existing lawn. Sometimes that is not enough, though, and replacement is called for, especially with old lawns (they don't live forever). First you must know what is growing out there—what your lawn is made up of. If it's a recently planted lawn, it may be a tall fescue, but most likely it's Bermuda or Kikuyu grass (or both mixed together!). These two warm-season grasses—they grow during warm weather—are spreading grasses that send out runners in all directions. In winter, they may go completely dormant, and that is where the practice of overseeding them with an annual winter grass, usually annual rye, comes from. The annual rye cosmetically covers the dormant grass from November through March.

WEEK

13

Bermuda and Kikuyu grasses should grow "low and close," according to Bob Cohen, of the Green Scene, a lawn care company in Tarzana that has serviced some 5,000 lawns in the last 20 years. Over time, however, these grasses may grow too tall so that when mowed only the brown bases of the plants remain. Renovation for a too-thick, too-cushiony lawn is straightforward, if you have the right equipment. A vertical mower, or dethatcher, rips out mounds of old runners and thatch and gives the lawn a fresh start. This machine can be rented, but make no mistake, it is a big job. Among other things, you'll end up with heaps of clippings. To have someone else do it, the cost may be $200 to $500 per thousand square feet of lawn, according to Cohen.

After renovation with a vertical mower, the lawn needs a good fertilizing and probably a pre-emergent herbicide to keep weeds from sprouting (crabgrass in particular). Two to three weeks later, the lawn is low, lush and green again. From then on it should be mowed at a height of about one inch for Bermuda and three-quarters of an inch for Kikuyu. The time to renovate a lawn this way is in spring, from late February into June.

For a lawn that is struggling along, full of weeds and dead spots, this kind of renovation may also be the ticket. But sometimes these problems point to conditions that do not suit the common Bermuda or Kikuyu, both of which need lots of sun and warmth. Perhaps trees have grown and are now shading more of the lawn; this is a case where the lawn may need to be replaced. But before you do that, says Cohen, "cooperate" with what's there. He suggests trying to get the existing grass to grow this spring and summer, with proper watering and fertilization, plus weed control, and perhaps dethatching. Then, by late summer, if things have not improved, consider killing off the old lawn and replacing these grasses with another perennial grass, most likely one of the modern, turf-type tall fescues that are doing so well in Southern California. Or St. Augustine if the yard has become too shady. It is the most shade-tolerant grass.

To kill off the existing grass, it costs, ballpark for a thousand square feet, about $45, and then $250 for a vertical mowing that rips most of it out (so the seed can come in contact with the soil), and then about $100 for the new seeding, fertilizing, weed control and soil conditioning. Do this in late summer or fall—at that time, when the warm-season grasses are actively growing, the herbicide (Roundup) works best, and the new lawn has the cooling days of fall and winter to look forward to.

You can also go deluxe: Have the soil tilled at that time and sod installed, for a total cost of about $1,000 for a thousand square feet. Interestingly, Cohen thinks most Southern California soils are just fine for lawns if properly watered and fertilized. He has seldom seen the need for aeration—the removal of plugs of soil to let water and air penetrate—or for adding organic soil amendments, though he says there are pockets of sandy soil that require the addition of organic matter (he favors peat moss), and he does add chemicals to loosen clay soils.

Improper watering, not clay soils, is a lawn's chief villain, Cohen says. His recommendations on watering are going to surprise a few people: Water Bermuda, Kikuyu and the tall-fescue lawns once a week near the coast, twice a week in the inland valleys during summer, less in spring and fall (bluegrass, not recommended for Southern California, is another story). However, the water must soak in at least six inches, and this means watering for long enough. If the water runs off, water for five minutes, turn it off for 15 minutes, then on for another five minutes, and so on, until the water has soaked deep into the soil, with little or no runoff. Then don't water for a week. If it gets really hot one afternoon, turn on the sprinklers for a minute to cool the grass off (this doesn't count as an irrigation). To further help the water soak in, try wetting agents such as Pentrex.

Improper watering, not clay soils, is a lawn's chief villain.

In fact, if neither of the descriptions above fits your lawn, but it still does poorly, you may be drowning your lawn, killing off beneficial bacteria and starving the roots for air. Try watering less often. Just make sure it soaks in.

GETTING LAWNS THROUGH A DROUGHT

A drought every now and then is inevitable in California. Most gardeners, when asked to save water during dry years, look no farther than the lawn. It's the obvious place to cut back. Even if you let it die, a lawn can be replanted when rains return and look good again almost immediately; not so with trees, shrubs or even roses. But you may need only to water less. "Most grasses have a 20 percent built-in buffer," Victor Gibeault, turf expert at UC Riverside, once told me. So water and fertilize 20 percent less than optimum; you will not notice the difference.

If we are in a drought, this far into the year is not the time to replace a lawn with something else, or to switch to a less-thirsty lawn grass. Wait for a rainy year and do it in the spring, or make the change in fall, gambling on the return of wet weather. The one exception might be trouble-prone bluegrass (if anyone still has a bluegrass lawn in Southern California), but only if it is to be replaced by a warm-season grass such as Bermuda grass. Surprisingly, Gibeault said, the latest findings show that the much-touted tall fescues can use as much water as bluegrass. However, and this is a big however, because they are tougher and have deeper roots, they can survive with less water, much less if necessary, though their appearance suffers.

Gibeault said that good old Bermuda grass is still the most thrifty grass for Southern California, despite its long winter dormancy. Warm-season lawns, which spread by stolons during the warm months of the year, are proven to use 15 to 50 percent less water than cool-season lawns. There are newer warm-season grasses, such as seashore paspalum, 'El Toro' zoysia and the buffalo grasses, but, said Gibeault, "Bermuda grass is still tops" for toughness and saving water. Except in the mature, shady garden. Here St. Augustine grass is probably best, though tall fescues and 'El Toro' have shown shade tolerance. Bermuda does not like shade at all.

Bermuda grass especially, but other grasses too, tends to build up a thick layer of thatch, and this makes watering difficult. If it gets thicker than a half to three-quarters inch, it repels water. This excess height can be removed with a vertical mower. At the same time, if you suspect that the soil under your lawn is dense and compacted, you might have it aerated, using a machine, seen on golf courses, that pulls out plugs of soil so water can penetrate.

Other measures you can take to save water are much simpler. Start by turning off automatic systems and watering only when the lawn needs it. No lawn should be watered every day, and most need water only every three to five days, depending on soil type and where you live.

In general, an inch of water will soak only six inches deep in a clay soil, one foot in a sandy soil. You want to encourage roots to grow at least a foot deep, so you need to water long enough to fill a cup or coffee can with one to two inches of water. Set a container out on the lawn and keep track of how much water you are applying.

Once you know you have applied enough water, wait as long as a week before watering again. If you notice that grass growing in sun does not spring up after being walked on, you have waited too long and it is time to water. An even better method is to buy a soil probe that takes a core of soil out of the ground so you can examine it and see how dry the soil is a foot down.

What if the water doesn't soak in? This could be because of thatch or compacted soil, but it also might be that the soil is hydrophobic, which means it's water repellent. Nurseries sell special wetting agents, or saturants, that help the water soak in. Or try watering in cycles. Turn the water on, then off while it soaks in, on again, then off, until you have filled your coffee can to the proper depth.

Some parts of the lawn may get much more sun and heat than others. Instead of watering the whole lawn when these suffer, use a portable sprinkler to water only these areas more frequently. Gibeault didn't recommend watering the lawn just to cool it off on hot days, nor did he see any benefits to mowing grass taller than normal (to shade the roots). Common Bermuda should be mowed so it is 1 to 1 1/4 inches tall, hybrid Bermudas 1/2 to 3/4 inches tall, and 1 1/2 inches for tall fescues.

Cut back on fertilizing, but don't stop. Lawns need nitrogen to maintain growth and stay healthy, but too much nitrogen causes excess growth that uses more water. Cool-season grasses, including the tall fescues, need fertilizing now and in the fall but not in summer. Warm-season lawns (including Bermuda) need fertilizer in late spring and summer.

Beyond these cultural practices, look for the obvious sources of wasted water—sprinklers so covered with grass that they don't spray properly (trim grass away by hand or replace with high pop-up sprinklers), sprinklers that water the street or sidewalk (adjust the nozzles by turning the screw on top), leaky valves or broken sprinkler heads.

If you want to cut down on the size of the lawn, or replace it entirely, fall is the time to undertake such ambitious projects so, at this point in the year, you have plenty of time to think it over.

Using a steel soil probe, or sampler—which pulls a plug of dirt from the garden—is the best way to actually see how well you've watered.

TOO EARLY FOR TOMATOES?

Just when should you plant tomatoes? If you visit a nursery this weekend, you'd certainly think now is the time because packs of little tomato plants line the benches. If you listen to conventional garden wisdom, however, you might wait until the weather is warmer in most areas, April inland and perhaps May near the coast, though some gardeners can definitely start now.

Most gardeners plant regular tomato varieties too early and then wonder why their plants have flowers but no fruit. The answer is that the flowers on most varieties of tomato don't make fruit until the weather is reasonably warm. If the first flowers open during the foggy, cool weather of May and early June, they aren't likely to produce tomatoes. Although daytime temperatures are relatively unimportant, night temperatures must be between 55° and 75° for fruit to set. If the nights are cooler than 55°, there will be no fruit, but you also get no fruit if the nights are warmer than 75°, which is why blossoms often drop off in midsummer, a common occurrence in the San Fernando Valley.

In areas not threatened by frost, or too close to the beach, you can start right now with the early varieties, which don't need as much nighttime warmth to set fruit. Two of the most obtainable are 'Early Girl' and 'Sweet 100'. 'Early Girl' is a normal-sized tomato, a determinate type, which means it grows only so tall (usually about three feet, so it does not need a large cage) and then stops. 'Sweet 100' is a cherry tomato that is indeterminate, which means there is no stopping it until frost blackens its foliage. Indeterminate tomatoes can grow as tall as a house and frequently do.

WEEK
14

Knowing if you are planting a determinate or indeterminate tomato variety is essential. While the one is quite manageable, the other requires massive support, or pruning. Unfortunately, this information is seldom on the plant label or even in seed catalogues. Of the common tomato varieties I've seen at nurseries in recent years, these are determinate: 'Pearson Improved', 'Ace', 'Celebrity', 'Roma' (for paste) and 'Patio' (for containers). Requiring only short stakes or small wire cages—the kind usually sold at nurseries—these are the least work to grow.

If you want lots of tomatoes in little space, grow the indeterminate varieties—'Better Boy', 'Big Boy', 'Golden Boy', 'Beefsteak', 'Beefmaster', 'Champion', 'Husky Red' and 'Pink Ponderosa'—on big wire cages. For each cage, use an 80-inch length of five-foot-wide concrete reinforcing wire with six-inch mesh openings (so you can reach inside for the tomatoes). Form each into a cylinder (which it tends to do on its own) about two feet across, fasten the ends by bending them over, and support it with two sturdy two-by-two-inch stakes so wind doesn't topple it. If it looks too big, it isn't. I've had 'Champion' tomatoes and even the squat 'Husky Red' grow over the top and halfway down the sides by the end of the season.

If you've had troubles with tomato diseases in the past, try planting in a different spot and stick with the top six varieties listed in the table below, which all proved to be at least moderately resistant. 'Sweet 100', 'Husky Red', 'Husky Gold' and 'Better Boy' showed especially good resistance to the various wilts and viruses.

So, when you plant is determined by where you live and what variety you plant. In most areas you can plant the early varieties this weekend and hope for the best. Near the coast, wait another month or more on the main-crop varieties. In the hotter interior climates where fruit set is a problem in summer, plant any variety this weekend, though April might be safer.

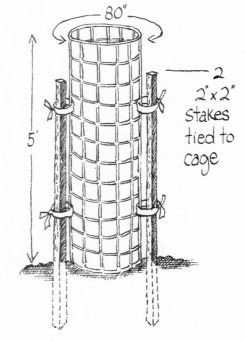

Although this weekend is the beginning of the tomato-planting season, it is by no means the end. Every few weeks, plant a different variety, beginning with the early types, and continue into August. If you start now, you should have tomatoes from mid-May until it just gets too cool in the fall to set fruit. Near the coast, I've had tomatoes still slowly ripening in December, though they never get as red as in summer.

This five-foot-tall welded-wire cage for indeterminate tomatoes is the best way to support these plants, which get huge by the end of summer.

In the most favored climates in Southern California, it's even possible to have tomatoes all year, at least in most years. In Santa Ana, longtime *Los Angeles Times* vegetable garden columnist Bill Sidnam keeps tomatoes coming all year by planting 'Early Girl' in the middle of February (he figures his last chance of frost is in January or early February). Those plants give him tomatoes in April or at least by Memorial Day. Meanwhile, he makes additional plantings in spring. The important planting, though, is in late August, when he plants 'Celebrity' or 'Champion', which begin fruiting in fall, bear all winter, sometimes lasting into June, when he replaces them.

He's found that the determinate 'Celebrity' and indeterminate 'Champion' don't seem to need the warm nights to set fruit, and if an actual frost threatens, he covers his tomato cages with a sheet, taking it off in the morning. Sidnam figures this technique works for all of Orange County, except in areas close to the beach. Incidentally, I'd listen to him when it comes to selecting varieties—by his own reckoning, he has grown more than 600 kinds of tomatoes and still prefers these three.

You can start tomatoes from seed (indoors for very early plantings), but since most of us need only a few plants, buying them as seedlings at nurseries makes more sense. How do you plant a tomato seedling? Deep. After preparing the soil, adding compost or amendments and mixing in some fertilizer, plant the seedling so that all the stem up to the first set of leaves is buried. Some gardeners even remove that first set of leaves so they can plant still deeper. This would instantly kill most seedlings, but a tomato forms roots all along that buried stem and is better off for it. In experiments carried out by Ortho, vines planted deep were twice the size after 30 days. Be sure to firm the soil down so there are no air pockets (but don't break those brittle stems), and water thoroughly.

From then on, water thoroughly (tomato roots run very deep), but not too often. Do not cut off any foliage. Tests have shown that pruning or pinching hinders production. If you did a good job on the soil—adding lots of compost or amendments and fertilizer—there's probably no need for additional fertilizing. Too much fertilizer might even reduce production. Sidnam uses Best's slow-release fertilizer tablets in his planting holes, so nutrients are always available.

THE BEST TOMATOES FOR SOUTHERN CALIFORNIA

W hich one of the current main-crop tomato varieties tastes best, produces the most or makes the biggest hamburger-smothering slices? That's what gardeners are debating now over the back fence, at nurseries, at the office. Those who have had problems in the past also want to know which kinds are the most resistant to those cursed tomato diseases that can shrivel plants before their time.

While everyone may have an opinion, some 4-H kids and parents in Orange County decided to gather some hard facts. During the summer of 1995, the Fountain Valley Cloverdale 4-H Club put 18 plants each of 13 different tomato varieties to the test—that's a grand total of 234 tomato plants. They grew them in the loamy fields of the UC Cooperative Extension Field Station at Irvine, a nice average climate—

TOP TOMATOES

Taste Ranking	Taste Test Points	Variety	Fruits Per Plant	Average Fruit Weight (Oz.)	Type
1	100	'Champion'	30	4.5	Indeterminate
2	91	'Sweet 100 Cherry'	n/a	0.5	Ind.
3	86	'Husky Red'	32	4.0	Ind.
4	82	'Better Boy'	18	4.9	Ind.
5	75	'Supersteak'	19	6.4	Ind.
6	72	'Husky Gold'	16	4.9.	Dwarf Ind.
7	23	'Big Girl'	23	5.3	Ind.
8	60	'Big Beef'	27	6.0	Ind.
9	54	'Gardener's Delight Cherry'	n/a	0.5	Ind.
10	46	'Heartland'	21	5.3	—
11	40	'San Diego'	19	4.8	—
12	38	'Celebrity'	17	6.0	Determinate
13	6	'Beefmaster'	24	8.3	Ind.

not too different from your own, not too hot, not too cool. With help from horticultural expert John Kabashima at the field station, they kept careful track of size, productivity and resistance to disease.

Then in September they took lugs of juicy, summer-ripe fruit to a farmers' market at the Orange County Fairgrounds and had some 179 shoppers rate them for taste. The accompanying table shows the results (it turned out that the variety 'Champion' was indeed the champion). That the 'Sweet 100' cherry tomato came in second shouldn't surprise anyone who's grown this tasty tomato. But neither may be the variety you'll want to plant, because a relatively new and unknown tomato was more resistant to diseases, so easier to grow. 'Husky Red' was the surprising choice for "overall most successful variety," while still garnering 86 points for taste on the group's 0-100 scale, coming in third. Equally surprising was how low the beefsteak types rated for taste. The supergiant 'Beefmaster' came in dead last with only six points, even though individual fruits *averaged* an incredible 8.3 ounces each.

All the tomatoes trialed were main-crop varieties, planted in late

'Husky Red' was the surprising choice for "overall most successful variety."

155

spring for a summer crop (which is why the popular 'Early Girl' was not included, though it has twice won informal *Los Angeles Times* office taste tests). May is probably the best time to plant tomatoes: The 4-H'ers planted on May 27, though they had hoped to plant in early May. They started with plants in four-inch pots just like those available at nurseries. After polling other wholesale growers to find which varieties were being shipped to nurseries, Gary Hayakawa, of Three Star Nursery, then grew all the young tomato plants. The 4-H kids planted them deep, burying about two-thirds of the stem underground—typical tomato-planting practices. They trained them on a commercial-type pole-and-trellis system since they were growing a field-full.

You can take comfort in the fact that their tomatoes had their share of problems, even in near perfect soil with the UC Cooperative Extension personnel watering at precisely the right times. A plant pathologist identified verticillium wilt (caused by a fungus that lives for years in the soil), curly top virus (transmitted by leafhoppers), blossom-end rot (a complicated physiological problem), spotted wilt virus (transmitted by thrips) and tobacco mosaic (transmitted by touch and pruning).

Despite all these diseases, the kids, aged eight to 18, managed to grow and then test some 1,500 pounds of tomatoes. Their efforts should help us suburban farmers figure out which ones to plant in our little plots.

April

SUMMER FLOWERS

NOW, OR AS SOON AS THERE'S ROOM IN THE garden, is the time to plant summer flowers. But what to plant? For ideas, I asked two experienced nursery people who also happen to be avid home gardeners: Frank Burkard, Jr., of Burkard Nurseries in Pasadena, and Cristin Fusano, color specialist at Roger's Gardens in Corona del Mar. Their answers are similar, but not the same. These two nurseries are in distinctly different climates—summers in Pasadena are quite different from summers at the beach. The questions I posed are typical of those overheard at nurseries.

Question: What bedding plants last a long time if planted now?

Answer: While impatiens may be the champ, the following will last into fall (and maybe beyond): ageratum, blue bedding salvia, cosmos, dusty miller, French marigold (if old flowers are picked off), gloriosa daisy, golden fleece, lobelia, nasturtium, nicotiana, petunia, red salvia, 'Telstar' dianthus, vinca rosea (*Catharanthus*), white nierembergia and zinnia.

Our experts singled out the cosmos 'Sonata' strain, new, very pretty and long lasting, especially the white, which was a Fleuroselect winner in Europe for its big blooms and short (two-foot) stature. For hot inland gardens, many new types and colors of vinca rosea are long lasting.

Q: I like pink and lavender flowers. What can I grow in summer?

A: Summer flowers are best known for their flashy colors—especially yellow and gold, which look so good in the summer sun. More subdued bedding plants to plant now include: alyssum, aster, cosmos, impatiens, petunia, phlox and 'Telstar' dianthus. Blue flowers that blend with these pastels are lobelia and blue bedding salvia.

For the softest schemes, don't buy seed mixes—shop for separate colors so you can pick the more subtle shades. Better nurseries sell many common annuals this way. "I suggest planting three different shades of impatiens, instead of a mix," says Fusano. "Try two shades of pink and a white, avoiding the oranges and reds. People are surprised at how much more pleasant this scheme is.

"Bedding dahlias can be added to the list," she adds, "if you buy them in four-inch pots, so you get only the light pinks, peachy pinks and corals. I know that some people are already doing this because on Monday morning at the nursery we often find only red and yellow dahlias left on the bench!"

Q: It gets very hot where I live. What can take the heat?

A: Amaranthus, blue bedding salvia, celosia, cosmos 'Sensation' and 'Sonata', gloriosa daisy, golden fleece, portulaca, red salvia, sanvitalia (creeping zinnia), vinca rosea and zinnia. Burkard thinks even the 'Telstar' strain of dianthus can take heat. Fusano adds marigolds and petunias to the list. For the shade, try *Begonia* 'Richmondensis' and bronze-leaf begonias.

Not too many people plant celosia. But take a look at one called 'New Look', about two-and-a-half feet tall, with red plume-like flowers and stunning reddish leaves. It will grow even in Palm Springs in summer. Try it with the old-fashioned amaranthus, grown for its stunning red and maroon leaves, a scheme popular in the Victorian era.

Q: My garden is very shady. Can I grow anything other than impatiens?

A: Apparently, many gardens are shady, because impatiens outsell any other bedding plant (they command an incredible 58 percent of the market). The experts suggest also bedding begonias, *Begonia* 'Richmondensis', coleus and forget-me-nots (best near the coast).

To liven up shady schemes, they also suggest using several perennials. Upright fuchsias are one, and several do well even inland, such as 'Gartenmeister Bonstedt', 'Jingle Bells', 'Marinka', 'Swingtime' and 'Voodoo'. (They say the fuchsia mite is not the pest it was a few years ago.) Try to include other perennials such as coral bells, sweet violets and the new small hydrangea 'Pink Elf', a shrub that grows only to bedding-plant proportions at about 18 inches tall and as wide, and is covered with bright pink flowers in summer.

Q: What can I grow that won't need a lot of water or care?

A: The toughest bedding plants are alyssum, blue bedding salvia, gloriosa daisy, golden fleece, marigold, petunia and the semisucculent portulaca.

The 1891 catalogue of Germain's, a Los Angeles seed company, offered more than 18 different kinds, or colors, of portulaca—this was before the advent of sprinkler systems, so proves their toughness. They are again available as separate colors—if you can't visually handle the common wild mix.

Water all of these almost every day the first week after planting, then about twice a week for the first few weeks. After that, they should be able to survive on once-a-week soakings.

Q: I'm tired of the same old summer bedding plants. Is there something else I can try?

A: Here are several suggestions for the jaded gardener: browallia, or amethyst flower (beautiful blue flowers on plants 18 inches tall in part shade); cleome (fluffy pink or rose flowers on plants to four feet tall); monarda (a three-foot-tall perennial with feathery pink to crimson flowers that attracts butterflies); *Nicotiana sylvestris* (sticky tobacco-like leaves and long, slender, fragrant white flowers, five feet tall), and nigella (intricate blue, pink or white flowers, 18 inches tall). For a different look in a very common flower, Burkard suggests finding the new pale apricot alyssum. Or mix perennials in with the bedding plants (grow them as annuals, or bear with them through the winter).

If you still want to plant impatiens, try the New Guinea hybrids in shady spots. 'Spectra' is the hot new series, with colors more vibrant, flowers larger (though fewer) and foliage sometimes colored, often a deep burgundy.

Here's one more piece of advice: Plant any of these flowers before June or July, so they have time to make the roots necessary to flower all summer long.

SUDDENLY, SUNFLOWERS!

Suddenly, sunflowers are everywhere—at florists, printed on trivets and towels, starring in television commercials, even planted in nice gardens, where they have taken on a new dignity and position as ornamental flowers. No longer are sunflowers relegated to the back 40 to rest their droopy heads against the alley fence or grow beside the corn.

Sunflowers "came from nowhere to become the best-selling flower in our catalogue," says Shepherd Ogden, of The Cook's Garden [*P.O. Box 5010, Hodges, SC, 29653, (800) 457-9703; www.cooksgarden.com*]. Its catalogue lists 17 varieties, including one that will grow to make that huge head full of edible seeds.

The new ornamental sunflowers are grown for their colorful flowers—velvety red, mahogany brown, golden yellow, burnt orange, creamy yellow, even calendula orange.

The new ornamental varieties are grown for their colorful flowers—velvety red, mahogany brown, golden yellow, burnt orange, creamy yellow, even calendula orange. These stunning varieties hail from Europe, where interest in this old native American favorite has increased because cut flowers are big business and cut sunflowers are trendy. Some of them have even won Europe's coveted Fleuroselect award.

Vincent van Gogh may very well have been the inspiration for the sunflower craze here. "I fell in love with sunflowers after seeing *Vincent and Theo*," says landscape architect Mike Swimmer (one scene depicts van Gogh painting in a huge field of sunflowers). So in a narrow little space between the driveway and his neighbor's fence in his West Los Angeles garden, Swimmer grows a whole forest of ornamental kinds, and not only for the colorful flowers. When the flowers are finished, he lets them dry, then hangs the seed heads by their stems in his aviary where his birds fish out their own seed snacks.

Florist Kathy Orlando, of Rita Flora in Los Angeles, is sure that everyone started wanting sunflower bouquets right after the exhibit of van Gogh's later paintings at the Metropolitan Museum of Art in 1987. "It seems like it's been building since then," she says.

At least two distinct types of annual sunflowers are out there, says Ogden, though there are some 110 species known to grow in the Americas, including many perennials. One type he describes as "stiff," the other as "scroogy-woogy," or lax and "all over the place."

The sunflowers closely related to the seed sunflower (such as 'Mammoth' and 'Giant Grey Stripe', with their big golden yellow discs) look like that inhabitant of the vegetable garden. They make a fat, sturdy stem with big, thick hairy leaves. Some produce but one huge flower; others may make as many as half a dozen, and good-sized seeds are sure to follow flowers. One, 'Evening Sun', with flowers half a foot across, can be a deep mahogany with golden edges and a chocolate-brown center.

'Sundrops' (a bright yellow), 'Chianti' (a dark red) and several others grow into lax, branching, soft-leafed plants with thinner stems but a profusion of smaller three- to four-inch flowers. 'Italian White' is one with light creamy-yellow rays surrounding a dark purple-black center. These do make seed—however, they are small and not what one thinks of as sunflower seed.

Either kind can be any height—you'll have to trust the catalogue descriptions. While 'Evening Sun' or the common 'Mammoth' seed sunflower may grow eight to 12 feet tall, the similar 'Big Smile' and 'Sunspot' grow just a foot or two.

In various seed catalogues you can find all sorts. 'Sunbeam' has a green eye at its center; 'Sunrise' is a fashionable pale lemon yellow, and 'Silverleaf' is more fashionable still with fuzzy, slightly silver foliage. 'Sunrich Lemon' and 'Sunrich Orange' have no pollen to rub off on clothing while you are making a bouquet (though the pollen on others doesn't seem to stain). 'Stella' looks like a very tall black-eyed Susan; 'Music Box' includes all sorts of colors on three-foot-tall plants; 'Prado Red', like 'Chianti', is very dark, and 'Orange Queen' and 'Tangina' are calendula colored. There are even doubles that hardly resemble sunflowers at all—'Teddy Bear' and 'Sole d'Oro' look like suns gone supernova. In the W. Atlee Burpee & Co. seed catalogue [*Warminster, PA 18974 (800) 888-1447*], you can even find a mix called Fun'n Sun that includes a bunch of these. Renee's Garden Seeds in the Santa Cruz area offers many interesting sunflowers, available at nurseries or directly at *(888) 880-7228* or www.reneesgarden.com.

Nothing could be easier to grow—even the birds can do it (and, in fact, they do plant many a sunflower)—or faster. "Talk about Jack and the Beanstalk, you can *watch* sunflowers grow," says Shirley Kerins, who has grown many for the Huntington Botanical Gardens' annual May plant sale. Some even turn to track the sun, the flowers following it across the sky. Children find the seed easy to handle and plant; the sunflowers grow quicker than kids lose interest and soon tower above them. When the flowers are finished, children can eat the seed or feed the birds.

Sunflowers do need full sun, the hotter the better, but they grow in coastal gardens just fine. The cool, breezy Ocean View Farms community garden in Mar Vista is full of sunflowers in summer. They thrive in almost any soil and need to be watered at least every week.

Plant them as early as April, or later in spring or early summer. From his several years of experience, Swimmer is sure that sunflowers can be planted at almost any time of year in coastal Southern California, even though most are supposedly day-length sensitive, needing long summer days to make buds (some new varieties, such as 'Sunrich Lemon' and 'Sunrich Orange', are day-neutral, for the cut flower busi-

The cool, breezy Ocean View Farms community garden in Mar Vista is full of sunflowers in summer.

ness). April is probably the best month to sow seed.

If you want to save seed, be prepared for ugly plants. Once seed sets, plants yellow and wither quickly. Don't pull them out until the seed is ripe, usually when the back of the flower turns completely brown.

Keep the "scroogy-woogy" kinds going a little longer by cutting off the flowers as they fade. These kinds may need staking since they can get pretty floppy, and edible seed is not likely.

There is one possible problem. Sunflowers produce substances that inhibit the growth of other plants. Allelopathic plants, they have been known to control weeds in their vicinity. No hard data or lists exist, but if you notice that plants close to the base of sunflowers are struggling, that might be the reason.

COTTAGE GARDEN FLOWERS

C ottage garden flowers, full of old-fashioned charm, have survived for centuries in England. As put to me by W. George Waters, British-born editor of *Pacific Horticulture*, the owners of cottage gardens were "immune to the fashion in flowers," so these plants tended to remain in their front yards (the location of all cottage gardens) as though in a botanical preserve. Cottage gardens "contained no pretense whatever," he says, and their owners planted anything that came their way. When they had something special "they tended to pass it around a bit," he says. Thus these flowers came down to us.

Waters also notes that the tenders of these humble plots, being farm folk, had a good deal of manure on hand, which undoubtedly accounts for the legendary profusion of flowers.

WEEK

16

A quick survey of Southern California nurseries right now will turn up quite a few cottage garden treasures, full of innocent exuberance, just like the illustrations in children's books.

Hollyhocks, in shades of red through yellow, are perhaps the definitive cottage garden flower, certainly the tallest and most picturesque. (There is no denying the simple pleasure of growing a flower taller than yourself.) Hollyhocks were brought to England from the Near East by the returning crusaders; this makes them one of the oldest of cultivated garden flowers.

They are available at nurseries as small plants, or as seed, from

which they grow very quickly (though it may take two years to flower from seed sown in spring). In Southern California, though, the best are probably grown from seed collected from alleyways or old gardens. Here, hollyhocks are extremely susceptible to rust—a plant disease that looks just like its namesake and can completely defoliate a hollyhock before it has finished flowering. It would seem that near-wild plants are not so susceptible. If you want one that is resistant, you may have to find such a plant and collect your own seed, or ask the owner to save you some, though even leafless, hollyhocks manage to flower and be impressive.

Cup-and-saucer, one of the campanulas, is a storybook flower found at nurseries with just a little searching, or it can be grown from seed. Described by one English author as having long been a "quaint inhabitant of cottage garden borders," it is a flower that children notice because its bright blue or lavender flowers do indeed look like cups sitting on tiny saucers. It is supposed to send up spires, but I have never succeeded in getting one to stand upright. Be prepared to stake them or give them room to lie down, a pose that makes them look quite quaint.

Cup-and-saucer, *Campanula medium*, is one quaint, old-fashioned flower that children adore.

Another blue flower of ancient history is the forget-me-not, which was "worn by Henry of Lancaster, later to become Henry IV, believing that whosoever would wear it, would never be forgotten," according to Roy Gender is his encyclopedic "The Cottage Garden" (Pelham Books, London). The tiny blue flowers are adorable; the botanical name, *Myosotis*, means "mouse ears" and refers to the small, fuzzy foliage. This is a cottage garden charmer for somewhat shady areas, but not deep shade. Try it with foxgloves, another cottage garden favorite for the shade.

Bachelor's button, also blue, but in white and pink as well, can still be found as seed and sometimes as small plants at nurseries. Some gardeners feel it is better planted in fall, but plants are mostly available now, for spring planting. This one grew wild in the farmers' fields, hence its other common name of cornflower, though at one time it

163

was known as hurtsick, "because it hindereth the reapers by dulling their sickles in the reaping of corn," according to Gerard, the original herbalist. Unfortunately, the plants sold today tend to be much improved, forming dense, ungainly heads of flowers; the unimproved kinds are much more graceful plants, if less floriferous. You might find an older variety growing in a seed-saver's garden, or let your own go to seed and save it. The W. Atlee Burpee seed catalogue [*Warminster, PA 18974 (800) 888-1447*] offers one named 'Tall Blue Boy' that it claims grows like the old-fashioned kinds, to almost three feet tall.

Love-in-a-mist (*Nigella*) dates to Elizabethan times, when it was taken there from the Near East—not for its lovely flowers, but for its seeds that were used in various concoctions, including a cure for freckles. One of the most unusual flowers, it has dainty petals of blue, pink or white partly hidden in a filigree of greenery. An annual, it is most easy to grow.

The flowers of love-in-a-mist can be cut and dried, as can the seed pods of honesty, so named because the seeds show through the transparent pods. Honesty, dating back to at least Tudor times, is available in most seed racks as *Lunaria biennis*. It, like cup-and-saucer, hollyhock and forget-me-not, is technically a biennial, which means it grows one year and flowers the next, though in Southern California biennials tend to flower immediately. Nursery plants should bloom the first year.

OTHER OLD-FASHIONED FLOWERS

These can still be found at California nurseries:

Bleeding heart—for shade, but not long-lived here

Borage—from the Celtic *borrach*, meaning "to have courage"

Daylily—from Shakespeare's time

English daisy (*Bellis perennis*) — the *daeyeseage* of Chaucer

Four o'clock—sometimes a weed in Southern California

Foxglove—or finger-flower, the origin of the botanical name *Digitalis*

Lavender

Leopard's bane (*Doronicum*)

Oriental poppy—these barely survive here

Pinks and sweet William—the perennial and annual dianthus

Primrose—of old, called cowslips or oxlips

Scabiosa—or pincushion flower

Scarlet campion (*Lychnis chalcedonica*)—with the most flagrant magenta flowers imaginable

Stock

Thalictrum

Thyme

Violet

Yarrow

Thrift, once aptly called ladies' cushion for its dense grass-like tufts of foliage, was once used for edging knot gardens. Currently it is enjoying a revival at nurseries, where several kinds are available, all with little pink pompon-like flowers atop wispy stems. A perennial, it is easy to grow.

CAN WE GROW CLEMATIS?

C lematis is one of those plants seen in eastern catalogues that we can't grow here. Or so some used to say. Others have discovered that clematis do just fine here, thank you, and more are showing up at nurseries.

These showy deciduous vines, beloved back east, in the Pacific Northwest and in England, may not cover cottages here (as they sometimes do in England), but perhaps that's just as well. In Southern California, clematis are well-mannered vines that produce more than their fair share of spectacular, usually flat-faced flowers, up to nine inches across, colored from pink and purple to a respectable blue.

Ann Gilboyne, who has raised a bunch for the annual May plant sale at The Arboretum of Los Angeles County, began growing them in her Glendale garden because, "I grew them in Wisconsin, and after I moved, I didn't know any better," she says, not knowing that few gardeners did grow them, at least as successfully as she now does. In all, she grows 25 different kinds.

Clematis is not one of those eastern plants that grows inland where winters get chilly but not on the milder coast. The variety 'Nelly Moser' has been growing in Gilboyne's garden for more than 12 years. Her mother has grown it for almost as long in her Laguna Niguel garden. This particular variety is a favorite—flowers are about eight inches across, with each light pink petal having a darker stripe down the middle.

English garden writer Christopher Lloyd describes clematis as "an extra, the gilt on the gingerbread," in his book "The Well-Chosen Garden" (Harper & Row, New York). "The fact to remember about them," he continues, "is that they don't need a special place to themselves. And so, to find a place for a clematis requires no more effort than to find an established shrub on which a clematis is not growing. . . . You merely need to match the vigor of your shrub with the vigor of the clematis that is to run through and over it." Which is exactly how, and where, to grow them in California—twining up something else.

In the Gilboyne garden, they climb bougainvilleas and climbing roses, honeysuckles and Costa Rican nightshade (*Solanum wendlandii*). One scrambles up a copper beech, another grows on the mailbox—clematis need not be tacked to a wall or trained on a trellis. Growing clematis with something else hides its shortcoming—it definitely has an off-season when dormant. Most get about six feet tall, though Gilboyne has a few that clamber up 12 feet, one right to the top of the chimney.

They grow unusually well with roses. Lloyd again: "A clematis with a rose is a particularly happy match because both plants are greedy and enjoy the good things in life."

Gilboyne especially likes the bluest of the clematis, 'General Sikorski', and 'President', which she calls the "bloomiest," because it flowers from April into December in her garden. Most don't bloom this long, becoming brown by November and going completely dormant until March. When clematis go dormant, the leaves seldom fall off on their own. Cut them off (pulling is liable to break the vine), or blast them off with a spray of water, which is what Gilboyne does.

The secret to growing clematis, Gilboyne says, is to pamper the roots: "Plant them deep, protect them, and shade them." Few plants are as finicky this way, the root system and crown being very sensitive. When planting, carefully tap them out of their pots—don't try to untangle the roots, and handle them gently. Plant a couple of inches deeper than they were in their containers, "like tomatoes," says Gilboyne. Or, she suggests, leave them in their nursery containers and cut off the bottoms with a serrated knife, planting pot and all so the lip of the container is flush with the soil surface. The pot helps protect the fragile crown from feet, hoes, digging animals and careless commercial gardeners. Gilboyne plants them in a rich, amended soil, the only kind she seems to have in her garden.

The old admonition "Keep their heads in the sun and their feet in the shade" is absolutely true. They need sun to flower, but the roots must be kept cool. Gilboyne puts a small boulder on the south side of most vines so the sun doesn't beat down on the root area. You could also use broken concrete or a stepping stone.

Clematis don't need as much water as some people think. Gilboyne successfully brought hers through the recent drought without going over her allowance. She fertilizes in early spring with blood meal; in April she pushes two Jobe's tomato stakes into the ground about 18 inches from either side of the plant. These slowly release nutrients through the summer.

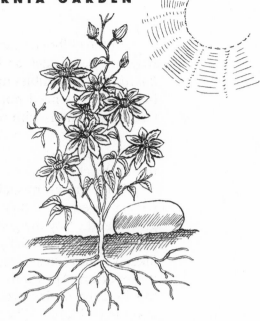

Gilboyne thinks the vines should never be pruned, though you can count on some dieback every summer. "I know I'll lose some entire stems in July," she says. "But I just cut those off, and they bounce back. The plant has as many lives as a cat." Be sure to cut some of the flowering stems for indoors. Gilboyne cuts several feet of flowering stems and lets them trail out of an arrangement, a very pretty picture.

The French Connection, a new group of deciduous clematis, originated in southern Europe and supposedly does fine in even the warmest areas—and their roots do not need to be shaded. Said to grow vigorously eight to 12 feet, they need regular watering and a little pruning in winter to control size. Hybrids of *Clematis viticella*, 'Alba Luxurians' is a white, 'Madame Julia Correvon' is a clear wine red, and 'Etoile Violette' is a deep violet.

Do not confuse deciduous clematis with the evergreen *Clematis armandii*, a much bigger vine with small white flowers, sometimes grown along fences in Southern California. It needs frequent pruning and training once it takes off, and leaf edges are often an unsightly brown.

Clematis roots really do need to be kept cool. A stone placed on the south side of the plant will shade and cool the roots.

SUMMER VEGETABLES

This is the month to start your own summer vegetables—fresher, free of pesticides and probably better for you than store-bought. You may even save some money in these tough times. Totally ripe tomatoes, crisp lettuce and cucumbers, beets and baby carrots, and corn so sweet it makes your teeth hurt—all of these can be grown in surprisingly little space in your backyard, and even in containers.

Try to pick a place that gets a full day of sun; only a very few vegetables can get by on less. If you plant in rows, run them from east to west. Plant from seed, sown directly in the garden, then thin to the suggested spacing. Some kinds are better started

WEEK
17

167

in small pots and then transplanted into the garden when four to six inches tall. These you can also buy as small plants at nurseries; the selection is getting better every year. A couple of summer crops take up lots of space, pumpkins, for instance. If you have small children and little space, they'll definitely prefer a jack-o'-lantern to cooked squash.

No space for a garden? Try containers.

To prepare the soil for planting, most people turn the soil with a spade, spading fork or rototiller and then mix in a two- to three-inch layer of organic matter or homemade compost along with a complete fertilizer. There are many methods, from "no till" to "biointensive." Robet Kourik's "Designing and Maintaining Your Edible Landscape Naturally" (*Metamorphic Press, Santa Rosa, 1986*) explains all the options.

As indicated in the following list, some crops do best planted in rows, either single or double. Make furrows and mound the soil in the space between. Plant on these slightly raised rows and flood the furrows to irrigate, or use drip. Making three- to four-foot-wide mounded beds, made fluffy with added organic matter, is a good way to grow small crops in very little space, or root crops that need a soft soil. Adding organic matter improves fertility so you can space plants close together, so close they choke out weeds. The added organic matter also raises the bed so excess water drains away, a good idea in heavy clay soils. To water, use a sprinkler or porous drip tubing.

No space for a garden? Try containers. You can grow almost any of the vegetables listed in a container (corn might be a challenge), as long as it's big enough. Try half oak barrels or the similarly sized pulp containers, and water and fertilize more often. One barrel should hold one tomato, one squash, one pumpkin or one cucumber, or two peppers or two eggplant, or a few bean plants. Lots of lettuce or carrots or similar small crops will also fit.

If you don't want to eat beets (or any other vegetable) every night for a week, don't plant too much seed at once. Plant a few seeds, or a few feet of row one week, then plant more a couple of weeks later to spread out the harvest.

Summer vegetables need lots of water. As long as the soil is well aerated, fluffed with organic matter and not compacted, it is difficult to overwater vegetables. Don't drown them, but don't let any vegetable dry out—fruit and blossom drop or a bitter taste often result. It's usually enough to add fertilizer when preparing the soil. Some may need more, especially those growing in sandy soils. Others, including tomatoes, produce less fruit if given too much fertilizer.

Plant fast-growing vegetables between slower-growing kinds to get the most out of your garden space. For instance, try beets between the peppers and tomatoes, or lettuce between the tomatoes and beans. They'll be ready to harvest before the larger, slower crops need the room.

You can grow several crops of the same vegetable in one place during this season, but next year play musical chairs—plant everything in a different part of the vegetable garden so diseases don't build up in the soil. This is especially important with tomatoes.

There are more insect pests in spring and summer than in fall and winter so have some controls standing by. Products safe to use in the vegetable garden include: BT (*Bacillus thuringiensis*) for tomato and other "worms" (most are moth larvae); D.E. (diatomaceous earth), which kills slugs, ants and grasshoppers; insecticidal soaps for aphids, scale and whiteflies, and the new refined horticultural oils that smother aphids, mites, some larvae and caterpillars, thrips and whiteflies. The best information on current pest control practices that I've found is the University of California book "Pests of the Garden and Small Farm," by Mary Louise Flint; call *(800) 994-8849* and order publication 3322.

Though there is little scientific evidence that certain plants contribute to the well-being of others, or that they help control pests, there is a rich folklore, very little of which has been explored by the scientific community. Some is worth trying, but be aware that the competition from companion plants can dramatically lower yields. For instance: Marigolds do repel nematodes, but in such a small area that it really doesn't effect nearby vegetables. Pole beans aren't supposed to get along with beets, but bush beans will (you figure). Basil is reputed to be a good companion for tomatoes, worth trying since they go well together in the kitchen too.

Here is a list of some favorite summer crops.

Beans (snap and lima): *Plant in full sun or partial shade; March through August for snap, May and June for lima. Sow seed in ground in rows 30" apart; thin seedlings to 8" apart. Harvest snap in 60 days, lima in 75 days.*

If you want the maximum amount in the minimum space, grow the pole-type beans on eight-foot poles or an eight-foot trellis. The bush types are for people who have a lot of room. Lima beans are picky about planting times, snap beans more versatile, but you have time for both. Plant a quarter of a row to snap beans in early March, another quarter of the row in April, another quarter to limas in early

May and the last quarter to limas in early June. As these wear out, replace with plantings of snap beans. Limas don't like the hot weather of late summer; the new plantings of snap beans will cruise into fall. Both kinds are susceptible to smog, which causes blotchy leaves, and the later planting dates run into the smog season in inland areas. Pick frequently to keep beans coming, just before pods begin to bulge. Should the beans get ahead of you, let them dry on the vines and harvest later as dried beans.

Beets: *Plant in full sun or partial shade; year round near the coast, inland January through September. Sow seed in ground in rows 18" to 24" apart; thin seedlings to 2" apart. In beds, keep 4" apart. Ready in 60 days or less.*

Plant every few weeks for nearly continuous harvest, though curly top virus can be a problem on midsummer crops. If so, plant in spring and again in fall. Beets are best picked when about two inches across, but can be left in the ground a long time, becoming only a little bitter and tough.

Carrots: *Plant in full sun, year round. Sow seed in ground in rows 2' apart; thin seedlings to 2" apart. In beds, keep 3" apart. Ready in 60 to 70 days.*

Plant short sections of rows every few weeks for a nearly continuous supply, though seeds get a little hard to germinate in late summer since they need cool, constantly moist soil to sprout (try shading the seeds or cover with damp newspaper). Gourmets say the young carrots are the best, but you won't get much crunch for your change, so let some grow larger and slice them up. Don't leave carrots in the ground too long—they get tough and crack. In heavy or rocky soils, try the shorter kinds to avoid deformed roots.

Chard: *Plant in full sun or partial shade; near the coast year round, inland February through May. Sow in ground in rows 2' apart; thin seedlings to 1' apart. In beds, keep 8" apart. Ready in 50 to 60 days.*

Another year-round crop near the coast, but susceptible to curly top virus inland in summer. Ruby chard adds a little color to the garden. Pick outer leaves first or they become tough and stringy.

Corn: *Plant in full sun, March through July. Sow seed in ground in rows 3' apart; thin seedlings to 1' apart. Ready in about 75 days.*

If you want full-kerneled ears, plant corn in blocks so wind can cross-pollinate plants. Four rows are the minimum. Make each row five feet long, and you'll have more than enough since it all ripens during the same week. For best flavor, eat within milliseconds of picking. Or grow popcorn, so you can dry and store your harvest. Corn earworms can be a problem, but they usually eat only the uppermost rows of kernels, leaving plenty. Fend off worms by applying 20 drops of mineral oil with a medicine dropper at the base of the silks, three to seven days after silks appear.

Cucumbers: *Plant in full sun or partial shade, April through June. Sow in ground in rows 4' apart; thin seedlings to 2' apart. Or plant several seeds in "hills" spaced 4' to 6' apart in every direction. Start harvesting after 50 to 70 days.*

Nowadays there are many kinds of cucumbers: burpless, the new crispy Saudi types such as 'Amira', other slicing cucumbers, pickling cucumbers (made to fit in a jar) and dual-purpose kinds. Varieties such as 'Salad Bush' are designed for container growing. Pick slicers when six to eight inches long. Harvest lasts several weeks. Cucumbers planted late in inland areas probably need a little shade, so some experts grow them on the east side of corn. Cucumbers can also be trained up a trellis, or cornstalks.

Eggplant: *Plant in full sun, April through May. Space transplants in rows 3' apart, spaced 18" apart. Ready in about 60 days.*

Each full-sized plant yields about five or six fruit if thinned to one to each main branch. Smaller-fruited "oriental" varieties produce more fruit and don't need thinning. All like a rich soil. Look for the beautiful 'Purple Blush' and other new hybrids, some naturally small, some white like an egg. When plants are young watch out for flea beetles; protect with floating row covers. Pick when glossy and firm.

Leaf lettuce: *Plant in full sun or partial shade, year round. Sow seed in ground in rows 2' apart; thin seedlings to 6" apart. In wide beds, keep 8" apart. Eat thinnings, start cutting in 30 days; finished in 50 to 70 days.*

Lettuces prefer fall, winter and spring where it gets hot, but with a little luck, or a little shade, you can have plenty to go with the tomatoes. Near the coast, growing lettuce is a snap. Plant several feet of a row at a time to spread out the harvest. Inland, try planting between rows of corn or between tomatoes and beans, where they are shaded from the hot summer sun. Harvest as it grows, beginning with thinnings and then the outer leaves.

Melons: *Plant in full sun, April through May. Sow seed in ground in rows 5' apart; thin seedlings to 2' apart. Ready in 70 to 120 days.*

Melons need a lot of space and a good deal of heat. Since each vine produces only a few fruits, melons really aren't a good bet in most gardens, especially near the coast. In hot, interior areas, however, they can be treat. To save space, look for bush-type watermelons. Harvest cantaloupes when a slight crack appears all around the stem where it joins the fruit.

Peppers: *Plant in full sun, April through May. Space transplants in rows 3' apart, spaced 2' apart. Start harvesting in 70 days.*

There are hundreds of kinds to choose from; try several. Culture is the same for all kinds and very similar to that of tomatoes and eggplant (they're all cousins). Cook, use fresh, or cut with an inch of stem attached and hang in the sun to dry.

Pumpkins: *Plant in full sun or partial shade, May through June. Sow seed in rows 6' apart; thin seedlings to 4' apart. Bush kinds in rows 3' apart; thin to 2' apart. Ready in about 100 days.*

Bush kinds, such as 'Bushkin', produce only a few 10-pound fruits, but they are large enough for a decent jack-o'-lantern and spread just six feet. Others get huge. To be ready by Halloween, plant seed June 10 through 15. Cut from the vine when stems are hard and dry and the plant begins to die.

Summer squash: *Plant in full sun or partial shade, April through June. Sow bush types in ground in rows 4' apart; thin seedlings to 1' apart. Or space transplants 3' apart in all directions. Ready in 50 to 60 days.*

For most people, one zucchini plant is enough, so grow several kinds of squash: yellow crookneck, yellow straightneck, scallop types or one of the entirely new types such as kuta and 'Sun Drops', with its tiny three-inch fruit. Pick fruits when young for best taste, at six inches long or less. Plants keep producing for several weeks.

Sunflowers: *Plant in full sun, March through July. Sow seed in ground in rows 3' apart; thin seedlings to 18" apart. Ready in 80 days.*

Nothing's taller, often growing to 10 feet, so plant on the north side of the garden so they don't shade other crops. Inland gardeners sometimes train heat-sensitive beans or cucumbers up the stalks to protect them from the summer sun. Dry heads in the sun only after backs of flowers turn completely brown.

Tomatoes: *Plant in full sun, April through late August. Space transplants in rows 3' apart in all directions. Harvest begins in 60 to 80 days.*

See Week 14 for more information.

CAPERS AND SWEET POTATOES

Broccoli has gone to flower and pea vines are turning brown, sure signs it must be time to plant the summer vegetable garden. After planting the tomatoes and eggplants, cucumbers and beans, consider something to wake up those tired taste buds, to make this year's garden a little different: sweet potatoes and capers.

Sweet potatoes in particular are a real treat, but not because of their edible tubers that regularly appear around Thanksgiving. It's the leaves and young stems that are the tasty surprise. You can only grow your own; you can't find them at markets. As for capers, well, some people think they're delicious, just the thing to spice up tartar sauce or other sauces and salads. You don't even need a vegetable garden to grow these two. One can be trellised on a wall; the other can be planted in with other small shrubs or perennials.

Extremely easy to grow, capers take any kind of soil, as long as the ground doesn't become soggy.

The caper, *Capparis spinosa*, is a smallish, deciduous shrub native to the Mediterranean, where it grows in the company of carobs, grapes and olives on sunny slopes and rocky walls. Quite drought resistant, it is often seen in gardens from Spain to Israel, where the showy white flowers and fluffy violet stamens add a little summer color.

David and Tina Silber, of Papaya Tree Nursery in Granada Hills, believe the caper should be common in California gardens as well. In their backyard nursery, they grow capers at the top of a retaining wall where each gets about one-and-a-half feet tall, spreading and spilling to four or more feet. They also grow them in large terra-cotta pots (15 inches in diameter) and, of course, in nursery containers; contact them by calling *(818) 363-3680*.

Extremely easy to grow, capers take any kind of soil, as long as the ground doesn't become soggy. David Silber waters the plants in the ground only every two months, but he does water deeply. Plants briefly lose their leaves in late winter.

As with olives, the caper flower buds must be treated to lose their initial bitter taste, but this is an easy process. Pick the flower buds when they are about the size of a pea, says Tina Silber. The caper blooms all summer and into fall, providing many pickings. A three- to four-year-old plant will yield about a cup each time. Pour a cup of buds into a plastic bag, and cover with kosher or non-iodized table salt. Let them sit at room temperature for 10 to 14 days. Rinse and taste one bud to check that the bitter taste is gone. If it is ready, rinse

173

all the buds and use, or store them in a jar filled with one part vinegar and two parts water, in the refrigerator.

Everyone has grown a sweet potato stuck with toothpicks in a glass of water. They do even better in the ground, where they quickly make eight-foot or larger vines. Jimmy Bautista, raised on sweet potatoes in his native Philippines, still grows the sprawling vines in his side yard in Pasadena, where they are trellised against the house, close by the back door to be handy for cooking. He keeps them up off the ground so the young shoots stay clean because that is his favorite part of the plant. The tender new growth—leaves and stems, much tastier than spinach or chard—is used in many Filipino dishes. His wife, Hermie, makes *kamote*, a delicious salad, and *sinigang*, a soup of the leaves and pork spareribs. (In Filipino markets, you can also find Haloya Tropical Ice Cream, and a delicious purple cake, both made from the tubers of *ube*, the purple sweet potato.)

Bautista starts new plants from cuttings taken in late fall, when he cuts off 18-inch stem tips and sticks them in a pail of water indoors. Most winters, the tropical vines die completely to the ground, so he always makes sure new cuttings are standing by.

Tubers form along the roots, close to the base of the vine. In summer, each plant usually produces a few, which Bautista carefully digs up. It takes a lot of vine to get a few tubers, so the sweet potatoes themselves are considered a bonus. He dries them in the sun for a couple of days before cooking. If you want to grow the vines for tubers, he recommends planting the cuttings about six inches apart. Choose a sunny place because these vines love heat and moisture, being native to South America. They are not, incidentally, related to regular potatoes and are not yams, which are native to the Old World.

Young plants are sold through seed catalogues but can't be shipped to California. The best way to begin, then, is to sprout a store-bought tuber in a jar of water, the way you did when you were a kid. When the sprouts are about a foot long snap them off and plant. Once you have a plant going, cuttings are the quicker, easier way for succeeding years.

And, once you've tasted *kamote*, you'll want to make sure there is always a vine near the back door.

NEW FABRICS FOR THE GARDEN

D esigned to get down and dirty, garden fabrics may never make an appearance on a Paris runway (though you can never be sure), but they can make gardening a whole lot easier. Judging from the gardeners I've talked to, some kind of garden fabric is probably in your future, especially if you grow edibles. The different kinds protect plants from pests, sun and weeds, make seeds a snap to germinate and bring in the earliest melons and tomatoes on the block.

Floating row covers: The most exciting of garden fabrics are the new flyweight floating row covers that look like gauze but are made of spun-bonded polypropylene, polyester or other woven plastic. Invented on the East Coast and designed initially as season extenders, they raise the temperature underneath by 10° or more. Almost by accident, though, it was discovered that they also completely exclude pests, even those as tiny as aphids or flea beetles. They let in almost 100 percent of the sunlight hitting them, and they are so lightweight they can be laid directly on top of plants, which simply push them up as they grow. You can water right through the fabric, by hand or with a sprinkler.

In San Marcos, Richard Borevitz uses floating row covers to bring in early crops of cucumbers, squash and melons for his Gourmet Gardens roadside stand. However, there's a downside to this warming ability. If daytime temperatures rise above 90°, "you can really a crisp crop," cautions Mike Heuer, of Harmony Farm Supply [3244 Hwy. 116 North, Sebastopol, CA 95472 *(707) 823-9125*; www.harmonyfarm.com], one mail-older source of garden fabrics. Floating row covers are best used here during the cool months.

Gardeners on the East Coast find them indispensable. Kip Andersen, the gardener for television's "The Victory Garden," says cucumbers can't be grown in Massachusetts without a floating row cover—but it has nothing to do with the short growing season. Cucumber beetles transmit a wilt disease that kills plants before they can set fruit. Covering the plants with a row cover until they begin to flower excludes the beetles, and plants survive long enough to produce good crops.

California farmers use them in a similar way in the Central Valley for fall cucurbit crops that get mosaic and other diseases, according to UC Cooperative Extension farm advisor Manuel Jimenez of

Visalia. Transmitted by aphids and other insects, these diseases can ruin cucumbers, melons and squash. Row covers keep the disease-carrying critters out, if applied right from the start. They even keep slugs and snails away from tender new plants. In the home garden, when plants begin to flower, remove the fabric so pollinating insects can get to the flowers.

Floating row covers help seeds germinate by holding in a little moisture and raising the temperature.

Floating row covers also help seeds germinate by holding in a little moisture and raising the temperature. A few adventuresome gardeners have found them the best way to start hard-to-germinate carrot seed. One is Master Gardener Joyce Gemmell, in the program at El Cajon. "Floating row covers are unbelievable on carrots and salad greens, wonderful on cole crops," she says. "I'd never garden without them." She lays floating row covers directly on top of seed beds for carrots and salad greens, like the mesclun mixes, and watches the plants push them up as they sprout and grow. Simply spread them loosely over the seeds or transplants and bury the edges in the soil.

For other, taller crops she makes tunnels of the row covers by draping them over six-foot lengths of nine-gauge wire bent into half-circles and stuck in the ground (or use half-inch PVC pipe). These arches, spaced about four feet apart, are all connected at the tops with light nylon rope. To keep the wind from whipping the fabric around, she secures it to the rope with spring-type clothespins. The edges touching the ground are stapled to one-by-one-inch pieces of wood so they are easy to lift up when working with the plants underneath.

Gemmell uses these tunnels in fall and winter for cole crops such as broccoli and cauliflower, where they provide extra warmth and protection against cabbage looper and snails. In spring she starts tomatoes, eggplant and peppers underneath, removing the tunnels when the plants hit the top. They add heat and completely exclude the tiniest of pests, such as flea beetles, which can make young eggplant look like it has been blasted by a shotgun. Borkevitz cautions: "Plant and cover immediately." Otherwise, you may trap pests inside.

Most row covers last several years if you're careful with them. Brands such as Reemay, Tufbell and Agrofabric are easy to find in mail-order catalogues in lengths small enough for home gardens.

Prepare to be amazed at the growth going on under the row cover. "It's truly phenomenal," says Andersen.

Shade cloth: Woven fabrics that shade the garden have been used by some for years, on structures over fuchsias and cymbidiums, for instance. You've seen them at nurseries where they protect the shade-loving plants. Shade fabrics have improved—they are now able to stand up to the sun for more than a few years and are stronger so they don't easily tear. You can find them in different densities, from light shade to quite dark, at nurseries and in catalogues.

In the garden, they can be attached to overhead structures to shade large areas, or used on little trellises in the vegetable garden to grow crops that like cooler temperatures in summer. One catalogue suggests 80 percent shade for shade-loving ornamental plants, but only 47 percent for lettuce, spinach and other crops that need some summer cooling in hot areas.

Weed barriers: Woven fabrics that keep weeds from growing undoubtedly have their uses in Southern California, but, so far, most who have tried find them less than amazing. They are used extensively by East Coast gardeners, who roll out the fabrics over prepared soil, then cut Xs and plant right through them. Then they cover the barrier with a mulch—not only to make it presentable but also to protect it from the sun. But most East Coast weeds are perennials, which get trapped underneath. Here, Heuer and others say, annual weeds find a way to sprout and grow in the mulch above the barrier. Heuer adds, "They won't stop Bermuda grass."

After a few years, the barriers "float" to the surface and begin to degrade. Picking up the old barrier and laying down a new one is difficult and messy. Heuer thinks they're "fairly effective" if they are pinned to the ground and a good thick mulch put on top. A variety of special pins are now sold for this purpose. Mulches—gravel or chips from a tree service—should be at least three inches thick. Chunky bark probably makes the worst mulch on top of a weed barrier.

For the experimenter, there are many new kinds of weed barriers worth trying. One, Ewemulch, is a natural, light brown, permeable wool blanket, suitable for short-term uses because it is biodegradable. To learn more, contact Appleseed Wool Corp. P.O. Box 101, 55 Bell St., Plymouth, OH 44865, *(419) 687-9665*; www.appleseedwool.com.

Bird netting: Nylon bird netting is the ultimate way to keep birds and other larger pests away from fruit. Because it can be hard to get on and off of fruit trees and berry bushes, some gardeners build large, aviary-like structures. Bird netting is a necessity over beds of strawberries; here you simply drape it over the plants.

Some gardeners have found that placing bird netting over a newly prepared or planted bed prevents cats from using that nice loose soil as an Olympic-sized litter box.

Woven fabrics that keep weeds from growing undoubtedly have their uses in Southern California, but, so far, most who have tried find them less than amazing.

A Tune-up for Roses

L ike cars, roses need periodic maintenance—minor tune-ups, if you will—to keep them growing and flowering. These should occur after every cycle of bloom (rather than after every 15,000 miles). While a rose will not quit and leave you stranded on a freeway should you miss one tune-up, it will better cruise through summer.

Though roses seem to be perpetually in flower in Southern California, the blossoms actually come in fairly distinct cycles. The first flowering is in early April, the next usually in late May, one in early July, and so on, right up to Christmas. This varies somewhat with the weather and certainly the neighborhood.

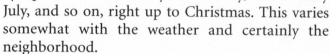

To speed this process, remove spent flowers promptly after each cycle; otherwise, much energy goes into the production of seeds, in the form of rose hips, or fruits. The rule for cutting off spent flowers couldn't be simpler: Make your cut just above a five-part leaf (this true leaf appears to be five smaller leaves). Fine-tune this technique by making the cut above a five-part leaf that faces in the direction you want the new growth to point, usually out from the center of the plant.

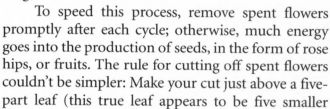

Also, look for weak growth and dead or damaged canes. Cut these out, or back to the first strong five-part leaf. Strip off any yellowed leaves.

While most serious rose growers fertilize every month of the growing season, it is sometimes easier to fertilize at the same time you cut off the spent blossoms. There is no end to the recommendations on how and what to fertilize roses with—all you really need to do is fertilize them with *something*. I've seen abundant roses on plants fertilized with fish emulsion, a rather weak fertilizer that usually contains only about five percent nitrogen. I also know people who fertilize with very strong stuff such as ammonium sulfate, which contains about 21 percent nitrogen (it's a real bargain but is strong enough to burn plants if too much is used). Easiest is to scatter a granular fertilizer around the base of the plant in a circle about six feet across, or apply a liquid fertilizer, following label directions, and then thoroughly water to push it into the soil. Don't apply right at the base of the plant since most roots are farther out.

Never underestimate how much water a rose wants. It can get by on very little, as countless roses growing on abandoned properties attest, but it will only thrive with lots. On the other hand, don't drown it—let the soil dry a little between irrigations. A thorough watering twice a week during spring and fall is usually enough. Summer usually calls for three irrigations a week, at least inland.

Be a little careful with new roses planted this past winter—they need less fertilizer (some people say none) and less water.

When you're finished, rake up any fallen petals and leaves and loosen the

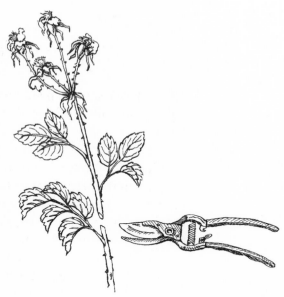

Promptly cut faded flowers from roses, making the cut just above a five-part leaf.

very surface of the soil around the bush for water and air to penetrate. You might want to add a mulch around the base. Bandini 101 planting amendment is a frequent recommendation—it is full of acidic shavings that help reduce the natural alkalinity of our soil.

If on subsequent tune-ups you notice that canes are getting old and woody and that no new growth is coming from the bottom of the plant, try a trick that helps roses make basal breaks, a term for new sprouts that come from the base of the plant. (Don't confuse these with suckers, sprouts coming from the roots. Suckers should be snapped off, basal breaks encouraged.)

To encourage basal breaks, add this regimen to your after-bloom routine: Sprinkle one tablespoon to a quarter cup (the recommendations vary) of Epsom salts around the base of the bush. Jon Bastian, editor of *Santa Barbara Roses*, the excellent publication of the Santa Barbara Rose Society assures me that this is not just so much folklore. Epsom salts is usually sold at pharmacies for soaking feet or as a laxative, though it can also be found at some nurseries. It is not to be confused with table salt or any other salt. The blue Epsom salts is magnesium sulfate–it will not add to the salt content of the soil (which is harmful to plants.)

Should you get exceptionally strong new growth from the base of the plant, you might try this other trick Bastian learned from an Italian gardener. Snap off the top of the new cane when it reaches about mid-thigh—it will break with a *snap* just like an asparagus stalk. This will encourage the shoot to branch and flower sooner.

Now you're ready for another 15,000 miles.

CAN ROSES GO ORGANIC?

E ver since roses first leafed out in early spring most gardeners have been contending with aphids. The unfortunate have already seen leaves dusted by powdery mildew. In time the undersides may become dotted with a bright orange disease, appropriately called rust. When it gets warm enough, nearly invisible thrips may stipple petals, and microscopic mites will web the undersides of leaves. Downy mildew may lay siege, and a humid summer will bring on the dreaded black spot. And these are just the seven most common rose problems.

Roses are subject to so many pests and diseases, it is a wonder so many of us grow them. But there are a few gardeners who manage nearly defect-free plants without even resorting to the common chemical controls and fertilizers. Call them lucky, or conscientious, but they have forsworn Miracle-Gro and malathion.

For more than 10 years, landscape designer Ivy Reid has been growing large, luscious roses in an island bed in her Pacific Palisades backyard with "no problems, pests or diseases at all," she says. They are surrounded by a great many other flowers, and the whole effect is of a wonderfully huge bouquet. Hers is a completely organic, Bio-Dynamic garden, following the techniques developed by the founder of this organic movement, Rudolf Steiner. If any plant should put these practices to the test, it's the rose.

This didn't happen overnight, Reid warns. It took several years to wean the garden from Osmocote and other chemical fertilizers. She carefully picked off every leaf that became diseased and every bug she discovered. "Now the garden is full of butterflies and ladybugs," she says. "The flowers even smell better." But patience and perseverance are necessary—expect a few problems while you better the soil and pesticides wear off so natural controls can take over.

Reid believes, as do most organic gardeners, that a healthy soil makes for healthy plants: "Healthy plants, like a healthy body, fend off problems." She begins her organic rose-growing year in January, when she carefully prunes all 30 plants and adds compost around the base of each. For every five plants, she uses about a one-cubic-foot bag of specially ordered Bio-Dynamic compost, enriched with manure and other organic and mineral products.

In April, early summer (after the second bloom) and again in early fall, she adds more compost to the soil surface. That's about it. "I've never found an easier, more effective way of growing roses," she says.

In Malibu, Andy Lopez claims to know of at least 6,000 organic rose gardeners out there. An organic gardening consultant who sells organic compost (enriched with llama manure and rock dusts), he organized The Invisible Gardeners, a club for organic gardeners, and started The Organic Gardening Bulletin Board; call *(310) 457-4438,* or log on to *http://invisiblegardener.com.* For him, organic gardening is a lifestyle. "It's no quick fix," he says. "Like cooking, you get better at it," as you improve the soil and avoid chemical fertilizers and sprays.

Lopez believes that high-nitrogen fertilizers are a soil's worst enemy. He uses compost as his basic soil improver and fertilizer, as well as other organic fertilizers such as alfalfa meal or compost tea (steep a sack of compost in water for five days). He is convinced that high-nitrogen fertilizers actually attract pests. "Ninety percent of the time, the real problem is nutrition," he says. The soil needs improving, with compost.

Andy Lopez believes that high-nitrogen fertilizers are a soil's worst enemy.

If pests do appear, his favorite remedy is a homemade soap spray, though his recently published book, "Natural Pest Control" (The Invisible Gardener, Los Angeles), suggests all sorts of non-chemical controls. He mixes a tablespoon of Dr. Bronners Peppermint Soap in a gallon of water, sometimes adding a couple of squirts of Tabasco, to control all kinds of pests, from aphids to mites. Especially wary of ants, which tend to bring other pests onto rosebushes, he uses this spray at the first sighting. He prefers to spray late in the day, just as the sun sets, so it sits on the leaves as long as possible and doesn't dry out. On hot days, the solution should be less concentrated (or simply wait for a cooler day). "You do have to be diligent," he summarizes. "You can't just ignore the garden until a pest or disease is out of control and then try to remedy it."

In his Altadena garden, Tom Carruth, horticulturist at Weeks Roses in Upland, has developed some interesting defenses against pests and diseases, though he admits that his techniques are not totally organic. By watering early in the morning, he manages to wash off powdery mildew before it has a chance to form. Although it grows in the dew of morning, he says, it can't stand being totally wet. Watering early in the day also prevents black spot, caused by foliage being too wet too long, or the air too humid. His rosebushes are spaced and positioned so that they have plenty of air circulating around them. This way, the leaves stay fresh and dry later in the day. "Those of us originally from the East Coast learned not to wet the foliage on roses," he says. "But that's not the case in California."

He has found that placing his sprinklers so they spray up to the undersides of leaves has dramatically reduced the microscopic web-forming spider mites. "They easily drown," he explains. Aphids are as easily dispatched (just wash or rub them off), though he hasn't found a way to battle summer's thrips, which damage flower petals.

For rust and downy mildew (a misnomer, for there is nothing "downy" about this disease that disfigures leaves and stems with dark purplish blotches), he suggests a dormant spray containing zinc or copper. Applied when roses are leafless in winter, it heads off diseases, reducing them by 90 percent, he figures.

The secret to using fewer chemicals, or none at all, in the rose garden, according to Carruth, is: Plan ahead, be persistent, and "learn to deal with the fact that everything's not going to be perfect."

BEWARE OF FALSE GARLIC

One of the worst weeds in the garden, right up there with nut-grass, is actively growing now and soon to flower and set seed. If you didn't know it, you might think it a pretty little wild onion. *Nothoscordum inodorum*, or false garlic, does look much like one of the *Allium* clan of onions and garlic. It has slightly grayish bulb-like foliage and a dainty cluster of little white flowers atop stems a foot tall or taller. That is perhaps how it escaped unnoticed in my garden for so long.

When digging out false garlic, make sure you get all the little baby bulbs at its base.

Having proved itself on the beaches of Bermuda and much of the southern United States, it has rapidly spread throughout Southern California, by seeds and by little bulblets so prodigiously produced by parent bulbs. These little bulblets quickly mature, form a brown skin and separate from the parent. Because they are no longer attached, the best systemic herbicides, including Roundup, cannot touch them.

And because they are dirt-brown, they get left behind when you attempt to get rid of the parent plant by digging it up.

There are no known chemical controls, short of fumigating the soil with methyl bromide (which kills everything, even tree roots, must be applied by professionals and is on the verge of being outlawed). The only way to get rid of false garlic is to dig it up. Working in a moist soil with a wide trowel, carefully dig up every parent plant and excavate a nice-sized pocket of soil surrounding it (to make sure none of the microscopic bulbs remain). Then send it all to the dump.

At this time of year, this is relatively easy. I've successfully eradicated quite a large stand from my garden, but it took three springs of watching and digging (in winter it is dormant and invisible). Never let any seeds form—every one is sure to germinate. The seedling bulbs are quick to make little bulblets themselves, and in no time you have a small forest of false garlic. Watch out!

SPRING CLEANING

F or some spring flowers, the show is just about over. Their petals litter the garden like the spilled popcorn in theater aisles. The ranunculus, tulips and daffodils have had it, and their untidiness needs attention. Though it always seems too soon, it's time to start clearing out and cleaning up for the summer ahead. Fortunately, not all spring flowers finish up at the same time. Otherwise, the work would be overwhelming.

Ranunculus might come back if you leave them alone and don't water much in summer, but most gardeners just pull them out. Tulips seldom come back with much conviction in Southern California, so dig them up while the leaves still clearly mark their locations and toss them. If you planted them as deeply as you should have, much digging is required.

Whether you are digging up or pulling out, have a sack of soil amendment and fertilizer on hand and replenish the soil. Products like Gromulch are useful for this purpose. A mix of bark and other organic products, they fluff up a soil, and, in the case of Gromulch, which contains recycled sewage sludge, add fertilizer value (and helps recycle the stuff).

Other bulbs, including many daffodils, and certainly most of the South African bulbs such as freesia, ixia and sparaxis, definitely return to flower again next spring, even multiplying in the meantime (some say even anemones return). These bulbs need to have their foliage cut back—but only after it turns completely brown, not before, no matter how untidy. To keep it from becoming an eyesore just when the rest of the garden comes into full flower, you must figure out how to disguise it. Some tie it in a simple overhand knot, which makes it lower and neater. (Done with a little care this knotted foliage is actually quite interesting, a sign that the gardener is good at his or her craft.) Others simply bend and hide the fading foliage under the leaves of a nearby plant. You can also dig up bulbs and temporarily plant them somewhere else until the foliage fades, but this is a major job.

After the foliage is cut back, most gardeners in California leave the bulbs in the ground. Some, though, dig and store them in a cool, dry, airy place—a corner of the garage, for instance.

Pull out spent annual flowers. Some, such as calendulas and snapdragons, may only be past their peak at this point—you might want to enjoy them for a few more weeks. Cutting off the dead flowers, or dead-heading, helps them last longer and make the garden look tidier. My wife is a champ at this chore, pinching off primrose blossoms to keep them going, even pansies. Dead-heading, like weeding, can be a very pleasant pastime, fit into those short periods of time when bigger projects are impossible, just before sunset, for instance. (Primroses, incidentally, can be left in the garden since they are generally perennial in nature, though they look pretty shabby in summer. Many gardeners prefer to replant them each year.)

A thorough watering helps revitalize the garden, especially if this has been one of those nearly rainless years. With all the flowers in bloom, you may be reluctant to water—laden with droplets of water, they may start to lean and topple. But it is time to begin watering in earnest. Smart gardeners disturb nothing by watering from underneath, with already installed drip lines or by laying the hose on the ground and flooding it a bit at a time. If you insist on using sprinklers, stake any plant that might fall over. Foxgloves, delphiniums, dahlias, gladiolus and others may come into flower without the benefit of stakes, but when you turn on the sprinklers, you are likely to lose a few just when they are at their best.

The touch of melancholy that accompanies the pulling out of spent flowers is quickly cured by a trip to the nursery, where you will find all the makings for a summer garden. Be sure not to buy spring flowers, in stock now for instant effect. What you want now are the little packs of tiny summer flowers, the smaller and younger the better. These will have the time to develop good root systems before flowering.

Dead-heading, like weeding, can be a very pleasant pastime, fit into those short periods of time when bigger projects are impossible.

May

SOME LIKE IT HOT

HOW ABOUT SOME HOT COLORS FOR THAT hot weather ahead? This is not the season for soft pink and misty blue. What's needed are colors that shimmer in the heat, that won't disappear in the glare of the midday sun, that burn with hidden fire. Flaming red, ember orange, molten gold, sun yellow—colors as hot as the sand at the beach. These also happen to be the colors of the annual flowers that grow best in summer, so there are plenty at nurseries now.

You may also see pansies, dianthus and a few others, which do better planted in the fall. You can coddle them all summer and they will grow and bloom, especially near the beach. But why bother? They're much prettier in the gentle light of spring.

WEEK
19

What you want now are celosia, coreopsis, cosmos, gaillardia, gayfeather, gloriosa daisies, marigolds, petunias, portulaca, salvias, verbena, zinnias and the like—there's lots to choose from. Is it too late to plant? Not at all. These summer flowers grow fast and will bloom through all the hot weather ahead, well into fall. They'll be in full flower during that time of year when people spend the most time outdoors, barbecuing, around the pool or playing croquet.

Just be sure to water them every day the first week or so, until they get their roots into the soil. Watering is more critical now than in fall.

Since most of summer's most striking flowers are annuals, you plant them now and then pull them out in fall. A few are perennials—you can plant them and pull them out with the annuals, or leave them and bear with them through winter when they look ragged at best. The brightest schemes mix a great variety of both. There are just too many summer flowers to plant only marigolds and petunias—a grand bouquet is possible.

Compose the garden at the nursery. Try flowers out in the shopping cart or on the ground in the aisles to see what looks good with what. Almost all the annuals and perennials at nurseries now already have at least one flower open, so there's no guessing about color. With any luck, the heights of the plants are on the labels so you can tell where to put them in the garden bed—toward the front or back.

Almost all zinnias are bright and sunny, like their native Mexico, even the pinks and roses. If mildew is a problem in your garden, be forewarned—zinnias get it. However, the new, almost fluorescent 'Classic Gold' doesn't get all the pests and diseases zinnias are prone to, mildew in particular, according to Lillian Greenup, of Sperling Nursery in Calabasas. It's a slightly spreading plant about 15 to 18 inches tall. About the same height is 'Rose Pinwheel', and, in true zinnia fashion, it's a Day-Glo shade of this normally muted color. It is mildew resistant, if not ironclad. There is also a cream in the 'Classic' series, with more colors on the way. Look for the taller zinnias, for those back-of-the-border plants.

'Lady in Red' is the hot ticket, says John Bauman, of the Palos Verdes Begonia Farm in Torrance. A dazzling orange-red, this recent salvia is an All-America Selections and Fleuroselect winner. Its growth is more open and upright than that of other bedding salvias, more like one of the perennial sages, but it tops out at about 15 inches. Greenup points out its one drawback: Like many salvias, it tends to be brittle. When you plant, be careful not to break off the branches, and don't let Rover run through the flowers.

The common, old-fashioned red bedding salvia may be even more brittle, but it's as red as ever. 'Red Hot Sally' is the best of these, says Lew Whitney, of Roger's Gardens in Corona del Mar. Cristin Fusano, color specialist at Roger's, says that if you bump a salvia it will break, but it "blooms forever." The news here are the more muted shades, such as the very handsome 'Burgundy' that mixes wine-red flowers with purple calyxes.

Another old favorite, the flame-like celosia (not the one that looks like a coral reef formation) has a 'New Look'. This strain has not

At the nursery, try flowers out in the shopping cart or on the ground in the aisles to see what looks good with what.

186

only bright red feathery flowers, but red leaves as well. You simply can't get any hotter—unless it's the 'Lady Bird' cosmos. These are what Bauman calls "the other cosmos," not the pink, lavender or white kinds so common in gardens, but those descended from *Cosmos sulphureus*. The colors do look like a sizzling sulfur spring—deep mineral yellow, oranges and reds.

To add a little height and strength to a garden of bedding plants, Fusano says, use a few perennials such as the deep red 'Garnet' penstemon. "People go right past the pink penstemon when this one is in bloom," she says. A sunflower relative named *Heliopsis* 'Summer Sun' is so bright, she says, "you can see it from the other side of the nursery"—and Roger's is a *big* nursery. It definitely brings height to the garden, growing to four feet with masses of two-inch flowers. Try planting it with one of the perennial heleniums, such as *Helenium autumnale* 'Sunshine Hybrid'. With flowers in bright autumnal colors (including that same mahogany hue found in gloriosa daisies, as well as bright yellows and golds), these help the summer garden slide into fall.

Then there are the quick-blooming perennial coreopsis, perhaps better used as annuals because they get so shabby in winter. 'Early Sunrise' is the best of the bright sun-yellow, double-flowered forms, to about 18 inches tall, but 'Baby Sun' is cuter and smaller, to only a foot, with single flowers.

One of Fusano's favorite annuals is golden fleece. "It looks like someone turned a spotlight on it," she says. This is a short, front-of-the-bed flower, staying under six inches.

Even marigolds seem to be getting brighter. Take a look at 'Flame' and 'Red Marietta'. 'Bonanza Orange' is one of Greenup's favorites—a brilliant pumpkin orange. She has even found a hot little vining thunbergia named 'Little Suzie', a shocking, not-to-be-missed orange, that grows to about four feet tall and will bloom until Thanksgiving, even in the San Fernando Valley. You figure out how to use it—spilling out of pots maybe?

With so many choices, isn't it about time you turned up the heat in the garden?

A Strategy for Summer Color

This is the weekend to make decisions for summer. I don't mean when to take that vacation, or which camp to send the kids to, but what to plant in the garden to make sure it is as colorful as spring's. The light of summer is very different from the light we are experiencing now. On cloudy, overcast days, pink and lavender and other soft colors look vibrant and spring-like, but as the overcast burns off for the summer, the light becomes strong and bright and soft colors melt into their surroundings. Strong colors are called for, at least for those sunny areas. This is why marigolds, gloriosa daisies and zinnias are such popular summer flowers.

Now is perhaps the best time to plant. We can usually count on a month or more of overcast weather still to come, which gives the plants time to take hold before the weather turns consistently hot. The spring flowers are pretty much finished, making space available in the garden.

Before you head for the nursery, or turn a spadeful of soil, work out your color scheme. Because summer flower colors are so striking, they do not always harmonize with one another and, without a little planning, can end up looking like so much splattered paint. Here are some simple tricks that can make a summer garden colorful and easy to live with.

It's Even Hot in the Shade

Bedding plants for shady parts of the garden can also be bright, if not sunny.

Impatiens certainly keep getting louder. For the brightest look, Lew Whitney recommends planting the mixes. Lillian Greenup suggests the 'Dazzler' series, 'Punch' in particular, and the 'Super Elfins'. Both groups have fade-resistant lipstick colors and a very uniform habit of growth. She describes 'Punch' as "not red and not coral—it's just a lovely color."

Whitney also likes the 'Nonstop' begonias, which are not tuberous begonias, though the flowers are nearly as large and certainly as colorful, and not ordinary bedding begonias. "They are much more floriferous than tuberous begonias," he says. "Keep feeding, and they keep flowering."

The leaves of coleus seem to glow in the shade.

&- Let one color dominate. The easiest is yellow—so many summer flowers are yellow or gold. Two of the best, marigolds and gloriosa daisies, are annuals and like hot weather. Coreopsis, a yellow gold, is a perennial that will flower all summer. Several yarrows bloom yellow or gold, including one barely two inches tall and some that tower three to four feet. For the foreground, there is the dainty but sturdy golden fleece, another golden yellow.

&- Add some subtle variations on this one-color theme. Gaillardia, a summer-flowering perennial, is mostly yellow but has touches of maroon (there is also a wonderful brick-red form). Certain marigolds have maroon in them, and gloriosa daisies are touched with mahogany, or are entirely that rich color.

&- Plan for a variety of heights. A garden of flowers that are all the same height looks like the landscaping at an industrial park. Using tall gloriosa daisies (not the new short kinds), the tall yarrows, perhaps daylilies or midsized sunflowers guarantees a great variety of heights.

Do not arrange all the flowers as though they were sitting on bleachers at the ball game. It makes sense to keep most of the tall flowers toward the back of the bed, and most of the short flowers in front, but here and there break this regimen and let some flowers stand out from the crowd. You might think of it this way: Most of the flowers are sitting on bleachers so they all get a good view, but here and there a few are standing up and cheering wildly, perhaps for your brilliant stroke of composition.

&- Add another, perhaps contrasting, color to liven things up. Those flowers called "blue" (but are really some shade of violet or purple) are a good bet. Blue bedding salvia (*Salvia farinacea*), usually labeled "blue bedder," is a traditional spoiler—it flowers most of summer and fall and is just tall enough to stand above marigolds. Lobelia is a popular blue for the front row.

&- Once you season this scheme with some subtle variations, and some contrast in height and color, you can confidently add more colors, perhaps the pinks and reds of petunias and zinnias, or the low-growing wildly colored portulaca—as long as they are in the minority. Rather than scattering these through the bed, concentrate them in little colonies of several plants so they become bays of color in a sea of sameness.

&- Should you begin to worry that the colors will clash, use the best trick of all: Plant white flowers between the potential offenders. White is called the "peacemaker" because it quickly cools color conflicts. White-flowered varieties of nicotiana are a favorite for summer

189

gardens, and white feverfew also works well. Other useful white flowers include good old alyssum and candytuft—low enough for the front row—and the white forms of petunias, lobelia, verbena, zinnia and even marigold (which comes in a passable creamy white).

How do you get the right colors when so many flowers, especially annuals, are sold as mixes? This is perhaps the toughest trick of all. More nurseries are beginning to sell flowers in packs of separate colors—all pinks, for instance—but it is still an uncommon practice. You could grow some from seed yourself—seed catalogues are full of separate colors. It is certainly not too late to sow seed—directly in the ground where they are to grow—of marigolds and zinnias, and others.

Most likely you will have to buy some plants in flower and in individual pots, and some that are young and in packs of several. Suppose we make a garden out of the plants just mentioned. We could let marigolds be the mainstay—they are easy to find in separate colors. So are blue bedding salvia, gloriosa daisies, golden fleece and lobelia. Zinnias are hard to find in separate colors, so look through the quart pots, and buy those with color showing, perhaps selecting only tall red ones. Do the same when buying a few petunias; pick through the nursery shelves looking only for the color you want.

There you have it—a colorful, sunny composition for summer with enough variety to make it interesting and a good balance of young, eager-to-grow plants and those older ones of which you can be sure of the color. Lay them out in the bed, still in their containers, and move them around until they look right. Then plant. Remember to keep them thoroughly watered the first few weeks.

Have You Watered the Garden Lately? Thoroughly?

T his should be the greenest, growingest time of the year; virtually everything is putting on new leaves. Gardens should look lush. If lawns, even those common Bermuda-grass lawns that are still coming out of winter dormancy, aren't thick carpets of green, suspect a dry soil, especially if we had little rain during the past winter. If shrubs look a little peaked, if flowers are not growing as they should or are blooming poorly, suspect a too-dry soil.

On inspection, you are likely to discover that the soil is as dry as dust—maybe not on the surface, but a few inches down, where most of the roots are. You will also probably find that getting the soil wet again is not easy. Soils tend to become water repellent if they get too dry.

It is important to realize that this can happen even if you feel that you have been watering. The mistake was probably made way back in February when it seemed to be raining often enough to carry a garden through. In some years, storms leave very little moisture behind, and following each is a hot dry period of Santa Ana winds. Since plants weren't growing much, the lack of water wasn't noticeable. Once the soil dried out, it became like a duck's back—shedding water instead of absorbing it. Think of how difficult it is to rewet a sponge that has become too dry—you get the picture.

A soil sampler, or probe, is a tool that I consider indispensable for checking my soil. Larger nurseries carry these rather expensive devices. It is a simple hollow tube, with one side cut away, that you push into the ground (if you can—if you can't, that's a good hint in itself). Pull it out, and you have a core of soil to examine for signs of moisture. If you want to save the considerable expense of buying one, use a spade; push it in and then lean back on it to examine the slice of soil exposed. However, the soil sampler disturbs the garden less.

Rewetting lawns and garden beds can add up to a weekend project because it requires many short irrigations to give the moisture time to soak in. The solution for a water-repellent soil is not to turn on the sprinklers and let them run for an hour. Instead, run them in short bursts. Turn them on for five or 10 minutes, then off. Wait half an hour. Turn them on again, then off, and then wait. And so on. The water will soak in a little deeper each time. Turning them off and on keeps the water from running off—into the street, into a low spot, into softer ground somewhere. As the day progresses, keep checking the soil with the sampler, until you have forced the water at least a foot deep, preferably 18 inches.

Research shows that most of a plant's roots, whether they belong to a flower or a tree, grow between three and 18 inches deep. The only way for water to soak this deep is to use a sprinkler or some kind of soaker device. You cannot water with your thumb clamped over the end of the hose, no matter how tempting and refreshing that may be on a warm day.

On inspection, you are likely to discover that the soil is as dry as dust.

NOW'S THE TIME TO PLANT CITRUS, AND OTHER MYTHS EXPLODED

June has always been the traditional citrus-planting season in Southern California. According to Dr. Mary Lu Arpaia, UC Cooperative Extension subtropical horticulturist at UC Riverside, however, it's on the late side. "April and May are best," she says, "but June is better than September." The idea is to get citrus in the ground after the last possible frost but before hot weather descends. Planting in the

WEEK
20

spring gives citrus plenty of time to get comfortable in their new surroundings before coping with the chilly winter weather (young plants with tender new growth are the most susceptible to frost). I had always heard that the reason June was a good time for planting was that citrus needed warm soil to grow in. So it turns out that while they may like heat, they don't at planting time. This was only the first citrus adage to fall under the ax.

Citrus do most of their growing in spring, and that is the best time to fertilize—though this is not the time often recommended. Fertilize, instead, in late February or early March, when new growth is just beginning, and then again after the trees have flowered, in late spring, but not while the trees are blossoming, says Dr. Arpaia. As an alternative, fertilize a little each month. Do not fertilize navel oranges and winter-fruiting mandarin oranges after July with any fertilizer high in nitrogen, or you may effect the December-to-January crop.

Citrus do most of their growing in spring, and that is the best time to fertilize.

Another maxim states that citrus, like most trees, need infrequent but thorough watering: "Soak it once a month" is what I've heard. Research shows that most citrus roots are in the top 18 to 24 inches of soil, which is relatively shallow for a tree. Citrus need watering more than once a month; the soil should always be moist a few inches down, but never soaking wet. Precisely how to water is difficult to spell out because it varies so much depending on soil and climate, but with roots so shallow it is easy to check. Dig a little hole a few inches down to check that the soil is moist but not wet.

Should you err on the side of too little water, soak the tree. It will probably rebound if you then keep it moist. Citrus are pretty tough trees, according to Dr. Arpaia. Too much water is more likely to be fatal, bringing on root diseases. Sickly, yellowish leaves are often a sign of too much water. Yellowish leaves with veins that remain green are chlorotic, which means the plant is missing one or more trace elements. Trees are more likely to be chlorotic in alkaline soils. To cure this deficiency, fertilize with chelated iron and other trace elements, available at all nurseries.

Dr. Mikeal Roose, assistant professor of genetics at UC Riverside, debunked another citrus myth: There are dwarf citrus. "There are no true dwarf scion varieties, like there are with peaches of other fruits," he says. It was nurseryman Don Durling, of Durling Nursery in Fallbrook, who had put me on to Dr. Roose. Durling is trying to get the dwarf question straightened out so people are not misled by nursery tags and labels. Citrus labeled "dwarf" are actually semidwarf. Citrus grow smaller only when budded onto rootstocks that slow their growth; they are not "naturally" dwarf. If you were to take a cutting from a "dwarf" tree, root it and then plant it, you would get a full-sized tree.

The citrus that should be labeled "dwarf" are budded onto a rootstock called Flying Dragon.

The rootstock most commonly used is Rubidoux trifoliate, which reduces the size of oranges, tangelos and 'Dancy' tangerines by about 45 percent and grapefruit and 'Owari' (Owari Satsuma) mandarins by about 70 percent. Expect citrus on this rootstock to reach nine to 14 feet in about 10 years. To keep the trees even smaller, grow them in containers, or prune yearly. These trees—the ones that should be labeled "semidwarf"—produce excellent fruit in a wide variety of soils and climates, and really aren't all that large.

The citrus that should be labeled "dwarf" are budded onto a rootstock called Flying Dragon. Although these grow to six or eight feet in 10 years, there are some catches. First, the process of growing the rootstock is tricky. Then, it is an expensive operation since the plant grows so slowly. Nursery customers are likely to think they're getting gypped because they have to pay so much for such a small tree. As a result, these dwarf citrus are not easy to find. Also, there is a stronger tendency for citrus budded onto Flying Dragon to become chlorotic in alkaline soils. They need water more often because they have smaller root systems and do not do as well in sandy soils or where the water is especially saline. However, they have proved to be fairly cold tolerant and are resistant to many citrus diseases.

So, should you decide to plant citrus now, expect to find trees at nurseries that are semidwarf, no matter what the label says, unless it clearly states that the plant is on Flying Dragon roots, or the nursery person can assure you that it is what the plant is budded on. Otherwise, expect a tree to grow to 10 or more feet and allow enough room. Or plant it in a pot. Citrus are one of the better choices for containers.

A Lemon by Every Door

No Southern California garden should be without a lemon by the back door, even if it is only in a container, or even if it is in a less than ideal spot. What other fruit does a cook require as often? What other fruit is always there, waiting patiently on the tree until needed? Lemons, like most other citrus, do not ripen, nor do they drop, their fruit all at once. Unlike a peach or a plum, the harvest is not over in a week, and you are seldom inundated with fruit. Fruit can hang on the tree for as long as six months without deteriorating, getting sweeter all the time. For this reason alone, lemons and citrus can be said to be the most useful trees in the garden.

Convinced? Then you are in luck because this is the perfect week to plant any citrus. Of all the citrus, lemons are the most adaptable. I know of plants that grow in shade and bear fruit (even one that grows in the shade of a live oak!) and plants that have lived in containers for 10 or more years, bearing fruit the whole time.

The ideal, of course (and essential for other citrus), is a sunny, warm spot, though lemons need the least heat of any citrus. For this reason, for instance, they grow very well as a commercial crop in Ventura County, not far from the beach.

If you are going to try one in a container, start with a large one, at least 18 inches across. Cover the drainage holes in the bottom with squares of window screen (to keep out slugs and sowbugs while keeping in soil), and use any good commercial potting soil.

Lemon varieties to look for include: the market lemon ('Eureka'), which bears all year; 'Improved Meyer', which bears round, thin-skinned fruit that is not as acidic on a naturally smaller tree, and the thorny 'Lisbon', with fruit that comes mostly in the fall. 'Frost', a new lemon that stands more cold and heat, is a good choice inland. If you seek the unusual, consider 'Ponderosa', the King Kong of lemons, with fruit that can weigh two pounds, though most of that is the thick rind. There is even a variegated lemon, with leaves (and occasional fruit) striped cream and green, very ornamental—like most citrus it can be a handsome landscape plant as well.

In the garden, plant lemons and other citrus in a generous hole, even if they come in one of those tall skinny containers. To the back-fill, add some amendment, some fertilizer and some extra iron in the form of iron sulfate or iron chelate. Citrus often get yellow leaves (though the veins remain green)—a lack of iron is usually the cause.

Watering is the most important part of citrus culture, and this is where many go wrong. Too much water (or fertilizer) can cause fruit drop and splitting, though so can the weather. After planting, mound up a basin wider than the tree (to be sure the water soaks down to the roots), and fill it with at least three inches of water. Water twice a week for the first few months of summer. For the remainder of the tree's first year, water every seven to 10 days. Water container plants every few days.

GENUINE GERANIUMS

I t's as close to a gardening craze as you're likely to find, this sudden interest in the genuine geraniums. Phenomenally popular in England and virtually unknown in Southern California, where they were seldom seen until a few years ago, they are now the talk of avid gardeners, and nurseries seem to add a new kind every week. "It's the flavor of the month," says Robin Parer, who runs a geranium nursery in Northern California in explaining the craze. Many Southern Californians have made the trek to her nursery, Geraniaceae. You can also order plants directly from the catalogue or web site [*122 Hillcrest Ave., Kentfield, CA 94904, (415) 461-4168; www.geraniaceae.com*].

True geraniums—plants with the botanic name of *Geranium*—are quite different from what we usually call geraniums. The pretenders, the Martha Washington, ivy, zonal and common "geraniums," are technically pelargoniums, native to Africa. True geraniums are found worldwide, from the Arabian Peninsula to Australia, England to the Hawaiian Islands. The confusion over names began in 1753, when Linnaeus lumped the two together as *Geranium* in his "Species Plantarum." When later botanists noted the obvious differences (one is that the flowers of geraniums are symmetrical while those of pelargoniums are asymmetrical), they separated them into *Pelargonium* and *Geranium*. But the damage was done and, amazingly, persists to this day. While it is hard to beat a pelargonium, especially in a pot, the genuine geraniums

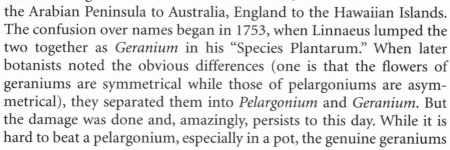

WEEK
21

also have their place in the California garden.

The place for the most commonly available, *Geranium incanum* (which is one of the few true geraniums from Africa), is unquestionably on slopes or in planters, where it can tumble and spill. Laguna Beach landscape architect Jana Ruzicka used it as a water-thrifty ground cover in a Corona del Mar garden just blocks from the seaside bluffs, where it swirls and foams around other plants—a 'Gruss an Teplitz' rose, statice, Santa Barbara daisies, tulbaghia and valerian. At a nearby condominium, they bubble out of a planter box on a balcony railing. In the misty ocean air, the flowers are especially vibrant.

They look nearly as good in the garden of Anne Williams in much drier (and hotter) Glendale. Williams has grown all the true geraniums she can lay her hands on, though it is only a fraction of what's out there—true geraniums are numerous enough to have inspired entire books on the subject. Two of the best are "Hardy Geraniums," by Peter F. Yeo, and "The Gardener's Guide to Growing Hardy Geraniums," by Trevor Bath and Joy Jones. First published in Great Britain, they are available from Timber Press; call *(800) 327-5680.*

Most of the true geraniums are small plants with smallish flowers. They are almost wildflowers; in fact, many are, including one named *Geranium californicum* that grows in the San Bernardino Mountains. Most bloom only in spring and perhaps early summer. On the other hand, they have virtually no problems with pests or diseases and many will flower in some shade, definite pluses. Don't expect the punch of a pelargonium—these are what Parer calls "linking, filler plants," best used in those spaces between other, bolder plants, such as roses.

Geranium sanguineum tops Williams' list of favorites because it's just so easy. It finds its place among other low plants, interweaving with them—a perfect filler along a path or in the front row of a flower garden. It almost disappears for the winter, but from early spring on there is a steady succession of nearly neon flowers a shade of magenta purple. For gardeners who are less gutsy with color, the variety *Geranium sanguineum lancastrense* has soft pink flowers, and it stays as a small spreading mat only inches tall.

Williams thinks the place for geraniums is in front of or even under roses because they can take the watering roses get and the smattering of shade thrown by the bushes—and they help hide the roses' knobby knees. One of her favorites for this use, *Geranium macrorrhizum*, is a dense foot-tall ground cover with flowers held well aloft. It even flowers in half a day of shade, according to Los Angeles land-

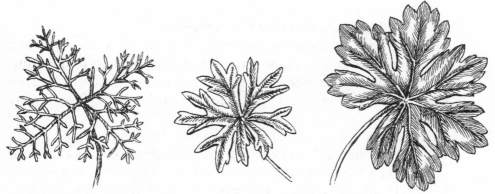

scape designer Christine Rosmini, who has used it as a small-scale ground cover under tall trees in a number of gardens. Parer says it will grow under oaks with little water (important for the health of the oaks) and that deer don't eat it. There are several kinds, with white, pink or deep rose flowers.

Williams doesn't recommend 'Ballerina', with elegant veining on the flowers, which grows well in England, preferring the very similar 'Lawrence Flatman', which does fine in our climate. Others that have thrived in her garden include *Geranium endressii* 'Wargrave Pink', the pearl-gray blue flowers of 'Mrs. Kimball Clark', and the hybrids 'Claridge Druce' and 'Biokovo'. In particular, 'Biokovo' seems to be a winner in Southern California, so much so that it is quickly becoming common in quart pots at nurseries. The very soft pink flowers are about an inch across, and there are lots of them. In one Westside garden it blooms furiously from March and into June, with a sprinkling of flowers through summer. Rather than dying to the ground in winter, it shrinks in size. Parer says that 'Claridge Druce' can stand the heat of the Central Valley—if the true geraniums are sensitive to anything, it's summer heat.

Some true geraniums come very close to true blue, a color gardeners covet. England's 'Johnson's Blue' is the purest (though not as blue as some catalogue photos would have you believe), but it's a poor grower in most gardens here. Williams has lost it several times. Better suited to our climate is *Geranium pratense*, which grows to two feet or more with near blue flowers. It does best when its roots are kept cool, similar to clematis, says Parer. Because it goes completely dormant in winter, mark its spot in the garden, or you're likely to accidentally dig it out come bulb-planting time. A more intense blue is found on *Geranium ibericum*, which also disappears for the winter. Less blue (more violet), but equally easy, is *Geranium magnificum*, an 18-inch bushy perennial.

The true geraniums not only have pretty flowers, they also have finely cut leaves that often resemble paper snowflakes.

Geranium maderense has staked its claim in the shade. It quickly forms a burly trunk several feet tall, typical of many plants from the islands of Madeira. The dramatic foot-wide leaves look like green paper snowflakes—there is probably no more dramatic plant for shady situations. After a couple of years in the garden, this biennial produces a single huge head, two-and-a-half feet wide, of small magenta-pink flowers. It then dies, although it usually reseeds. This is one the English struggle to grow in greenhouses. It won't be found in the 1,290 pages of "Hortus," the ultimate plant dictionary, nor, for that matter, at too many nurseries here, but it and many genuine geraniums are out there, waiting to take their places in the California sun.

MUMS FOR THE GARDEN

Many of us have forgotten that chrysanthemums are good garden plants, not just florists' fare. They certainly were in my grandfather's garden, where they stood proud and tall. Now they are so common at supermarkets and florist shops that their garden value is often overlooked. That value is great, however: "Sunset Western Garden Book" goes so far as to call chrysanthemums "the most useful of all autumn-blooming perennials." True perennials, they reliably flower in the fall and come back year after year.

There was a time when nurseries carried small cuttings in two-inch pots in the spring, but those seem to have gone the way of tail fins on cars. Instead, we suddenly find mums in full flower all year, but especially in the fall. Those called garden mums, naturally small flowered and small of stature, are used like other bedding plants, for temporary color. Others have larger flowers and bloom on plants treated with chemicals to keep them short. These are usually tossed after they finish flowering just like the florists' mums (though you can save them). And there are those fantastic cut flowers seen at florists. With flowers that look like spiders, or that imitate anemones and dahlias, or with petals that look like little spoons, these are exhibition mums, originally bred for competition at flower shows.

All will grow in the garden as true perennials, if cut back after flowering and then nurtured through the next spring and summer. If you buy them in flower in any season other than autumn—when they are naturally inclined to flower—they may be confused for a while, but they adjust and come back.

If you want to do it right, as my grandfather did, plant now and start with small plants. The best source is Sunnyslope Gardens [*8638 Huntington Drive, San Gabriel, CA 91775 (626) 287-4071*], which has been selling chrysanthemums for more than 50 years at their nursery and through their catalogue. They offer every conceivable kind and color (but not true blue), and a great variety of sizes from very short to towering. There are those wondrous cascading mums. There are flowers with petals that are thread-thin, or massed into pompons.

Sunnyslope sells the traditional rooted cuttings. These little plants will grow to full-size, even towering, mums by fall if planted in a good, rich soil that would suit any other perennial. As soon as the plants are in the ground, pinch off the very top of the stem to force it to make low branches.

Pinching the growing tips of plants such as chrysanthemums encourages them to make a multitude of flowering stems.

To keep plants low and bushy, pinch off the tips of the resulting growth several more times during the season (most florist plants have been pinched repeatedly). As an experiment one year, Anna Benson of Brentwood decided not to pinch back the mums growing in one of her borders. "I was hoping they would look a little wild and more natural," she says. "I was surprised at how tall they got," and they did make a wonderfully wild kind of tall meadow, but required staking.

Like roses, mums need regular watering and fertilizing (at least three times before they flower) and protection from aphids and mildew (some people use rose systemic insecticide/fertilizers). The kinds other than the small cushion mums and garden mums also need staking—Benson stakes hers after they are about a foot tall. Every year right after they flower, she cuts them back right to the ground.

When they stop flowering well, dig them up and divide them in early spring. Toss out the old center of the plant, and save and replant only the newer stems at the edges. This is the other way of starting mums, from your own, or someone else's, divisions.

To save potted mums from the house or received as gifts, follow a similar procedure: Cut the flowers off, leaving a few green leaves on the stem. Take the clump out of the pot, split it into separate plants and plant them in the garden. When new growth sprouts from the base, remove the old stems. Some will come back a lot taller than they were in the pot, once they outgrow the chemical dwarfing treatment.

If you want a garden like my grandfather's—in fall, full of perfectly grown mums with outrageously different flowers and autumnal colors, all nicely staked and staggered for height—it's best to start with rooted cuttings so you know what you're getting.

IMPATIENS—OR
COLEUS AND CALADIUMS

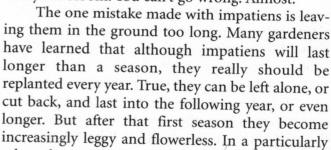

For some, impatiens are far too common to consider; for others, they are a godsend. In this country, they are the single most popular flower grown, but for good reason: They are the only flower that thrives where there is little light. No green thumb is required, just water. If they look a little as if they are molded from plastic, it is because they nearly always look good and are nearly always in bloom. You can't go wrong. Almost.

The one mistake made with impatiens is leaving them in the ground too long. Many gardeners have learned that although impatiens will last longer than a season, they really should be replanted every year. True, they can be left alone, or cut back, and last into the following year, or even longer. But after that first season they become increasingly leggy and flowerless. In a particularly cold year, you may lose them altogether to a frost. In that case, you must start over, because they will not come back.

Many professionals replant impatiens every spring, pulling them out in October or November and replacing them with *Primula obconica* or something similar, which looks good all winter. In the spring, out come the primroses and in goes a new batch of impatiens. It's a neat switch since the obconica primroses are similarly colored and grow in the same conditions as impatiens, but they look their best in winter, while the impatiens look best in summer.

Be careful with impatiens color. While you can't really go wrong, most plantings can use a little fine-tuning. For anything other than a very small bed, avoid the orange-colored ones that often come in a mix, and the bicolored, saving these for containers or where they can stand alone. Designers prefer to use only the reds and the many shades of pink, plus a lot of whites. It makes a more harmonious scheme.

WEEK
22

Avoid alternating colors too abruptly, which creates a speckled look; plant several of each color in a mass. To be sure of the colors, buy plants that already have at least one flower open, or buy plants by color, not as a mix. In small plantings, you can try using the oranges and salmons and even the bicolors—there are not enough plants to clash—but with lots of white, which softens any differences.

Break up the plantings with patches of green. The low-growing, shade-loving baby's tears is a favorite, often mixed with bronze-leafed ajuga. A surprising combination mixes common parsley and impatiens. White azaleas, such as the tried-and-true variety 'Alaska', are another good companion plant, as is the bright blue 'Cambridge' strain of lobelia, though it won't take the same depth of shade.

It's the fancy, multicolored leaves of caladiums and the taller coleus that make them an attractive alternative to impatiens.

Or, rather than impatiens, why not coleus and caladiums? Where summers are warm, these two plants—grown for colorful foliage, not flowers—thrive in the shade. At Villa Abondanza, a private estate in the Hollywood Hills, these two tropical-looking plants filled the beds with luxuriant, even exuberant, color all summer long.

Several years ago, the late Patrick Turnbull and Collie Valadez, garden designers and true plantsmen, told me they had made this discovery "after we became bored with impatiens": Caladiums and coleus grow in the same situation and with the same amount of shade as impatiens. Every spring they replanted the beds as if these two perennial plants were annuals. There was no attempt of keep the coleus and caladiums year round, which is possible with impatiens. The caladiums shrivel in the real cold, though they can come back from their underground tubers when warm weather returns.

Turnbull and Valadez were quick to point out that the Villa Abondanza is a warm garden with a southern exposure and that the tree-like pittosporums above the coleus and caladiums got trimmed high (the lowest branches were seven feet up) so the shade was not dark and dreary. They reported similar success in a Brentwood garden and at their home in Monrovia, but suspected that where ocean breezes are more constant, and in the bottom of Coldwater and other cool canyons, coleus and caladiums might not find quite enough of the warm sultry days and evenings they so obviously enjoy. In these situations, others have had luck planting them in more sun. Coleus are poisonous plants, they also noted, so are not a good idea in gardens visited by small children.

"We feed them to the point of almost burning the foliage," said Collie Valadez.

Pampered as they were by Turnbull and Valadez, the standard coleus used in the centers of these beds grew to four feet by summer's end. Around them grew the caladiums, and at the edges were the lower, spreading kinds of coleus. The coleus was planted in spring as soon as space appeared in the beds, and the caladiums a little later, just before the coleus grew together and touched.

"The caladiums won't grow until the soil is almost hot," said Turnbull. "So we may buy the tubers earlier, but we don't plant them until May or June." Caladiums are available as tubers from January through May. The caladiums sold as tubers grow 18 to 20 inches tall; the small potted plants that sometimes show up at nurseries don't grow as well or as tall. (Plant the tubers in holes two inches deep, and make sure they go in right side up, the rounded end facing down.) Turnbull and Valadez used the all-green and the all-red-and-green kinds but did not mix them.

Every coleus plant was hand-picked. "Some coleus colors can really clash," said Valadez. "So we are careful to pick only those that go together. Too much variety makes the eye very nervous." Added Turnbull: "They can look terrible, like colored popcorn." They bought the coleus in color packs or quart pots, as small as they could find them, because an important part of coleus culture is pinching. Every week the growing tips must be nipped to encourage bushiness; left alone, the plants tend to get tall and leggy. When the standard kinds in the centers of the beds were about 16 to 18 inches tall, they were tied to stakes so overhead watering would not flatten them later on.

And Turnbull and Valadez fed and fed, first at planting time, when the soil was heavily amended with organic matter (for every 100 square feet they used a two-cubic-foot bag of planting, not potting, mix), a preplant fertilizer (one with numbers like 2-10-10 or 2-12-8 on the label) and a peppering of the slow-release fertilizer Osmocote. The plants were then fertilized every week with a liquid fertilizer used at half-strength. "We feed them to the point of almost burning the foliage," said Valadez. "They are very hungry plants." The beds were protected with snail bait because "snails love coleus."

All coleus flower buds were pinched off until about two weeks before Thanksgiving, when they were allowed to bloom. By that holiday the plants were covered with pretty blue flowers that looked good for about a week. When coleus flower, they are finished and the leaves begin to drop. By then it was time to plant the spring garden, and out they came.

Though this combination of coleus and caladiums was a fair amount of work, Turnbull thought it "worth the extra effort because it is such high drama," something that is too much to ask of the trusty but commonplace impatiens.

In May, Add a Touch of Gray

Gray plants look completely at home in our Mediterranean climate. If you do not grow any, you really should—for their sunny disposition, their leavening effect and their fascinating foliage. I was reminded of their value when visiting a garden by the late Westside landscape architect Robert M. Fletcher. Though the garden was less than a year old at the time, the gray-leafed plants were already stunning.

Fletcher used gray plants in most of his gardens. His reason was simple enough: "They provide contrast," he said. "For most clients, gray plants are a new idea because most people tend to think green." In the garden I was visiting, the gray-leafed plants lined the paths, and even on that overcast day, they marked the way as clearly as landing lights at an airport. In other gardens, he planted gray plants in drifts that "move through the space with a rhythm," contrasting with the green plants.

WEEK 23

He was especially fond of the gray plants that reflect sunlight—the ones with almost silvery foliage—they are so bright in the garden (other gray-leafed plants absorb light and have more of a matte finish). These silvery plants reflect moonlight, he noted, and are as interesting at night as they are during the day.

Which of the many gray plants was his favorite? "Plain old dusty miller," he once told me, referring to *Senecio cineraria*. He planted it as an annual in beds of pink, blue and purple flowers—the latter two are perhaps the most satisfactory companions for gray foliage. Purple petunias, verbena and pansies with dusty miller are possible combinations. Gray is also elegant next to true pink and even orange. *Centaurea gymnocarpa* is a dusty miller that's a little harder to find, but what a show it makes, with gray, gray leaves and lovely, soft, thistle-like pink flowers. Easily spreading to three feet, it gets only a couple feet tall and can be trimmed back after flowering. This one becomes a fairly permanent plant.

It is not surprising that many gardeners still "think green." Until only a few years ago, plain old dusty miller was just about the only gray-leafed plant to be found at nurseries. Not so now—most good gardeners are very aware of gray plants, and nurseries are certainly full of them, though some of the most interesting may still be a challenge to find.

Quite common at nurseries are the grayer lavenders, a sure sign of the new significance of gray foliage, and lamb's ears, one of the best. Lamb's ears grows quickly to make clumps several feet across and six to eight inches tall, with leaves as soft and downy as a—lamb's ear. Nothing looks better at the front of a flower bed during spring, summer and fall, though this is not a long-lived plant. Clumps tend to die out after a few years and are best replanted, and they are a little shabby looking in winter.

Lychnis coronaria, one of my favorites, looks a lot like lamb's ears, but it's much slower and more permanent. I prefer 'Alba', the variety with white flowers. (The common one has the brightest magenta flowers you will ever see—the very definition of that color.) It is even good at self-seeding about my garden, though it is anything but a pest. Cerastium, also called snow-in-summer, used to be sold only in flats as a ground cover, but that much gray can be a little tiresome. However, it is one of the best gray plants used in smaller patches, with its tiny leaves and crisp white flowers that bloom in spring and summer.

Convolvulus cneorum, understandably better known as bush morning glory, makes a shrub-like mound, two feet tall by perhaps three feet across, covered with shimmery, silver foliage and white morning-glory flowers. Mine usually last several years; they then either die or become so awkward that I replace them. The gray leaves and purple flowers of common Mexican sage (*Salvia leucantha*) look stunning with the purple flowers of the princess flower (*Tibouchina urvilleana*). Both bloom at the same time, in summer and fall.

Several new gray-leafed plants are worth searching for. One I recently found at Turk Hessellund Nursery in Montecito is appropriately named silver sage (*Salvia argentea*). Its huge white leaves, covered with silver hairs, form a low rosette about 18 inches across. A biennial, it grows one year then flowers the next (and presumably dies thereafter). Whitish flowers come in late spring on spikes about four feet tall. Similar is *Verbascum bombyciferum*. Also a biennial, its big rosette of felty leaves sends up a tall spike of soft yellow flowers in spring and summer. Either of these newcomers will bring instant excitement to an otherwise bland garden—they look like living exclamation points.

Many gray and blue-gray grasses make exclamation points as well, albeit smaller. The native *Elymus* 'Canyon Prince' is one of the most silvery, but it spreads a little too aggressively for my garden. *Muhlenbergia lindheimeri*, however, is a perfect gentleman with wispy blue-gray leaves and nice flower spikes. Equally well-behaved are the common and uncommon kinds of blue fescue, especially a miniature named 'Moody Blue'. Blue oat grass (*Helictotrichon sempervirens*) is so blue as to be beyond gray. The list of gray grasses, so useful for their soft or striking contrast in the garden is almost endless. An excellent reference and pictorial is "The Encyclopedia of Ornamental Grasses," by Southern California nurseryman John Greenlee (Rodale Press, Emmaus, Pennsylvania).

Among the more difficult to find gray plants is silver sword (*Astelia nervosa chathamica*), a dramatic explosion of stiff, silvery three-foot leaves. It prefers a bit of shade inland. Another new and hard-to-find plant for slightly shady areas is *Plectranthus argentea*, a small, open shrub about three feet tall by four feet across. With big silver-gray leaves, it produces long spikes of white flowers in fall. Several salvias have handsome gray foliage, especially pretty when combined with their bright blue, jewel-like flowers, as on *Salvia chamaedryoides*. Full sun for this low, sprawling bush. For just a touch of gray here and there in the not-overwatered garden, search for the rosette-forming, powdery-white chalk dudleya (*Dudleya brittonii*), a big fleshy succulent usually found hanging from sheer rock faces in its native Baja. Of course, there are many gray-leafed succulents, but few make such a show, or are as near white.

You can even grow gray in the vegetable garden by planting artichokes.

Most of these are small plants that can be mixed with annuals and perennials. However, don't overlook large plants with gray foliage. It was a pair of existing sentinel-sized, blue-gray deodar cedars that inspired the use of gray in the Fletcher garden I visited. Elaeagnus, pineapple guava, *Pittosporum crassifolium* and the stunning *Acacia pendula* are a few other big gray plants, but that's another story.

SUMMER'S WORST WEEDS

Warm weather has brought up a whole new crop of annual weeds—purslane (the spreading one with the reddish succulent leaves), spurge (the flattest growing, with tiny leaves) and a host of grasses including crabgrass. Attend to these quickly—this young, they are easy to scrape off with a hoe. Do so in the morning so they dry up during the day. Wait too late in the day, and they may reroot during the cool, damp spring nights.

A few other weeds have also made their appearance, but they are not as easy to get rid of. Three out of four of the world's worst weeds are common in Southern California gardens; if we include the San Joaquin Valley or places such as Blythe, all four are present and accounted for. Which weeds are the worst? If you guessed nutgrass, you're right, though it is really nut*sedge*, since it's a sedge, not a grass.

Bermuda grass? You bet. And bindweed. Indeed. Number four, Johnson grass, is more of an agricultural weed, though it has been found in gardens. All of these are perennials, which means they come back year after year, spreading and conquering, which is why they are the worst. All are found worldwide, so we are not alone.

With all of these perennial weeds, prevention is the best defense, says Dave Cudney, weed scientist at UC Riverside. Don't let them even get started in your garden. Keep an eye on any imported soil and on newly arrived plants. Don't spread these weeds by putting them in the compost pile. Their bulbs or seeds will survive if the pile is not kept hot (this means it must be moist, deep, with added nitrogen, and warm to the touch). In my own garden, I have two weeding buckets—one for most of the weeds, which go in the compost pile, and one for these persistent perennial weeds and weeds that have already made seed, which gets emptied in the garbage. I take no chances.

Nutsedge is perhaps the worst of the worst, making little "nutlets," or tubers, underground. New ones form when the plant is still a youngster, right after it reaches the four- or five-leaf stage. It mostly spreads by its tubers—it seldom makes seed. To make matters even worse, tubers may be as deep in the soil as 18 inches, though six to eight inches is typical. Cudney offers one way to deal with nutsedge: Physically remove all the soil to a depth of 18 inches or more and send it to the dump.

If that is not feasible, then the tactic is to starve it to death; as long as the plant has no leaves, it cannot make food and eventually dies. Pull up all the plants. Every time new little plants appear, pull them out quickly, before they can make new tubers. Keep this up religiously for three years, and you will probably be rid of it. (This Cudney calls "a holy crusade.") Nutsedge often gets out of control when people go on summer vacation, which gives it just enough time to make new tubers. Be very wary from March through November, when it is actively growing, and keep pulling it out.

Little else will work. The herbicide Roundup will work partially but not completely. Even then it is difficult to treat only nutsedge when it is in among other plants. Any spray falling on other, more susceptible plants will harm them more than it does the nutsedge. As with all chemicals, read label precautions and directions carefully.

Cudney suggests one other means of control. He got rid of his nutsedge in his backyard when he laid four inches of concrete dog run over it, but on campus he has seen it break through a newly paved walk of asphalt. It's one tough customer.

Bindweed is next on the list of bad guys. It looks like a wild morning glory, with white cup flowers, and it twists around other plants in a vining fashion. It spreads underground on bright white roots; if you pull up only part of it, it resprouts from the roots. Roundup will partially control it. The best time to apply it is just as the vine begins to flower. This ensures that the chemical is carried back to the roots (while the plant is growing, all materials are carried toward the tip of the plant, not toward the roots). One way to apply Roundup on bindweed while avoiding other plants is to wipe it on the leaves with a sponge. Wear rubber gloves and follow directions carefully, even though Roundup is considered a relatively safe herbicide.

Other than that, the best method is again starvation—keep pulling it out, promptly, for about three years. Then it should give up, as long as there are no seeds present. Bindweed seeds can lie dormant

Nutsedge may be the worst weed in California. Attempt to dig up the slightly pleated leaves, and plants return from a "nut" deep underground.

for 40 years in the garden before sprouting.

By comparison, Bermuda grass (some call it devil grass) seems easy to get rid of. A real wuss, it is highly susceptible to Roundup, though it too can come back here and there, or from seed. You can also try to dig it all out, but there are lots of rhizomes below ground, and even a tiny bit left behind can resprout. Keep after it, perhaps spot spraying any stragglers with Roundup, and it can be vanquished. Tilling soil where Bermuda grass is present will only chop the rhizomes into little pieces and help it multiply quickly.

> The best method is starvation—keep pulling bindweed out, promptly, for about three years.

If you think you have number four on this list, Johnson grass, you can be sure if you find rhizomes underground as thick as your thumb. The grass itself, airy and graceful, quite tall, looks a lot like barnyard grass. Roundup works fairly well on it as a control. Or dig it out.

Gardeners with these weeds undoubtedly wish there was a quick, surefire control. Short of selling your house and moving on, however, you gain control only with persistence and patience, with three to four years' worth of both required.

June

LET'S HEAR IT FOR HYDRANGEAS

AS LONG AGO AS 1908, STANDARD PLANS FOR CALifornia gardens put hydrangeas on the east and north side of the house: In a sample plan for a small property designed by John McLaren, creator of San Francisco's Golden Gate Park, "roses, carnations and other flowering plants" are lined along the south and west exposures, while "fuchsias, hydrangeas, etc." are specified for the north and east walls. Though time has turned the trusty hydrangea into a garden cliché, it has not diminished its value in the garden—it is still the most dramatic of plants for these exposures. Nothing grows as full and lush against a north- or east-facing wall or fence; few shrubs have flowers as large, and not many bloom when hydrangeas do, or for as long. Hydrangeas come into full flower in June and can last easily into late summer and even early fall. The true flowers are gone, but the sepals, being modified leaves, live on, changing color as the flower heads fade. (Incidentally, these can be dried: Cut and hang them upside down in the garage.)

The hydrangeas we grow on the Pacific Coast are different from those grown in the rest of the country. Ours are cultivars of *Hydrangea macrophylla*, developed about the turn of the century mostly by the French to grow in pots on summer terraces or in greenhouses. Early varieties had names such as 'Triomphe de Lisle' and 'Mme E. Moulliere'. Early references called them by another botanical name, *Hydrangea hortensis*. Even further back, they weren't *Hydrangea* at all, but *Hortensia*, which explains why a famous planting of them in pots at the Villa Aldobrandini, at Frascati just outside Rome, is known as the Hortensia Terrace. Indeed, a favored, but almost forgotten, place for hydrangeas is in pots, where they thrive. They look most comfortable in Italian pots that measure about 18 inches tall and as wide. With several, you can have a Hortensia Terrace of your own.

Note that the colored parts of the hydrangea "flower" are actually sepals, modified leaves that protect the true flowers, found on close examination (they are tiny) at the bases of the sepals. On the standard big-flowered hydrangeas, all the flowers have sepals and are sterile. Some varieties of *Hydrangea macrophylla* have fertile flowers without the prominent sepals surrounded by sterile flowers with sepals. These are the lace-cap hydrangeas—the effect is graceful and airy. Some, including 'Bluebird', have flowers that can be turned blue. The flowers of 'Mariesii Variegata' can as well. With leaves splashed with cream, it is a very handsome landscape plant.

The hydrangeas available today are often labeled only "pink," "white" or "blue," which really isn't much help. "Pink" can be many shades of that color, from near magenta to a clear light pink, more pleasing to most eyes. Some pinks fade to an antique mauve that is handsome, even elegant in the proper setting. 'Pink 'n Pretty' is a more compact form, and 'Pink Elf' is a genuine dwarf, growing only two feet and as wide, perfect in pots and in the garden. (Your nursery can order these and the lace caps from Monrovia Nursery Company in Azusa.) 'Rose Supreme' is the huge-flowered hydrangea seen in gardens with the clear pink sepals; 'Red Star' has large brilliant pink flower heads, and 'Sister Therese' has white sepals fading to green. The latter three are offered by El Modeno Gardens, another wholesale supplier.

"Blue" is always suspect in a hydrangea. The blue color of a hydrangea is determined by the soil: In acid soils, like those of Seattle and New Zealand, blue appears in the sepals; in alkaline soils, which we tend to have, the sepals are pink. Dana Groot, son of a Holland-born grower with Dutch nursery acumen in his blood, knows the secret to turning hydrangeas blue in containers—he grew them for years for El Modeno Gardens, which also sells 'Kuhnert', capable of producing clear blue sepals in an acid soil; 'Merritt's Supreme', which can be made dark pink or blue, and 'Nikko Blue', which is hardier to cold than the others.

Not all hydrangeas can be turned blue, and you may be growing one that won't budge. You can always try, though, by adding the chemical aluminum sulfate, sold by the bag at larger nurseries, to the soil (it acidifies the soil, among other things). The sepals' red anthocyanin pigment then becomes blue upon complexing with aluminum, abundant in most soils, but unavailable to the plant if the soil is alkaline or if there is too much phosphorous. Nursery people try for a pH of 5.5 or lower.

Some hydrangeas, 'Kuhnert' and 'Merritt's Supreme', for instance, are easier to make blue than others. And some are blue with no apparent help from their owners. One must surmise that the soil is for some reason acidic, or that someone in the past had made an effort to turn them blue.

This is not something that happens overnight. "Your pink blooms won't change to blue before your eyes," wrote Californian Albert Wilson in his 1949 book, "How Does Your Garden Grow." "The results come gradually over a number of years and you will have to keep up the application at intervals." His recommendation (also that of the University of California at the time): For every square yard of ground, scatter half a pound of aluminum sulfate; for pots, dissolve three ounces in one gallon of water. A modern reference cited by Groot suggests adding the aluminum sulfate in September, months before flowers begin to form.

Equally important, according to Groot, is to use a fertilizer that does not contain much phosphorous, such as one with numbers like 15-2-10 or 10-0-0 on the label. For the clearest blue, use a fertilizer with medium amounts of nitrogen and lots of potassium, but little or no phosphorus.

When can you plant hydrangeas? Nurseries usually sell them only when they are in flower, so now is the best time to buy them. In pots, plant them right away. Otherwise, keep them in their nursery containers, and plant in fall, when watering them will be much easier.

That they do so well against the walls of a house hints at how much light they need. They will grow under the canopy of a tall, airy tree, but they prefer about half a day of sun (as found against an east wall) or at least a bright clear sky overhead (against a north wall with no trees nearby). They are not so much shade plants as they are half-shade shrubs. The 1915 reference "California Garden Flowers," by E.J. Wickson, suggests giving them "more or less shade, according to the fervency of the local sunshine."

Not all hydrangeas can be turned blue, and you may be growing one that won't budge.

One can only guess what plant the "etc." in McLaren's 1908 plan referred to, but the secret to a happy, healthy hydrangea growing in the ground would seem to be not to crowd it with other plants or with other hydrangeas, which grow at least four feet across, and many make it to six or eight feet. The best are most often seen growing nearly alone, or at least in clear control of the garden bed. Possible companions are fuchsias near the coast, or camellias anywhere. Pink hydrangeas and foxgloves or the foxglove-like *Rehmannia elata* would be a stunning combination.

> **HOW TO TURN HYDRANGEAS BLUE**
> ❧ In fall, add aluminum sulfate: 1 tablespoon per foot of plant height.
> ❧ Use a fertilizer without any phosphorous.

"The all-important requirement of these hydrangeas is water. They should never be allowed to flag for lack of it, especially if they are grown in pots, always in part shade; big pots can take a lot. Open-ground plants need less attention to watering, but even they are greatly improved by regular summer soakings," wrote Sydney Mitchell in the 1947 book, "Your California Garden and Mine."

In the future hydrangeas may become one of those pampered, cherished plants that get a little extra water in otherwise thrifty gardens. Around the Mediterranean Sea, where water is more precious than it is here, hydrangeas are usually showcased in pots, where they can more easily be watered. Although hydrangeas certainly aren't drought-resistant plants, it really doesn't take more than a watering can full to soak a pot or two thoroughly. Plenty of hydrangeas in the ground in gardens are obviously not watered often (you can tell because the nearby lawns are suffering).

It is not necessary to prune a hydrangea, as thousands of untended plants in gardens prove. To control its size, in the fall prune branches that have flowered, and nip off the tips of those that haven't. You can even cut back the entire plant by removing two-thirds of the length of all the stems.

For a container-grown hydrangea, Groot says, every year cut back the whole plant by mid-July, or as soon as the flowers begin to fade, leaving just six- to eight-inch stubs, which will all have buds. In about two to three weeks these will leaf out (you won't have a bare plant for long) and, by September, will make more buds that will bloom the following spring. Don't prune again, or you may lose next year's flowers, though you can thin out some branches in August for a better placed display of flowers. By summer, these nubbins will have produced a bush three to four feet around. Although hydrangeas lose their leaves in winter, that is not the time to prune hydrangeas in containers—you will lose future flowers. If all the leaves do not fall off on their own, pick them off in mid-November. This will help the flower buds develop and get rid of any mites, whitefly, powdery mildew or green peach aphids that may be waiting for winter to pass. These pests are the most common on hydrangeas, though seldom serious enough to warrant spraying.

PICKING AND PLANTING THE TRUSTY TERRA-COTTA POT

People have been growing things in *terra cotta* pots ever since the Egyptians first came up with the basic flared shape (so plants could be removed easily). It was the Romans who coined the name *terra cocta*, which means "baked earth," or *terra cotta* in modern Italian, though the clay doesn't start out as that dusty mineral color. It begins as an ordinary gray, and once fired it turns that distinctive terra-cotta shade, the perfect foil for foliage, flowers and fruit. The earthy color looks good, even natural, in the vicinity of the plant's roots. This is one reason terra-cotta remains the gardener's container of choice, despite challenges from glazed pots, concrete, plaster of paris and, most recently, plastic (which, in homage, is often molded in a terra-cotta color).

Good terra-cotta pots, hard because they've been fired in high heat, last a very long time. Beware of the less expensive kinds fired at low heat (often in a pile of burning tires). These feel softer, have a slightly grainy texture and may be a brighter red, and they weather away like the bluffs in Santa Monica, only quicker. Coatings, available at some nurseries, can prolong their lives, but these darken the shade of red so it is not as earthy.

Most good terra-cotta pots are made in molds, but some are still made by hand (and quite expensive). You can tell by looking inside. In a handmade pot you can see the coils that made up the pot, or the spirals, indicating it was thrown on a wheel. There are often even a few of the potter's thumb prints, where he or she pinched or teased the clay.

Some of the designs are as old as the process itself. The garlands, clusters of fruit and other raised designs on many pots today date

back to the patterns used on Roman sarcophagi. The elegant pots with the bulging rolled rims, copies of 600-year-old Italian Renaissance pots, are a distinctive, sturdy shape, and the thick rim makes it an easy pot to pick up.

Another thing gardeners like about terra-cotta is that it ages gracefully. Minerals in our water soon frost the sides (it does not seem to harm plants). Some gardeners consider the white blush of caked-on minerals that build up over time an essential part of the pot and speed up the process by painting on a mix of lime and water. Gardeners who don't can lessen it with a scrubbing of white vinegar, or scrape it off with a putty knife. Some of the newest pots sold at nurseries already look old, appearing to have weathered many a season in the garden.

Cover the drainage hole in a container with a tiny bit of window screen, to keep soil in and slugs and sowbugs out.

In particularly moist places, algae may grow on pots, and even moss, though the harder and denser the pot, the less likely this is to occur. Some gardeners like this look—so much so that one company, Moretti Moss Pots, is now making soft gray pots that already have algae growing on them—moss will probably follow.

Terra-cotta hasn't survived the centuries on looks alone. Plants like growing in the unglazed, porous clay, which, like a swamp cooler, keeps the roots cool by evaporation, even on ferociously hot days. It also lets the roots—which need oxygen just as leaves do—breathe. The porous clay wicks away excess moisture so potting soils seldom become waterlogged—which helps prevent root rot, another plus.

Most pots are taller than they are wide so there is plenty of room for the roots. Low pots are for shallow-rooted plants. The squat versions of the common flowerpot were once called begonia pots or, in larger sizes, azalea pots, because those plants don't need much root depth. The shortest, most shallow pots, often quite wide with near-vertical sides, are bulb pans. They were designed for growing bulbs only for one season (bulbs need almost no soil if you plan to toss them out after flowering). Today, gardeners usually plant bulbs in taller pots (and keep them for more than one season). Bulb pans are just right for small annual flowers and vegetables, such as pansies and lettuce, that you might want to cluster together.

When shopping for a pot, remember that it is possible to overpot a plant—that is, to give it more room than it needs, so the soil tends to get too soggy and the roots rot. The rule of thumb is never move a plant into a pot more than twice the size of the plant's previous home.

If you're willing to put up with a few defects, there are good buys at factory seconds stores. Stay away from pots with long, thin, hairline cracks; these will probably break in time. Short, open cracks are most likely okay; they're caused by the clay cooling too quickly. That little blemish is enough to cut the price in half.

Pots discolor paving and decking they sit on, but not if you put them up on the little "pot feet," also sold at nurseries.

Gravel in the bottom of a pot encourages rot and leaves less soil for the roots. Modern potting mixes are so porous that they require no additional measures to speed drainage. A better idea is to cover the drainage hole with a patch of window screen, to keep the soil in and slugs and sowbugs out.

WHY LEAVES TURN YELLOW

Why did the leaves on my _____ (*fill in the blank*) turn yellow? This is the question nursery people, professional gardeners, consultants and, yes, even garden writers hear almost daily. On occasion they even ask themselves, and it's not an easy question to answer. "There are a thousand reasons why leaves might turn yellow on a plant," says William Darlington, of Soil and Plant Laboratory in Santa Ana, which does tissue and soil analysis for growers and gardeners alike. "It's a very nondescript symptom."

Some reasons for yellowing are more likely than others, though even the experts don't agree on the most common causes. Ted Stamen, urban horticultural advisor for UC Cooperative Extension in Riverside County, thinks that 90 percent of the time the culprit is over- or underwatering. However, Darlington says yellowing is more likely due to a lack of nitrogen, if the whole plant is pale in color and the leaves turning yellow are older and at the base of the plant. It simply needs a high-nitrogen fertilizer, with numbers like 10-4-2 on the label. For quicker results look for one that has some of its nitrogen in the nitrate or nitric form (also shown on the label).

Mineral salts in our water and soil, which inhibit the uptake of nitrogen, can also be to blame. Steer manures are typically high in

It's easy to spot chlorosis by veins that stay green as the leaf turns yellow.

salts (so don't use them too much). In rainy years, though, salts in the soil shouldn't be much of a problem because rain pushes salts down below the roots. But lots of rain also washes out most of the available nitrogen, so fertilize more than in drier years.

UC Cooperative Extension horticultural expert John Kabashima in Orange County agrees that yellowing most likely indicates a nitrogen deficiency. The lower leaves yellow because the new top growth is pulling nitrogen from them in order to continue growing, since there is not enough available in the soil. And he also puts overwatering on the top of the list. "Anything damaging the roots [as too much water will] is effecting the uptake of nutrients," he says.

If the leaves turning yellow are near the top of the plant, on new growth, it is probably a deficiency of some other element, such as iron, zinc or manganese. This is chlorosis, in which the leaves turn yellow but the veins stay green. Most gardeners know to look for interveinal chlorosis as a sign that the plant needs iron or another minor element. "Nitrogen and iron are by far the most limiting elements in alkaline soils like ours," says Darlington. They're in the soil, but the alkalinity of western soils makes them insoluble, unavailable to the plant. A lack of either is the first thing to suspect, he says.

Garn Wallace, of Wallace Laboratories in El Segundo, which also runs tissue and soil tests for professional and home gardeners, is convinced that chlorosis is the culprit in a majority of cases, but adds some interesting qualifiers. While iron is plentiful in California soils (perhaps five percent of our soil is iron by weight), what makes it unavailable to plants is the soil alkalinity, which, he says, is caused by lime. (Gardeners who are from the East Coast, or who heed gardening books written by eastern authors, should note that lime is a problem here and should *never* be added to a soil. In the east, it is frequently recommended to tone down the natural acidity of their soils.) To counteract the lime in our soils, he says, every gardener should add gypsum to the soil every time it is turned or prepared for planting.

In addition, Wallace suspects that a number of heavy metals, such as copper, some found in soil amendments that contain sewage sludge, interfere with the uptake of iron, and that cold, heavy, waterlogged soils do the same. He always expects to see a lot of chlorotic yellowing after wet winters.

His solutions? Improve a soil where you are going to plant or replant by adding gypsum and organic matter. Gypsum has many benefits: It reduces salinity, subdues heavy metals, binds organic matter to the soil particles and the like. Add about 50 pounds for every 1,000 square feet. (Be careful, you can overdo it, especially if you live in Gypsum Canyon in Orange County!) Homemade compost is the best soil amendment, but if you don't have any, add mushroom compost, peat moss or other organic matter so it becomes about 10 to 20 percent of the soil volume. If you are cultivating to a depth of a foot, that would be a one- to two-inch layer. Wallace says manures are okay if you use only 10 percent by volume, because of the salts they contain.

Where there are yellowing permanent plantings, such as trees and shrubs, and you do not want to turn or disturb the soil, scatter chelated iron over the surface. Wallace favors a product called Sequestrine 138SE because it gets to work faster. He calls it a "designer chelate," because its formula was carefully designed years ago at UCLA. But all forms of iron chelate work with time.

"Vertical mulching" is another idea from Wallace for yellowing permanent plantings. Dig holes near the effected plants and fill them with improved soil, mixing in amendments such as homemade compost, sludge, mushroom compost, manure or—his least favorite—shavings and sawdust, the kind sold by the bag at nurseries. He has dug holes and then a few years later found them stuffed with roots, all able to take up nutrients needed by the plant. For trees, he suggests digging four or five holes, two to three feet deep and a foot wide, spaced evenly around the tree out near the drip line, the edge of the tree's canopy. You could even use a post-hole digger.

To help acidify the soil, which makes iron more soluble and usable, sprinkle soil sulfur on the surface and water it in. Again, Wallace has a favorite product, DisperSul Plus Fe Mg, which also contains some needed iron (and manganese), though it may be hard to find at nurseries. Follow label directions—it is possible to use too much sulfur.

If you think your problem is serious, or want to fine-tune your solutions, get a soil test or leaf tissue analysis done by a professional lab, usually listed under Soil Testing in the classified section of the phone book. A soil test costs about $70 and tissue analysis between $50 and $70. You might find that you actually have one of the 1,000 other reasons leaves turn yellow.

JUNE DROP, AND OTHER FRUIT TREE PROBLEMS

B e prepared for June drop, a phenomenon where deciduous fruit trees naturally drop small unripened fruit. Most of the complaints about June drop come from people growing apricots, peaches or nectarines in the greater Los Angeles Basin, which includes nearly all of Orange County. Some self-thinning is natural, but if a lot of fruit drops, blame it on the weather. In some locales, and in some years, these fruit trees don't get enough winter chilling—the weather's just too mild. Or it may be the age of the tree. In general, young deciduous fruit trees are a little more likely to drop fruit than older trees, so it might be that a tree will outgrow the tendency. Sometimes fruit drop is attributed to erratic watering or too much fertilizer, but these are unlikely causes, according to Jim LaRue, tree fruit farm advisor for UC Cooperative Extension. Weather is more likely to cause fruit drop than watering, but to be on the safe side, set up a regular watering schedule in which the tree gets a thorough soaking about every three to four weeks in summer.

Persimmons are more prone to fruit drop than other deciduous fruits, especially those planted in recent years that were budded onto a rootstock from a different persimmon named *Diospyros lotus*. Though this rootstock is more resistant to root diseases, in Southern California it apparently contributes to fruit drop. This tendency does diminish after the tree is five years old. Too much nitrogen fertilizer can definitely cause fruit drop in persimmons, says LaRue, who suggests not fertilizing the trees at all after the first few years in the ground.

Other complaints heard now include apricots that have mushy brown centers, and peaches and nectarines that are mealy or are not sweet. The brown centers in apricots are the result of pit burn. This too is due to the weather—in this case, days that are too hot. Fruit that is mealy or not sweet this year, may or may not be next year. Again, it's the weather. All one can do is hope for better.

After a tree has finished bearing fruit, it is especially important that it gets adequate water from then on and into the fall in order to build up strength before going dormant. Don't water at the base of the tree; soak the ground in the area where most of the roots are, from several feet from the trunk to several feet beyond the canopy of foliage. Fertilize only once a year, in late winter.

You can also prune a tad once a tree has stopped bearing. Take out any overly vigorous sprouts growing up from the center, and thin just enough to let a little light into the center. (Don't overdo it—bark sunburns.) This helps preserve the lower branches so that in years to come all the fruit is not out of reach. Heavier pruning is best done in winter, when the tree is leafless and you can see what you are doing.

GROWING GARDENIAS

Some gardeners are convinced that the most popular gardenia, 'Mystery', is so named for good reason, because it's such a puzzling plant to grow. Tempted by the heady, high-school corsage fragrance, many people try, only to give up when plant after plant yellows and dies. Yet Herbert Kelly, who grows 25 varieties (did you know there were that many?) at his nursery Kelly's Plant World in Sanger, says that gardenias are "relatively easy to grow." It certainly doesn't take too much searching in most neighborhoods to find old, thriving six-foot bushes covered in flowers.

Why do some plants yellow and die while others thrive? For one thing, says Kelly, "they need full sun," even in the sizzling Central Valley where his nursery is located. "I don't know where nurserymen got the idea that gardenias grow in shade," he says. "Yet I have many customers tell me that's where they were told to plant their gardenias." Gardenias love and need heat, especially at their feet. Except in the hottest climates, they can't get it growing in the shade.

WEEK 26

According to Conrad Skimina, retired research director at Monrovia Nursery Company in Azusa, one of the largest wholesale growers, a gardenia does poorly and turns yellowish in winter when soil temperatures drop below 62°. It can't take up iron from a chilly soil, so it becomes chlorotic (leaves yellow between the veins). If it gets too chlorotic, the leaves will never recover, no matter what you do, and they eventually fall off. To help emerging spring foliage, says Skimina, mix ferrous sulfate or iron chelate into the top inch of soil in spring and summer, when the soil is warm enough for the plant to make use of it.

Are you ready to try planting another gardenia? If you really want to make a difference, be prepared to make our naturally alkaline soils slightly more acidic at planting time. Gardenias need an acid soil—a

NEW GARDENIAS

'Mystery', growing to five or six feet tall by about three feet wide, with glossy green leaves and creamy-white double flowers, may be the most popular gardenia, but there are others.

'August Beauty': Similar (and as tall), it flowers a little earlier and a little later in the year, from May to November.

'First Love': A new variety from Monrovia Nursery that should be available at local garden suppliers, this too is similar to 'Mystery' but with bigger flowers (up to four inches across) and larger leaves. The flowers are probably the same as those grown for use in leis in Hawaii, which is where this variety originated. The leaves are a deeper green and, says Audrey Teasdale, Monrovia's botanist, less likely to yellow.

'Daisy': A new single-flowered variety from Hines Wholesale Nursery, this one is a compact three-foot ball with dark green leaves and fragrant, five-petal blossoms.

pH of 5.5 is about right. So before planting, mix soil sulfur (available at nurseries) into the soil, following package directions. Add organic amendments, which also help improve soil drainage since gardenias don't like heavy clay soils. A several-inch layer mixed into the top foot of soil should do it. Skimina recommends sphagnum peat moss (not sedge peat), the most acidic amendment. Just be careful not to let it dry out before adding it to the soil, or you will have a frustrating time rewetting it (with regular watering it is unlikely to dry out once in the soil). If you buy it dry, soak the loose peat for several days in a plastic garbage can. You can also use ground-bark type amendments, although Skimina warns against those with redwood bark. They may impede growth.

Gardenias need what Kelly calls "regular watering," which means not too much and not too little; they won't tolerate going dry. Fertilize several times during the growing season, starting in spring, and each time use an acid-type fertilizer (usually sold for azaleas and camellias) that contains an ammonium type of nitrogen, such as ammonium sulfate, ammonium nitrate or urea. This also helps acidify the soil. Kelly recommends putting down a thick mulch of ground fir bark (not redwood), or something similar, to keep the soil a little cooler in summer and warmer in winter in inland areas.

In a nutshell, then, gardenias need: full sun, acid soil, periodic fertilizing with an acid-type fertilizer, regular watering and a healthy mulch. That doesn't sound too difficult, does it?

MAKING CUTTINGS

Some of the plants I grow now have been with me for decades, moving from garden to garden as cuttings. Cuttings are one way plants are propagated vegetatively—that is, a piece of the plant, not a seed, begets a new plant. It is quite amazing when you think about it because many of the plants we grow are all pieces of the same original plant. They could, in fact, be considered—collectively—one plant.

If you have a *Pittosporum tobira* 'Wheeler's Dwarf' in your garden, it's the very same 'Wheeler's Dwarf' growing in mine, and the very same plant growing in thousands of gardens, all part of the original plant, presumably discovered in a Mr. Wheeler's nursery and propagated because it was more compact than *Pittosporum tobira*. Vegetative propagation is a form of plant immortality: It is possible that a plant you are growing is the same plant grown centuries earlier. The original plant may be long gone, but its bits and pieces have survived.

While most gardeners have grown something from seed, they may have tried taking cuttings only on a few dependable plants such as impatiens, geraniums and succulents. With the right gear, though, cuttings can be one of the easiest, quickest and most surefire ways to propagate plants. Spring through summer is an excellent time to give this a try—the warmth encourages the formation of roots on the cut stems. (In most coastal areas, some plants, such as fuchsias and helichrysums, also root quickly in the cool and wet of winter.)

Take cuttings from the growing tips of plants, not from stems that are about to flower. Cut off three to four inches. Then, using a single-edged razor blade, make a clean cut just below a leaf. Strip or cut off the bottom few leaves, leaving a few on top. If the remaining leaves are larger than a few inches long, slice off the top half with the razor blade. Some people dip the base of the stem into rooting hormone, but I haven't found that it helps much. More important is to keep the leaves constantly moist, as though they were in a humid greenhouse.

Fill a plastic quart pot with coarse perlite (also sold as Sponge

To make a tip cutting, cut the upper few inches of a stem that is not about to flower, then make another clean cut with a razor just below a leaf.

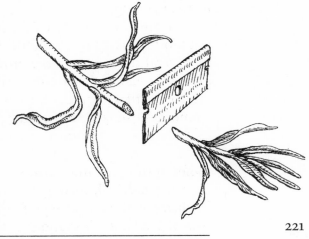

Rok) or coarse sand. Sand and perlite work best because they do not contain organic matter, which can rot cuttings while they slowly make roots. Push cuttings into this medium so that a couple of inches of stem, but no leaves, are buried. Wet everything down, let excess water drain away, then put the pot and cuttings in a big plastic bag and seal the top with a twist tie. The bag acts a miniature greenhouse. Keep the pot and bag in a bright place but not in direct sun. In a few weeks, open the bag and tug the cuttings a little to see if they've rooted. Keep checking until the cuttings root, or rot. This works on a surprising number of plants, though there seems no way to determine which plants root easily and which don't.

A better method is to set up a mist system. A gentle mist of water keeps the leaves from drying out while the cutting makes roots, but doesn't keep them so moist that they rot (the problem with the plastic bag technique). My first try at mist propagation was so successful that I found myself the recipient of all sorts of cuttings from others who wanted them propagated. I ended up with so many little plants that I soon had a miniature nursery going in the side yard, which ended up benefiting a horticultural society's plant sale, since there wasn't enough room in my garden for this bounty. Even good gardeners were amazed at my luck; yet the system was so simple I was embarrassed to reveal it.

All I did was buy a little brass mist nozzle (the kind with only one pinhole-sized opening, available at nurseries) and put it on the end of a hose. I tied the hose to a wooden stake so it was held well above the pots of cuttings. I turned the water on—barely—in the morning and off at night. Very little water came out of the nozzle so I wasn't using much, but the leaves were always moist. Most cuttings rooted in a matter of weeks, though a few did rot. I later added a special timer that turned the nozzle on and off throughout the day, so the cuttings didn't get too moist. I kept them in filtered sun, so they would not elongate from lack of light; this also helped prevent any molds or diseases. The cuttings were in pots or flats filled with coarse perlite, which kept the "soil" from becoming soggy—the water went right though it.

Thanks to this ability to make cuttings, I have saved plants that otherwise would have been left behind when I moved. I have also been able to grow all sorts of things I got from others that couldn't be found at nurseries. I even preserved an old cabbage rose that grew in my grandmother's garden, giving several to my children so it could enjoy another century of life.

BANANAS AND GINGERS

Bananas and gingers are two decidedly tropical-looking plants that we can grow in Southern California. Every gardener should give both a try, even if only in a container. Both are best planted now, while the weather is getting warmer. The trick is finding them.

Many nurseries tend to shy away from carrying tropical plants because they have been out of fashion for so long. There was a time when every Southern California garden looked a little tropical, and a few looked like jungles. Newcomers delighted in growing the most exotic things, and bananas and gingers (and, of course, palms and philodendrons) headed their lists. But garden styles changed, and now these big-leafed plants appear only briefly, if at all, at nurseries in summer, so this is when you have your best shot. Your other option is to beg a start from someone—bananas and gingers are ridiculously easy to start from the side shoots they make.

The exceptions are the Abyssinian bananas, the biggest of the bunch, which are easily recognized because they grow as a single spectacular plant, without any side shoots. *Ensete ventricosum* is the tallest (easily growing to 15 feet) with huge green leaves; sitting under one is like being under the big top. *Ensete ventricosum* 'Maurelli', with maroon leaves, is a little more squat. Most often called the red banana, it is perhaps the easiest to find at nurseries. It is also a first-class container plant, and growing it in a container will dwarf it considerably. One I kept in an 18-inch container for years never grew taller, or wider, than four feet. It can do much to enliven a patio or balcony garden. Both Abyssinian bananas die after they flower, but this takes at least five years when grown in the ground, much longer in a container. Then they must be replaced.

Other bananas, including the edible kinds, go under the botanical name *Musa*. They too die after flowering and fruiting but are quickly replaced by quantities of side shoots. (Remove most of these, or you will quickly have a jungle.) Your best chance at obtaining one of these bananas is by starting a side shoot. They are very easy to cut loose from the parent plant with a sharp spade or serrated knife, and can even be left lying around the garden for a few weeks before they begin to wither—but pot them up as soon as possible. For best results, take one that is about two feet tall.

There are many *Musa*, including one with maroon-blotched leaves. The most common, *Musa paradisiaca*, is unfortunately the least attractive. This is the tall one that grows around many older homes that always has wind-shredded leaves. Because it is so tall, it is difficult to tidy up (banana leaves are best cut off with a large, serrated kitchen knife; pruning shears get tangled in the stringy fibers). *Musa paradisiaca* produces fruit, but it is usually starchy or seedy. If you want an edible banana, you'll have to do some searching. Or join the California Rare Fruit Growers (*c/o The Fullerton Arboretum, California State University Fullerton, Fullerton, CA 92634*), which can help you find a source.

Growing your own bananas is a kick, and there seems no end to the variety. I've grown one called 'Dwarf Cavendish', which has excellent fruit that tastes and looks like tiny commercial bananas (each banana is about six inches long, but you get a bunch). The plant grew only to about six feet with an equal spread, and it was very easy to imagine turning the whole backyard into a plantation. Seaside Banana Gardens, just north of Ventura and visible from Highway 1, grows dozens of interesting, tasty kinds. Some they sell as plants.

Gingers are equally as exotic. Few things are as easy to grow, but again you will probably have to beg a start from someone. Gingers grow from fat, spreading tubers that can be severed from the clump with a sharp spade. Each spring these tubers send up new shoots, which flower in the fall; in winter, after they bloom, cut the old stalks to the ground to make way for the new.

Most grow to about six feet tall. They do splendidly in big containers, where they tend to stay a little shorter. The most common, the shell ginger (*Alpinia zerumbet*), is a tough plant, very tall, to eight or even 10 feet, and different from most in that the stalks persist for many years. If you want to avoid having a thicket, cut them to the ground after flowering. The beautiful, shell-like flowers are creamy on the outside, speckled yellow and orange on the inside—but the droopy blooms are almost hidden in the foliage.

Most of the other gingers for Southern California go under the botanical name of *Hedychium*, and the flowers are quite visible atop the foliage. *Hedychium flavum* has fragrant, creamy yellow flowers; *Hedychium coronarium* is similar, but the flowers are white. *Hedychium gardneranum*, the Kahili ginger, has the most spectacular flowers—foot-tall spikes of yellow petals with bright red stamens. *Hedychium greenei* has red flowers, but it's the maroon leaves that make it so decorative. This one produces little plantlets where the flowers were; these make good starts.

The edible ginger, *Zingiber officinale*, can be grown from the tubers sold at markets, though it is very cold-sensitive and not very vigorous. Because edible ginger grows only about two feet tall and doesn't increase much, ginger farming is not a real possibility in the backyard.

SUMMER

I HOPE YOU'LL PARDON ME FOR SHORTENING SUM-
mer to only two months. For California gardeners, though,
July and August make up a season unto itself, a time when gardening comes to almost a complete standstill. If it was not necessary to water and weed, you could almost take the two
months off. It's simply too hot to do much of anything, though there
are a few notable exceptions, such as planting bearded iris and sowing
seed of all kinds in August. Gardeners living farther inland and in the
San Fernando Valley might take exception to this short-summer
notion and suggest that the hot days begin quite a bit earlier (and last
longer), but they'll certainly agree that summer is no time to be working outside.

In much of Southern California, gardeners can keep busy until
about the Fourth of July, when, even on the coast (usually), the sun
breaks out from the June gloom of high clouds and summer arrives.
From now until fall, watering is a real burden if you plant anything,
since you'll need to water the young plants at least daily in the heat
until they become established, which may take a month or more. You
can still plant the occasional thing, a bougainvillea perhaps, or another
subtropical that does best planted when it's warm—just to keep your
hand in it. You can continue planting things in containers, for which
daily watering is necessary almost all year anyway. And you could plant
another round in the vegetable garden, because you're better off
putting vegetables in a few at a time so as not to be overwhelmed with
bumper crops. But other things had better wait until fall.

Our lazy, hazy summers are, in a way, similar to the eastern winter—a good time to browse through seed catalogues and make plans
for the garden, anticipating the return of planting weather in the fall.

If you feel sorry for your plants on really hot days, it's okay to go outside and spritz them with water. Contrary to an old gardeners' tale, it's as refreshing for plants as it is for people. However, when it's time to irrigate the garden, do so thoroughly—a thumb clamped over the end of the hose just doesn't cut it. Use sprinklers, soakers or drip systems, and water long and deep, but not too frequently. Too-frequent irrigation encourages roots to grow close to the surface, where soil is subject to extremes of temperature and rapid drying. If you water less frequently, but for longer intervals, you force water deep in the soil where it is safe from evaporation. This also coaxes roots deeper, where they can stay cool and comfy.

One way to dramatically cut down on watering is to heavily mulch the garden.

Frequent irrigation is also likely to get you into trouble with plants that are sensitive to warm, wet soils, and that succumb to root rots in summer if kept too wet. A plant such as santolina that suddenly wilts in summer probably doesn't need water—it may be dying from too much. Water in the morning, and the foliage will dry quickly; wet foliage encourages diseases on the leaves.

One way to dramatically cut down on watering is to heavily mulch the garden, covering the soil with two to three inches of a coarse organic material. In my book, nurseries sell only one suitable mulch—shredded bark. Don't confuse it with those chunks of bark sold for mulching—they're more of a problem than a help. Shredded bark is stringy, soft and packs down into a good, water-conserving, weed-preventing mulch. Even better is the stuff that comes from a tree service's shredder, if you can talk one out of it. Some tree services, now realizing how valuable these chopped-up bits of trees and shrubs are, sell them; others can't be bothered. Call a few and see if they're willing. Incidentally, it's been proved that even a mulch of shredded eucalyptus improves growth and health, so don't be worried about what kinds of plants comprise your mulch.

My trees, shrubs (including roses and native plants) and some big perennials, such as lion's tail and salvias, are mulched with shreddings from a tree company. I mulch my bedding plants and most perennials with my own compost, pulling it from the pile when it is still coarse, so it won't blow or wash away. Since I am always planting and puttering in the flower beds, I prefer compost as a mulch because I don't have to move it aside when I'm working. I just dig it in, and when I'm finished for the day I add more on top.

You'll be amazed at what a mulch can do. Plants will be much healthier and happier in summer, and less splattered with mud in winter. You need only to keep it away from the very base of plants—if that sensitive area stays too wet, it can become diseased.

Be sure to attend to the weeding. Summer weeds are up and growing, and some are already setting seed. Most of them are deep-rooted so hoeing won't always work. A better idea is to use a hand weeder and pry the roots out. Put weeds that have already set seed in a bucket and then in the trash; you don't want seeds to spread or end up in the compost pile.

With the garden weeded, mulched and watered, you can head for the beach. Or sit in the shade of that tree you planted a few autumns ago, admiring the summer-blooming flowers you planted back in spring, and plan for fall.

July

ALL ABOUT BOUGAINVILLEAS

BOUGAINVILLEAS LIKE IT HOT. THAT'S WHY THESE plants, originally native to Brazil, do so well on top of toasty tile roofs or on sizzling, south-facing facades. Warm is their kind of weather, summer their time of year.

"Best planted in the summer" is the succinct but seldom-heeded advice given by landscape architect Roland Stewart Hoyt in his classic 1933 handbook "Planting Lists for Southern California." If this suggestion was followed more frequently, one might not hear so many complaints about bougainvilleas just sitting there sulking for as long as a year after planting. Certainly they can be planted at other times, but "bougies," as gardeners are fond of calling them, grow quickly and surely planted in early summer.

WEEK **28**

Unless, when you go to do so, you try to tap one out of its container in the conventional, rough fashion. If you do, you are likely to end up with a handful of soil and broken roots. This is the other reason newly planted bougainvilleas do not grow well. Their roots often do not knit together to form a solid rootball and so are easily damaged—"fragile" is one description.

This is not an old gardeners' tale. "You have to handle the rootball very carefully," says Lew Whitney, of Roger's Gardens in Corona del Mar, who planted hundreds when he managed the nursery's landscape division. "When they came in metal cans, we didn't even try to get them out. We cut the can and planted it along with the rootball [it eventually rusted away]. Now we carefully, very carefully, slide the rootball out of the plastic can. Ironically," he adds, "you can't kill an established bougainvillea. Try getting rid of a 15-year-old giant."

Daryl Hosta, who heads his own Santa Monica landscape design and installation company, has also planted his share of bougies. "Nurseries used to sell immature plants that simply fell apart when they came out of the pot, but now plants are more mature and better rooted," he says. "However, we are still very careful."

Another piece of classic bougainvillea advice: To encourage flowering, stop watering established plants about now. Whitney, in fact, suggests *never* watering bougainvilleas that have been in the garden for five or more years. Bougies are right at the top of most drought-resistant plant lists. "No heavy fertilization, either," cautions Hosta. "They don't need it."

More advice from old garden books: "Always prune drastically in spring." Pruning is necessary on most of the tall, vining kinds to keep them from getting too big and heavy. The tall, vining kinds include the bright red, house-smothering 'Barbara Karst' and 'San Diego Red', which is one of the best to espalier on a wall. Prune in summer, and there may be no flowers. Prune in fall or winter, and frost may nip new growth. Many say you can't prune a bougainvillea too much, as long as you don't denude it of foliage. And wear gloves; some bougies have nasty thorns. "Some hardly have any," says Hosta. "But others are rattlesnakes."

You can even prune a bougainvillea hard enough to shape it into a small lollipop tree. One new wrinkle in bougainvilleas is that they are now sold as small trees to grow in the ground or in a large container on a patio. Even the giant 'Barbara Karst' can be pruned into a tame little tree. Pruning the entire head each spring and cutting back any vigorous new branches throughout the summer will keep it this way.

Not all bougainvilleas are big vines. 'Rosenka' is a shrub, growing about three feet tall and five feet across, though you have to lop off the occasional six-foot stem. Its flower bracts start out gold, then change to pink. (The color is in the papery bracts; the little white botanically true flowers are at their base.) A new sport of 'Rosenka', 'Oo-la-la', has the more conventional purplish red flower bracts, but it is just as small and shrubby. Whitney can't say enough about these small bougainvilleas: They make good ground covers, they're great in containers, and they can go in a border of such shrubby things as lavender, *Pittosporum crassifolium* 'Compactum' and *Nandina* 'Gulfstream'—three of his favorite companion plants.

'La Jolla' and 'Temple Fire' are larger shrubby bougainvilleas, with

A BOUGAINVILLEA COLOR GUIDE
All of these are the tall, vining kinds.

WHITE	PURPLE	RED
'Jamaica White'	*Bougainvillea*	'Barbara Karst'
'Mary Palmer's	*brasiliensis* (labeled	(rampant growth)
Enchantment' (big,	also *Bougainvillea*	'Crimson Jewel'
strong grower)	*spectabilis* or	'James Walker'
	"purple")	(suffused with
ORANGE TO GOLD	'Don Mario'	purple)
'Afterglow'	(suffused with red)	'Manila Red'
'California Gold'	'Purple Queen'	'San Diego Red' (also
'Camarillo Fiesta'		sold as 'Scarlett
(suffused with	**PINK**	O'Hara')
pink)	'Cherry Blossom'	
'Orange King'	'Tahitian Maid'	
	'Texas Dawn'	

red flowers. 'Hawaii' (also sold as 'Raspberry Ice') has creamy, variegated leaf margins; 'Orange Ice' is a new version of this plant. All grow to about five feet tall and eight feet across, looking a bit like flowering haystacks. Hosta uses them as ground covers on hillsides. "They're great for hiding ugly old retaining walls or other eyesores," he says.

Another early California garden writer, Belle Sumner Angier, wrote in a 1906 book: "A misplaced bougainvillea can absolutely overshadow every other bloom in the garden, and make one sigh for the absence of color." In her time there were only the red and purple kinds. Today many of the newer colors are subdued and easier to work into gardens of more conventional color. There are calmer shades of red, some that could even be called pink. There are oranges, and golds that come reasonably close to yellow. Still, they are by no means quiet colors, anymore than Rio is a quiet town. The truly timid can always choose white.

A few gardeners have reported that these softer colors are slow, weak growers—wimps in the world of bougainvilleas—but this may depend on where they grow. Some suspect the soft-colored kinds like more heat and do better south of Long Beach and away from the lingering fog. They certainly grow fine in Hawaii.

Hosta calls these newer colors "manmade" and thinks that if a bougainvillea is not red or purple, it's not a bougie at all. "There's nothing like the reds and purples," he says. "They are stronger growers, and the colors are electric." Neon is what bougainvilleas are all about. At the beach, the reds and purples are the best choices, he adds, even in cool, foggy Santa Monica, where you see them espaliered on

The new colors are by no means quiet colors, anymore than Rio is a quiet town.

south-facing beach-house walls.

Hosta often even plants red and purple bougainvilleas together. Whitney, too, likes to plant two or three different vining kinds in the same hole, so they knit together to make a multi-hued vine—a white, pink and red, for instance. Two of his favorites together are the "almost yellow" 'California Gold' and the bronzy 'Orange King'.

If you do your shopping and planting now, you can usually find plants in bloom. Seeing the actual color helps avoid future shock or disappointment. Descriptions seldom do the bougainvillea flower bracts justice. One described as orange could be, but it also might have another color running through it—pink, for instance. Some of the mixes of color look better than they sound. The accompanying chart groups the vining bougainvilleas into admittedly loose color groups, but it should help narrow what has become a large field of summer-hot colors.

RED, WHITE AND BLUE
FOR THE FOURTH

This weekend many gardeners are singing "Hooray for the Red, White and Blue" with planting schemes that mimic those Fourth of July colors. It's not too late to plant such a scheme, since all the appropriate plants are now at nurseries, in flower, in quart or gallon cans. This is what those annuals sold in full flower are for—instant, last-minute color for special occasions, such as a Fourth of July celebration. Even a few popped into pots will brighten a front porch or patio.

Garden designer Jane Brooks, of Color Garden in Torrance, has planted several red, white and blue gardens for clients. In one she used shocking red annual salvia, blue bedding salvia and the little white daisy *Chrysanthemum paludosum*. (In warmer inland gardens, perhaps white vinca rosea and white zinnias are better choices—whatever you can find in flower at nurseries.) In another garden, Brooks used red and blue petunias with white lobelia. Red, white and blue petunias look great spilling from pots.

Purists might object to calling the petunias and lobelia blue, but these flowers come close enough. True blue flowers are very scarce indeed—there may be no flower that matches the dark blue found on Old Glory.

Ageratum, blue enough to go with red and white petunias, is also available now in full flower. This one can take coastal and inland temperatures. So can the petunias, though they might show some smog damage later in the season. The small-flowered multiflora type of petunia is more resistant to smog than the large-flowered grandiflora strains.

Because all of these are annuals and only last the season, there is no need to untangle the matted roots when you take them out of their nursery containers. You might actually set them back by doing so. What they do need is water almost every day at first, though not a whole lot. Annuals have shallow roots, so short, shallow waterings suit them fine. Those planted in pots will definitely need water every day once their roots begin to fill the containers.

WAYS TO WATER A GARDEN BED

Watering is a fact of life in California. For lawns, there is no shortage of information on how to irrigate. Brochures abound anyplace that sells sprinklers (and sprinklers are just about the only way to water a lawn, though there is some experimenting going on with underground drip lines).

But how do you water that increasingly prominent flower or shrub bed? Ordinary sprinklers throw a circle of water 10 to 20 feet in diameter. A garden bed is typically two to five feet wide, or deep, and a good deal longer. The length varies but the width is pretty much a given, since any wider and you can't get to the plants in back (unless you have an access path, sometimes used in big English borders). Any narrower just isn't wide enough to grow much of anything.

So one problem is the shape; another is that ordinary lawn sprinklers end up wetting whatever is behind the bed. If that something is the house, or even a fence, getting it wet is not a good idea. There are better ways to water these long, narrow beds. I talked with irrigation experts who suggested a number of ideas, including several kinds of drip systems, microsprays and minisprinklers, special strip sprinklers and a new generation of small-radius pop-ups. Each irrigation system has its pros and cons.

Circular pop-ups: These are taller versions of the common lawn sprinkler that use water pressure to pop up on six- or 12-inch risers

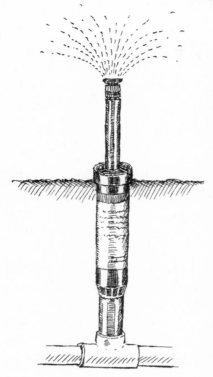

Pop-up sprinkler.

(an internal spring retracts the head). If you put these in front of the flower bed and make sure that the plants in front are low, when they pop up they will spray above them. Low-angle, almost horizontal, sprays work better than the high-angle sprays if there is any breeze blowing when you irrigate, though you may need the high-angle sprays to reach those tall plants in the back.

For even coverage, arrange circular pop-ups in a triangular or square pattern so the spray from one sprinkler head reaches the next head (as lawn sprinklers should). This would be difficult in most flower beds with plants of varying height, since the spray heads in the back would have to be taller than your tallest flowers. You would have to settle for simply overlapping those in the front, with less coverage toward the back. Or in the back, on top of very tall plastic risers, you could put only the nozzles (available separately)—but this is a bit of an eyesore.

The radius of circular pop-up sprays is usually quite large, to 15 feet, but there are new heads now that throw as little as a two-foot radius. You can adjust the radius to be between two and six feet with the little screw on top of the head. Or you can control it by changing the water pressure. One way of changing the water pressure, says irrigation consultant Bob Galbreath, of Garden Technology in Los Angeles, is with a nifty little adjustable pressure regulator made of engineering plastic that goes between the irrigation valve and the sprinkler line. It's manufactured by Bermad (PRV-075 is the one made for three-quarter-inch valves). Lower the pressure, and you shrink the radius. Galbreath likes to use pressure regulators on each sprinkler line, so he can control each system.

Regulating the pressure also stops misting. We've all seen lawn sprinklers that turn most of the water into mist that then blows off into the neighbor's yard. Reducing the pressure to what the sprinklers were designed to run at, usually about 30 pounds per square inch (p.s.i.), makes them much more efficient (typical house pressure is 70 p.s.i.; pressure at the street can be over 200 p.s.i.).

Finding these pressure regulators and the smaller-radius sprinklers (Toro makes the smallest) at nurseries or hardware and building supply stores is difficult. You will probably have to purchase them from irrigation supply dealers (look in the classified pages of the phone book under Irrigation or Sprinklers).

Strip sprays: Strip sprinklers sound too good to be true. Attached to risers or pop-ups, they water narrow rectangular areas, typically four by 20 feet, even two by six, though they must be spaced about 10 feet apart (or three feet apart for the smaller ones) so they overlap.

Choose from center strips, which sit in the middle of the bed, or side strips, which are placed along an edge. There are also side-end and center-end strips that are half the pattern of a strip, to cover the ends.

Actually, the pattern is more like a bow tie than a rectangle, says Rain Bird advisor Jim Worcester, but strip sprays do cover the area when overlapped, if a little less evenly than regular circular spray heads on a square or triangular pattern.

Today's better spray heads (strip and circular) have something called matched precipitation rate, which means that no matter what the pattern, the sprinklers within a given manufacturer's group put the same amount of water on the ground. In other words, a quarter circle will soak any piece of ground just as thoroughly as a full circle. Spray heads are now also putting less water per minute on the ground. According to Toro consultant Eric Shirley, this low-flow technology is where the big effort is being made by sprinkler manufacturers, since any runoff is pure waste.

Runoff is more likely in flower beds than on lawns and occurs when the ground can't soak up the water fast enough because it slopes or is a dense clay. Today's plastic sprinklers have a flow of about 1.5 to 2.5 gallons a minute, compared to old brass sprinklers that dump about four gallons on the ground each minute. If you have heavy clay soil or sloping ground, try to get the low-flow or low-gallonage nozzles, available for most sprinklers. You can also get sprinklers with pressure-compensating devices for hillsides. These even out the flow and pressure of sprinklers that are uphill or downhill from others.

Bubblers and streams: These are nozzles mounted on low risers that flood the garden bed either by letting the water bubble out or by spraying it in streams. They keep water off the foliage, which is important to some gardeners, including many rose fanciers. They put

---

WHICH IS BEST?

Which of these irrigation systems is best for you? Consider these points and which are most important.

- Saving water: Choose drip.
- Weeding less: Choose drip.
- Not digging trenches: Choose drip.
- Growing a great variety of plants, including those that spread by rooting stems or rhizomes: Choose microsprays or pop-up sprinklers; maybe drip.
- Seeing wet ground: Choose microsprays or pop-up sprinklers.
- Being out of the way and invisible: Choose pop-up sprinklers, or bury drip.
- Keeping everything uncomplicated: Choose pop-up sprinklers.
- No work at all: Have someone design and install one of these systems, putting everything on a controller (but remember to adjust the settings by season, and shut it off when it's raining).

---

on water quite quickly (about 1.5 gallons a minute), and except on flat, enclosed ground, runoff is inevitable. These were recommended against for home gardens by all the consultants, though they are quite common in commercial landscapes where concrete paving or edging encloses the beds.

If all of this sprinkler technology sounds hopelessly complicated, have Rain Bird design a system specifically for you. Ask for the material (you must draw a diagram showing the dimensions of your garden) at a Rain Bird retailer. Toro and Rain Bird have do-it-yourself planning and installation guides, and hotlines if you run into problems. Toro's is *(800) 367-8676*; Rain Bird's is *(800) 247-3782*. You can also call these numbers to request a guide.

Drip alternatives: Drip irrigation, of one kind or another, is the near-perfect way to water a long, narrow bed of flowers or low shrubs. It's easier to install than a sprinkler system (no digging trenches) and about 15 percent more efficient with water.

However, many people have a hard time maintaining or even understanding drip systems. "How long do I leave them on?" is the big imponderable question, since you can't see the ground getting wet. Others object to the visible tubing, which can get in the way of ordinary gardening activities, such as digging or hoeing. Also, plants that root along their stems or spread by rhizomes don't, because the soil surface remains dry.

"Drip Irrigation" [*Metamorphic Press, P.O. Box 1841, Santa Rosa, CA 95402 (707) 874-2606*], by garden consultant Robert Kourik, is an

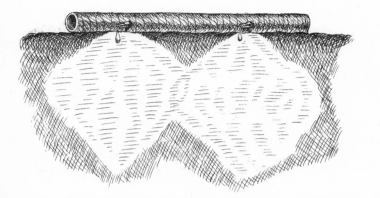

Inline drip.

excellent book that demystifies the subject. In it he covers all the details on choosing and installing a drip system.

Inline emitters: For a flower or small shrub bed, Kourik and Galbreath both suggest blanketing the bed with inline emitters, rather than using individual emitters on the ends of spaghetti tubing. Inline emitters are built into larger half-inch tubing and are usually spaced about a foot apart. If you cover the bed with rows of tubing spaced a foot apart, you'll end up wetting the whole bed. Applied slowly, as drip systems do, water spreads out underground, at least 12 inches wide in most soils, although the water is barely visible on the surface. This means that the roots get evenly watered but the surface seldom gets wet enough for weeds to sprout, another big plus for drip.

To hide the tubing, cover it with a water-conserving mulch. Some kinds can even be buried. However, buried inline drip systems must be activated every day, even if it is only for a minute or two, Kourik says, or deposits in the water will clog them. However, watering a little bit every day is the preferred method with any kind of drip. Each day, you (or a controller) replace the amount of water lost the previous day.

All the standard drip devices are necessary at the beginning of the line: vacuum breaker, check valve, filter and pressure regulator. You find these at stores more now than you did a few years ago, but you may have to look in Kourik's book for sources for the more sophisticated inline tubing, an unlikely find at home supply stores and nurseries. Although drip systems typically cost 20 to 30 percent more than sprinklers, according to Kourik, "the payback comes in only four years from water savings."

All the consultants recommended against the porous tubing kind of drip—it is prone to clogging. However, several gardeners I know use these inexpensive soaker systems and simply replace them every few years. In some cases, Worcester suggests using laser tubing,

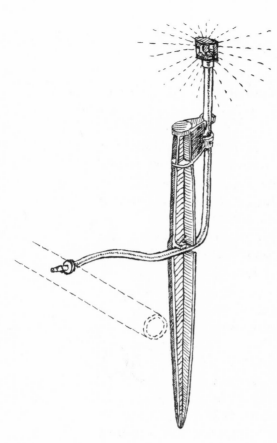

which has precisely drilled holes spaced six or 12 inches apart. He likes it for beds of annuals. Again, the idea is to blanket the whole area, but toss it out every year—it is designed to be disposable.

With true drip systems, fertilizing is more work. You can't just scatter fertilizer on the ground. You must either install a fertilizer injector on the system, water it in by hand (or fertilize just before a rain), or work it into the soil. To sprout seeds you also must water by hand.

Microsprays and minisprinklers: These little sprays and sprinklers are incredibly easy to set up, and you can see them wetting the soil. Attached to drip tubing, they put water on much more slowly than conventional sprinklers. Various kinds vary from five to 20 gallons an *hour*, compared to conventional sprinklers that deliver 1 to 2 gallons every minute. However, the

Microspray. droplets are so small that the spray is very much subject to the wind. And the nozzles, usually mounted on slender plastic pipes or tubing attached to stakes, are quite fragile—dogs and kids can wreak havoc. But the slim black pipes are nearly invisible in the garden, and many can be made any height you wish so they are above all the plants. There are adapters that let you mount them on risers of the sturdier standard PVC pipe, but then they become quite visible.

If the pressure is very low, they will water small areas, but even with 30 p.s.i., they have fairly large radiuses, up to 20 feet. They must be turned on for much longer times than regular sprinklers, but they wet the ground with no puddling, erosion or compacting of the soil. They are sure to germinate every seed you sow, plus all those lying dormant in the soil.

WHY NOT WATER LILIES?

Is a lily pond, or pool, really such an impossible idea for your garden, something only for large estates and public parks? "I think it's the word *pool* that scares people off," says George Knopf, who has grown water lilies for more than 28 years in his Sylmar backyard. Yet he grows these gorgeous flowers in "pools" as small as two feet across, and even in containers. "There's really nothing easier to grow," he says. "They're less work than cutting the grass, though you do have to follow a few rules and grow kinds that do well in Southern California."

At his former nursery, Knopf made a specialty of finding the kinds that thrive in our climate, varieties that bloom near the beach (where there is sometimes not as much sun and heat as water lilies like) and in the inland valleys (where there is plenty of heat but also the occasional cold of winter). Some of these varieties were his own hybrids.

He found that most of the blue-flowered tropical lilies freeze in his San Fernando Valley backyard, or are just too difficult to grow otherwise, though he does have one that has survived for many years. This one even made it through a particularly cold winter, surviving one night under an inch-and-a-half-thick sheet of ice.

Nearer the coast, many tropical lilies do fine. In my own ornamental pool in West Los Angeles I have grown a smallish one named 'Tina' for many years. It flowers from late spring into December, sending up one striking, vibrant purple-blue flower after another. It would be hard to imagine my pond without this tropical lily.

Knopf mostly grows what are called hardy lilies, which are not fazed by cold and do not need as much heat as the tropicals. They do not come in the tropicals' bright colors—most are shades of yellow and pink. The kinds Knopf grows—about 26 different varieties—begin flowering in March and keep at it until October. Anything less in the way of performance he weeded out long ago, though he continues to try the new varieties as they come along, most recently a batch out of France (they were a great disappointment).

As for the pools of water required by his lilies, they can be quite small. Miniature lilies—Knopf grows one named 'Pygmaea Helvola'—will grow in a large (18 to 24 inches) container or flowerpot with its drainage hole plugged. The tiny yellow flowers on this one are only

about an inch across; the leaves, staying in a tight circle, spread no farther than 18 inches.

Many more water lilies are small enough to grow in something the size of a half-whiskey barrel (which makes an excellent container for lilies but only after some laborious work, cleaning out the charcoal and leaching out any whiskey that remains), wine barrel or a similarly sized flowerpot. This is perhaps the best size for beginners. I, for one, can testify that you can grow lilies for years in these

Plant hardy waterlilies to one side of the tub so they have room to spread. They'll easily reach the other side by end of summer.

containers with practically no effort, though after a dozen years the bottom finally gave out on one of my oak barrels.

The ideal pool, the next step up, for medium-sized lilies (those with the biggest and most frequent flowers, the kind Knopf grows) measures about five by eight feet and is 20 to 24 inches deep. The depth is most important here because water lilies need a certain amount of water above their crowns. The minimum is about six inches; the maximum about 14 inches. My own pools are only 18 inches deep, the legal depth before the city building department considers a body of water a swimming pool, for which I would have had to abide by its rules and regulations. However, in my 18-inch-deep pool I grow the one tropical lily and three of Knopf's hardy hybrids, and they do just fine at this depth, as do the goldfish that live with them.

Should you consider making such a pool, Knopf recommends using plastic cement, not Portland cement, which is so porous that you will be forever filling the pool with water. Or make a pool out of regular cement, finishing the inside with plastic plaster to make it watertight. An easier alternative is to use a special flexible, waterproof liner; some are sold at nurseries.

You can plant a new lily at any time of year if you can find them, but summer is a particularly good time, because some nurseries carry them now. There are also several specialty nurseries: Van Ness Water Gardens [*2460 N. Euclid Ave., Upland, CA 91786-1199 (909) 982-2425*], a Southern California fixture for years, is a retail nursery that also does business through its mail-order catalogue. Sunland Water Gardens [*9948 Sunland Blvd., Sunland (818) 353-5131*] is another knowledgeable source to visit.

Lilies are planted in shallow plastic tubs (the kind sold at hardware stores for general utility use) that measure about 18 inches across by nine inches deep and have no drainage holes in the bottom. To plant, place three tablespoons of a complete granular fertilizer (any kind, with numbers such as 10-10-10 on the label, as long as it contains no weed or insect controls) in the very bottom and cover with ordinary garden soil, meaning dirt—do not use amendments or potting soil. Lilies seem to like the worst clay soil you can find in your garden; just make sure it is pulverized.

Many more water lilies are small enough to grow in something the size of a half-whiskey barrel.

You can center tropical lilies in the tub or container, but place hardy lilies off to one side so they have room to grow across the tub. Hardy ones grow from thick, horizontal tubers, which should be only partially buried, with the tops exposed. Don't bother to cover the surface of the soil with sand or gravel. If you thoroughly wet the soil before hefting the planted container into the pool (they get very heavy), you'll get a little muddying of the water but it will quickly settle and clear.

Don't worry if the leaves do not reach the surface. They will elongate and be floating on the water within 24 to 36 hours. Do not immediately pick off old leaves, even if unsightly—that is where water snails deposit their eggs and, in a pool, the more snails the better. Egg masses look like clear jelly and hatch in about seven days, so check for eggs and wait until they're gone before you remove the decaying leaves. You can control the size of lilies by picking leaves that spread too far, without effecting flowering.

Repot the fast-growing hardy lilies every year, preferably in March. This is a big job: Lift the heavy pot from the pool, find a place to dump the old soil, and then cut off the older end of the tuber, saving only the few inches from which leaves grow. Add fertilizer and new soil. Repot tropicals every few years; there is no trimming back to be done.

What about pool maintenance? This is where many beginners go wrong. Do not change the water once the pool gets started. Says Knopf: "We never clean our pools." This applies even to container ponds. In my own garden, I have grown water lilies in two large concrete containers and a half-whiskey barrel for well over 10 years, and in a large three-by-12-foot raised concrete pool for the last five, and I have never changed the water in any of them. Never use chlorine, and avoid pumps or fountains since lilies like still water. Filters are absolutely unnecessary unless you are trying to raise a lot of koi in a small pool, but then you can forget about lilies or any other aquatic plants because koi are voracious.

Fish and plants are the secret to a clean, clear pool. Knopf recommends using what pet shops call feeder goldfish—the kind that cost almost nothing and are destined to be dinner for a pet reptile. (Several in my own ponds were spared this fate when my older son bought too many for his snake; others were won at a school carnival.) Don't consider koi because they eat everything in sight, even the water snails. In very shallow pools or containers, guppy-like mosquito fish will control those insects, but they do not eat algae so are a poor second choice to common goldfish.

Goldfish, snails and water plants keep pools in balance, as long as the pool is small, or deep if it is large. Large, shallow pools are algae factories. Pools may turn green at certain times of the year—this is normal and is actually appreciated by the fish. If the green color persists, though, it is probably because not enough of the water's surface is covered by lily pads or other plants—they should cover 50 to 75 percent. No matter what, do not change the water; just be patient and wait for things to clear. Add water only to replace what is lost to evaporation. Every few years you may have to remove debris from the bottom of the pool, either by scooping it out or by using a special pool vacuum, but don't drain it.

EPIPHYTES

There may be times when your garden is so chock full that there just isn't space for another plant—frustrating your desire to try something new. At those times, consider epiphytes, plants that take their sustenance from the air (some people call them air plants), gathering enough water from rain or fog, using whatever falls their way and lodges in their leaves or roots for food. In the wild, they usually grow attached to other plants, though they are not parasites; some grow attached to cliffs or rocks. This is primarily what their roots are for—holding on. Leaves do most of the gathering of water and nutrients, though roots do contribute.

In the garden, then, epiphytes are not usually grown in pots. Instead, affix them to slabs of wood, tree fern fiber or bark, and then hang them on a wall, fence or patio post. This is what makes them valuable plants—not much else will grow on these surfaces.

WEEK **31**

In general, watering epiphytes can hardly be called "watering" at all. Simply mist them quickly with the hose, just enough to get them wet. The best time of the day is in the evening. If you want exuberant growth and no maintenance, consider putting in a drip system equipped with little mist nozzles (rather than the usual emitters) and controlled by an irrigation clock. Watering every three days is about right for most epiphytes, though those inland might need more, and close to coast, less. Most can't be grown too far inland because they are tender to frosts.

For bright, sunny spots, the toughest epiphytes are the mostly gray-leafed tillandsias, which are one of the bromeliads. In a pinch, most can go for weeks without water. A tillandsia is too dry when its leaf edges begin to roll up. The best way to water at this point is to drop it in a bucket of water for a few hours so it can soak up all it needs. Otherwise, water every few days with a quick blast from the hose, followed by another after the leaves dry. One sprinkle is not enough—tillandsias do not have time to take in the water before it evaporates.

Paul T. Isley III, of Rainforest Flora in Gardena, waters his personal collection of epiphytic tillandsias with a mist system. He grows hundreds attached to a long fence in full sun. At his nursery, they grow outdoors on a huge trellis, on benches, hanging from the rafters in a greenhouse and attached to the carcasses of giant old grapevines. If you want to know all about tillandsias, you can't go wrong with his authoritative and lavishly illustrated book "Tillandsia" (Botanical Press, Gardena), which also has lots of scanning electron microscope photographs of tillandsia leaves, so you can see the clever ways these plants catch and store water. Though grown mostly for their fascinating foliage, many also have stunning flower spikes. Some are even fragrant. *Tillandsia crocata* is one tiny, fuzzy-gray tillandsia with little spikes of yellow flowers that are powerfully fragrant for their size. I've found this one to be especially easy and long-lived in my garden.

Tillandsias are sometimes available at nurseries, though at Isley's Rainforest Flora [*19121 Hawthorne Blvd., Torrance, CA 90503, (310) 370-8044; www.rainforestflora.com*], you can pick through bins of these bromeliads, most of which are raised from seed on the premises.

Staghorn ferns are another epiphyte, and another specialty of Rainforest Flora. Staghorn ferns are simply spectacular once they get a few years behind them. Every bright but sunless north wall in the milder parts of Southern California should have at least one staghorn fern, if for no other reason than to knock the socks off out-of-state visitors. The most common kinds form clumps protected by papery

Staghorn ferns are simply spectacular once they get a few years behind them.

245

shields and antler-like leaves three to four feet across. They can be found at nurseries as small plants and should immediately be reattached with plastic tree tape to large plaques, about two by two feet in size, made from a couple of one-by-12-inch boards held together with one-by-two-inch pieces nailed to the back. In time, they will outgrow even the largest boards and will begin to cling to the walls of the house, or to a fence or tree trunk, though they can be peeled off if need be.

They require next to no maintenance near the coast, and only occasional watering. Though they look decidedly tropical, they are quite drought resistant where humidity is reasonably high (as far inland as Pasadena). As do other ferns, they need to grow in bright shade.

In part shade, try any of the various epiphytic orchids that will grow outdoors in Southern California. When I first moved from Northern California years ago, I was most amazed by the orchids growing outdoors in gardens here, attached to trees, just as they do in tropical South America—especially the oncidiums. I immediately bought and "planted" some. I tied them onto slabs of tree fern bark, which I hung from nails driven into the porch posts. Now their roots wrap around the posts, securely holding the clumps of leaves. Every fall, my amazement returns, as thread-thin stalks open delicate flowers that flutter like little dancing ladies in the dry autumn breezes. I believe the ones I am growing are, in fact, commonly called dancing ladies (*Oncidium gawerramsey*). They have inch-across golden-yellow petals, flecked maroon at the base, with the lower petal flared like a twirling skirt. I also grow *Oncidium enderianum* on a cajeput tree, though it may be a little more cold-sensitive. For me it blooms every fall with sprays of chocolate-colored orchids that even have a delicate fragrance. Earl Ross, the orchid specialist at The Arboretum of Los Angeles County, suggests another oncidium for those who live farther inland: *Oncidium sphacelatum* is hardy outdoors even in Arcadia.

Flowering in the dead of winter is the hardiest orchid of all, *Laelia anceps*, also worth looking for. Attach it to a tree or wall, and every year it will astonish you with spikes of lavender and purple orchids. It grows where it can get morning sun, shaded for the rest of the day by the porch or a tree. Occasionally, spritz it with water, and that's it for care.

> Every fall, my amazement returns, as thread-thin stalks open delicate flowers that flutter like little dancing ladies in the dry autumn breezes.

BEES AND WASPS

Don't confuse the long-waisted wasps, such as this Mud Dauber, that hunt larvae in your garden, with the aggressive short-waisted Yellow Jackets.

"Why do bumblebees suck your blood?" was the difficult question posed to a friend by a little girl returning from summer camp. It seems some boys had trapped a "bee" (it was probably a Yellow Jacket since it was hovering around their lunch) under a paper cup. Sliding a piece of paper under the cup, one boy picked it up and shook it up real good (something only a little boy would do). Then it escaped. Of course, it stung the little girl, not the boys.

Though they may sting, the wasps and bumblebees of summer are one of the gardener's best friends. As Southern California becomes more urbanized, the traditional pollinator of flowers, vegetables and fruit—the honeybee—is becoming ever more scarce. Bumblebees, and wasps to a lesser degree, have taken their place. Because honeybees live in large colonies, they need a good-sized space—an attic, shed, large tree—to build their hives. These places are getting harder for them to find. More often than not, they are forcibly evicted by agents hired by the owner.

Bumblebees (there are several kinds in Southern California), on the other hand, live in small colonies, usually in the ground. They seem to be on the increase, since suitable lodging is easier to find in urban areas. And they don't suck your blood—it is even difficult to provoke them to sting, unlike the common honeybee. I'm the only person I know who has actually been stung by one, and it was only when I pinched one by accident as I was about to pull a weed. I can verify what is said in the literature about their sting, that it is less painful than a honeybee's. My sons used to pet them, stroking their downy fuzz, without provoking them, and I, while bumbling about in the garden myself, have often rudely disturbed them without upsetting them. They seem to ignore my presence.

Bumblebees have a look-alike in the Carpenter Bee, though they are not closely related. While bumblebees are banded with yellow, the larger Carpenter Bees are pure jet black. They get their name from their wood-burrowing habits, drilling perfect dime-sized tunnels in old wood. These tunnels are quite deep and hold a number of baby bees, packed in one on top of the other like Pringles in a can (the first to hatch must wait until the last does before it can exit).

Only one bee could be considered a pest. Leaf-cutter Bees are the gals who are cutting those neat circles out of your rose leaves, but they seldom take more than a few chunks to line their nests.

Most wasps are also friends of the gardener, though they look very fierce and most unfriendly. The large, thread-waisted wasps that build homes of mud or paper are great hunters. While weeding I have seen them cruising low in the plants, to occasionally dive and come up with larvae of some kind, often of cutworms, unearthed as I work, or other larvae, such as cabbage worms feeding on leaves.

The most common big wasp is the Golden Polistes, which builds the small umbrella-like paper nests occasionally found on eaves of the house or in trees. These are the wasps that are striped and colored like a Yellow Jacket, but with long, narrow waists connecting thorax and abdomen. I've been told that they can be provoked and will sting, but they've never bothered me. The even larger Mud Dauber is mostly black with thin yellow bands. She builds the mud houses found in attics and garages. These wasps are not easily provoked and seldom sting. I have found them to be nice companions while working in the garden.

Even the Yellow Jacket does his share of hunting for garden pests, but he is the one to watch out for. Yellow Jackets seem to enjoy stinging, and, unlike honeybees, can do it over and over. Recent research has shown that if you squash one, it releases an odor that brings more wasps and incites them to riot. Yellow Jackets are usually very yellow and are shorter and more squat than the other common wasps. They are the ones that land on your hamburger just as you are ready to take a bite, that like fruit almost as much as meat, and that cause instant panic when they land on your child's soda-smeared face during outdoor meals. They have no table manners at all.

In my own garden, they are not welcome, though I have yet to find a way to get rid of them. There are some high-tech traps available, but these didn't seem to work when I tried them briefly. Though they slowly became filled with Yellow Jackets, more appeared to take their places. Yellow Jackets live in the ground, in colonies that get quite large by the end of summer—as many as 15,000 individuals according to "Insects of the Los Angeles Basin," by Charles L. Hogue (Natural History Museum of Los Angeles County), and heaven help anyone who comes too near. Just walking nearby sends tremors through the ground that bring them out in droves.

One other wasp occasionally seen scares gardeners to death. The Tarantula Hawk stalks those big spiders and is easily recognized because it is one of the biggest wasps in the world and is a striking blue-black with red wings. I used to frequent a pile of gritty soil dumped by the road to get the makings of a fast-draining potting soil. One day I found the husk of a dead tarantula lying on top. A few days later, I realized that I must have been digging in dirt that contained Tarantula Hawk nests. Sure enough, on my return I found them—cruising low over the ground and alighting near little tunnels in my mound of prized soil, which I promptly abandoned. Since I had been doing most of my pillaging in winter, they had not been active. But once the weather had warmed up, with it came the hawks. The sting is said to very painful (worse than the bite of the timid tarantula). But most people have sense enough to stay well clear of the Tarantula Hawk's activities.

Wasps and bumblebees are most plentiful now because the colonies start anew each year, dying out in winter. In the case of bumblebees, the queen alone survives, and she must begin a new colony all by herself in spring. Queens are often seen gathering pollen at the time fruit trees flower, pollinating them as they go. Bumblebees are not as sensitive to cold as honeybees so become active earlier in the year.

As pollinators, all bees are important—they can make the difference between having a crop of fruit or not. And wasps are an important part of pest control (though I think Yellow Jackets aren't worth the aggravation). As gardeners we should let them all be, and maybe whisper a quiet "Thanks" in appreciation when working alongside them.

August

THE BIG OPPORTUNITY: STARTING THINGS FROM SEED

A N EARLY GARDEN WRITER WROTE: "AUGUST IS the time to prepare for the second California springtime which the beginning of the rainy season ushers in."

Look in any old-time Southern California gardening book, and you'll find an interesting suggestion for something to do this month: Start plants from seed. As unlikely as it may sound, August is one of the best times to sow seed—for vegetables and annual flowers that bloom and ripen in the cool winter weather ahead. Starting seed now takes advantage of the warm soil; in a cold soil, seeds will germinate very slowly or not at all.

True, buying plants in nursery packs is quick and easy. Even gung-ho gardeners appreciate the convenience of small plants ready to go. But the choice of what to plant is very limited—especially for vegetables, because growers often use tired, old varieties even when exciting new kinds are available.

WEEK
32

Starting plants from seed is more of an adventure. Take a look in any seed catalogue to see the astounding multitude of vegetables offered as seed. Even with flowers, you'll find some fascinating stuff in catalogues that you'll never see at nurseries.

At this time of year, you can even begin perennials, trees and shrubs from seed, and then plant them out in the fall, that season best of all for planting. "One more August opportunity looks beyond the fall bloom," wrote E.J. Wickson in his "California Garden Flowers," published in 1915. "Biennials and perennials which bloom the second year in wintry climates count a year in California as good as two years elsewhere, providing they are started so that they can grow in the latter half of one year and bloom in the first half of the next. The list is too long to even name the plants which thus declare their joy in coming to California."

Perhaps the best selection of perennial plants to grow from seed is offered by Thompson & Morgan (it is, after all, an English seed house), and almost all are illustrated in color in its catalogue [*P.O. Box 1308, Jackson, NJ 08527-0308 (800) 274-7333*]. Following the lead of Professor Wickson, I won't try to list all the perennials that can be grown from seed. I will warn you, however, that not all those offered in Thompson & Morgan will succeed here, but therein lies the adventure.

Starting plants from seed may be an adventure, but it's not nearly as mysterious or difficult as it may seem. The requirements are simple: Seeds need a good soil and constant moisture, and they must be planted at the proper depth. Some also need warmth; this is why eastern publications always talk of starting seed indoors. Here, in mild Southern California, it is much easier to start them outside—in the ground or in containers. Indoors, seedlings are more prone to diseases and will etiolate—bleach and stretch for the light—which gets them off to a spindly start. Outdoors, seedlings remain short and tough, which makes for sturdy plants that don't topple or succumb to damping off, a disease that withers newly sprouted seedlings.

Starting seeds directly in the soil was much more popular at one time than it is now. Most of the early references speak of sowing seed in the ground at this time of year. Wickson again: "It is interesting to try many other things with an August start on irrigated land, and a beginner will often be surprised and delighted over his achievements if he dares to defy the warning of the wiseacres who tell him he must wait for fall rains."

Planted as seeds in the garden, many flowers will grow and then bloom in late fall, lasting into winter and early spring. Vegetables such as broccoli and lettuce can be harvested months earlier. Some vegetables grow best when sown directly in the ground, root crops, in particular, and so do a few flowers, such as larkspur and zinnias.

To sow in the ground, irrigate, wait a few days, then pulverize the soil, making sure there are no clods of any kind, and level it with a rake. Carefully make little furrows at the proper depth, following the recommendations on the seed packet. If there are no directions, plant

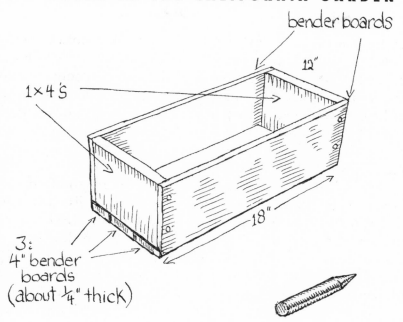

bender boards

1×4's

12"

18"

3:
4" bender
boards
(about ¼" thick)

seed twice as deep as it is thick.

It's difficult to space seeds evenly in the planting trench. Most people end up planting way too many, with the seedlings then wastefully clumped together. Once up, thin to the recommended distance apart (also specified on packets). Catalogues often sell gizmos that meter out very small seed, giving you more control. Colored organic coatings make seed more visible against the soil (nature tends to do the opposite, coloring seed like soil so it is invisible to birds). Coated seed is also easier to handle since it's slightly larger. Unfortunately, only some seed is coated, and catalogues seldom tell you which is.

To protect emerging seedlings from birds and bugs, use one of the new floating row covers, lightweight fabrics that let sun and water in but keep critters out. After sowing, cover the bed loosely, and tuck the edges into the soil. As plants grow, they push the fabric up. Most seed companies and some nurseries carry floating row covers under a variety of names, such as Agryl, Reemay and Tufbell.

There are some good reasons to sow seeds in containers and then transplant the seedlings into small pots and finally out in the ground. You can provide a better soil and better protect seedlings from bugs and birds. And weeds aren't a problem—out in the garden, it can be difficult to tell sprouting weeds from sprouting seedlings.

You can use all sorts of containers. However, it is hard to beat old-fashioned wood flats, which help insulate the soil and keep it moist. If you have a hand saw, hammer and a few nails, you can build

Make your own old-fashioned seed flats of redwood bender board and one-by-fours. Fashion a dibble by sharpening a dowel.

your own with redwood one-by-fours and bender board (the thin wood sold to edge lawns). Twelve inches wide by 18 inches long and about four inches deep (the wood is actually three-and-a-half inches wide) is a convenient size. Fill to within half an inch of the top with fresh potting mix (the kind sold by the bag at nurseries), and loosely pack it down with a leftover piece of wood. Make the furrows with a piece of leftover bender board.

Packaged potting mix is sterilized, which almost guarantees that damping off and other diseases won't affect seedlings. It's also just the right consistency to keep seeds moist but not soggy. This is another rule of thumb: Seeds must be kept moist, especially overnight, which means you may have to water them as often as twice a day. Some gardeners cover the soil with a tailored sheet of newspaper as a moisture-conserving mulch between waterings, removing it as the seeds sprout. Or use a cut piece of floating row cover, which also helps trap heat and moisture, speeding germination.

To water, use a very fine spray; use a special nozzle with lots of little holes, available at nurseries, or a mist nozzle (I use a special fine nozzle made for watering bonsai). Or get a watering can made for seedlings, such as the English-made Hawes watering can with the fine rose (the proper name for a watering can nozzle) that faces up. Water seedlings upside-down, that is, with the nozzle pointing upward, so the water goes up, arches and falls as naturally as a light rain.

Again, follow the seed packet's recommendation on how deep to plant seed. This is critical. The reason that seed doesn't germinate is usually because it is covered with too much soil. Err on the side of planting too shallow. And don't think that planting lots of seed close together will ensure that at least some will germinate. Unless the seed is old, almost all will sprout. A pinch is usually enough for a row in a flat.

Now water and be patient. It takes at least a week or two for most seed to sprout, if kept constantly moist. Keep flats in a partially shaded place in summer and early fall (in a sunny location in winter and spring). The more sun they get, the less likely they are to succumb to diseases or to etiolate. Keep them up off the ground, away from sow-bugs (which usually prefer decaying matter, but will nibble on very young seedlings), but especially snails and slugs, which relish them.

Patience is again required for the seeds to grow to transplanting size. This may take several more weeks. Move the seedlings from the flats when the first pair of true leaves appear. The odd round leaves that initially sprout are actually part of the seed and not true leaves. You can use a dibble—like a tiny trowel—to pry out each seedling,

---

A Few Good Seed Catalogues

🐌 The Cook's Garden, P.O. Box 5010, Hodges, SC 29653 (800) 457-9703.

🐌 Bountiful Gardens, 18001 Shafer Ranch Road, Willits, CA 95490 (707) 459-6410.

🐌 Nichols Garden Nursery, 1190 Old Salem Rd., Albany, OR 97321 (541) 928-9280.

🐌 Park Seed Co., Cokesbury Road, Greenwood, SC 29647 (800) 845-3369.

🐌 Seeds of Change, P.O. Box 15700, Santa Fe, NM 87506 (888) 762-1333.

🐌 Thompson & Morgan, P.O. Box 1308, Jackson, NJ 08527 (800) 274-7333

🐌 W. Atlee Burpee & Co., Warminster, PA 18974, (800) 888-1447.

---

and then punch a planting hole. You can make one from a piece of wooden dowel. The Widger, an improvement on this old, old tool, really does look like a little trowel (Ecology Action is one source for Widgers and kits to make redwood flats as well). Most gardeners move seedlings into old nursery packs or tiny pots. Peat pots are not recommended in California because they dry out too quickly.

A few weeks later still and the transplants should be ready to go into the garden. They'll look just like the little plants available at nurseries, but they are less likely to be rootbound or too big for their packs. The whole process takes about six to eight weeks. It's really not much of a mystery at all. The only real puzzle is how so much life can be packed into that little bundle called a seed.

Plant Sweet Peas Before Labor Day

S tart sweet peas now if you want to have blooms by Christmas," one early garden book says of August. Ernest Braunton in "The Garden Beautiful in California," published in 1940, elaborates: "This is the best month for sowing sweet peas for winter blooms. If left until next month they will not make bloom until spring."

The sweet peas I plant are the old-fashioned, tall vining kinds that produce masses of flowers with stems long enough to cut and that are often quite fragrant. I've always found the bush-type sweet peas a bit of a disappointment. If you think you haven't enough room for the big vining kinds, consider that sweet peas grow great in a pot—just the thing to brighten a wintry patio. Being among the earliest things you can plant in fall, they are also among the earliest to bloom.

For a number of years, I've planted tall vining sweet peas in large Italian terra-cotta pots (about 14 inches across), which I fill to within an inch of the top with bagged potting soil. Then I push in three or four eight-foot-long bamboo poles, and beside every pole I plant three seeds—so each container holds about a dozen plants. A neighbor of mine plants hers in the ground, against the south- and west-facing walls of the house, fastening commercially available sweet-pea netting to the eaves and to stakes driven into the ground. Though it's a distance of some 10 feet, the sweet peas easily reach the roof by late spring. Sweet peas need full, bright sun.

Soak the seeds in a cup of water for 24 hours before planting, or germination will be slow and possibly spotty. Push each seed one inch into the soil or potting mix. Keep moist by watering whenever the soil starts to dry. When they begin to flower, pick as much as you want to make compact little bouquets. Cut off all faded flower spikes. Though tedious, this really does keep them blooming much longer than they would if left alone.

Growing them in the ground is even easier if the soil has been enriched with homemade compost or bags of soil amendment. As an early expert wrote in a 1906 Los Angeles book, they "ask not much more than to be dumped on the ground in the winter season." They don't even need fertilizing, but keep them watered.

If you want to grow sweet peas the old-fashioned, labor-intensive way—where first a deep trench is dug—follow this advice from Braunton's book: "You cannot trench too deeply or make soil too rich for sweet peas if fertilizer is sufficiently mixed with the soil before replacing it in [the] trench. The last move should be putting [the soil] through a half-inch mesh sieve as it drops back in [the] trench; then it's mixed. Plant seeds in moist soil but do not water until plants are up."

For years, I grew the English 'Spencer' strains. They, and other English sweet peas, can be ordered from Fragrant Garden Nursery [*P.O. Box 4246, Brookings, OR 97415; www.fragrantgarden.com*]. 'Winter Elegance,' a strain sold by Renee's Garden Seeds, at nurseries and at *(888) 880)-7228; www.reneesgarden.com*, is bred especially for the cut-flower business for winter blooms. Other vining strains include a deliciously fragrant mix sold as 'Old Spice,' 'Early Mammoth' and the vigorous 'Multiflora Gigantea' series. For the most powerful fragrance and a decidedly old-fashioned look, search out the original named selection, 'Painted Lady,' developed in 1737. It has simple bicolored red and white flowers that smell like expensive candies. English catalogues, such as Thompson & Morgan, [*P.O. Box 1308, Jackson, NJ 08527, (800) 274-7333*] usually carry it.

Keep seeds away from children. Unlike edible peas, sweet-pea seeds are poisonous, another good reason to keep all spent flowers picked off so they can never set seed.

TALL BEARDED IRIS

In August, even diehard gardeners are more likely to be thinking about iced tea than they are about bearded iris. But this is the month to buy, plant and divide these pretty perennial plants. Now, when bearded iris are dormant, is the time to move the sweet potato-sized rhizomes, so this is when growers dig up their plants and send them to nurseries, and hobbyists plant or divide old clumps. August is the busiest month in an iris fancier's year, and iris societies often hold sales at this time, where members sell their excess plants.

Tall bearded iris have been out of fashion for a while, but because of their proven drought resistance, they are making a comeback. Gardeners appreciate their strong, vertical sword-like foliage—a good accent in a garden of mounded forms—and tall flower spikes that stand well above other flowers, exclamation points in a flowery composition. Bearded iris are called tall when they have flowering stems that reach 27 inches. Many are much taller, to four feet or so. The beard that gives them their name is the little fuzzy part in the middle of the flowers, between the upper petals, called standards, and lower ones, called falls.

WEEK 33

The parents of today's bearded iris came from the Mediterranean, that ancient area with a climate so similar to our own. *Iris florentina*, *Iris x germanica* and other relatives still grow wild in the dry hills of Spain, Provence and Tuscany. And so, bearded iris follow a cycle very similar to our own native plants, which bloom in early spring, grow during spring and early summer and then go almost dormant until fall when winter rains return. In California, tall bearded iris flower during a seven-week period in late March and April, do most of their growing in May and June, then become semi-dormant in July, August and September. Those called reblooming

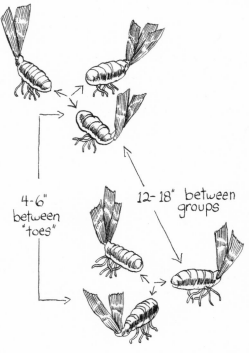

4-6" between "toes"

12-18" between groups

flower again in the fall. These are the kinds to search out if you only have room for a few.

Gardeners who already have large clumps of bearded iris that no longer bloom the way they used to should get the spade out and start digging right now. Tall bearded iris need dividing about every three years. "Just when a clump really looks good, it is time to divide," iris grower Jim Puckett says. "If you wait another year, you will regret it. Flowering drops off dramatically when the clumps become crowded."

Replant iris in tight groups with all the leafy ends of rhizomes facing out from the center. Space them about four to six inches apart in the groups, and space the groups 12 to 18 inches apart.

Save only the larger, healthier rhizomes with healthy root systems, from the outer edge of the clump. These are the most likely to bloom next spring. Shake the soil from the roots, trim the foliage so it is about six inches long (to compensate for the loss of roots) and then carefully replant.

It's a good idea to add a little amendment and fertilizer to the soil before replanting. Plant in small groups of three. The growing tips (the end with the leaves) should face out, and there should be four to six inches between the ends, or toes. Plant several such clusters of three, spacing each cluster about 12 to 18 inches apart in a random pattern. This arrangement will make a new clump that looks as though it has been undisturbed for years, and it allows for some room to grow.

Water the new plantings, and they will begin to grow new roots. In winter, the plants go briefly and completely dormant again. New leaves will follow, which prompt flowers in spring. Puckett says the August timing is critical because, if they are to flower in spring, the new or divided plants need six weeks to grow roots before going dormant again.

Planting the rhizomes that are available at society sales or nurseries now is a similar process. Bearded iris like a well-drained soil so add amendments. If your garden soil is a heavy clay, Puckett says, amend it and gently mound the whole bed to a height of two to three inches, to speed drainage. Plant the rhizomes so the tops are right at the soil surface, exposed. You can plant just one of each kind, and wait a few years for them to multiply and spread, but they are more dramatic in drifts of at least three of the same kind. Water the plants every seven to 10 days until they are established in the garden. The following summer back off on the watering after July, so the plants can go a little dry. In Puckett's care instructions, "Be sure not to overwater" is emphasized in capital letters.

Bearded iris planted in some shade will grow, but don't expect them to flower. They are happiest in our hottest, sunniest areas, one reason the San Fernando Valley Iris Society is such an active one. Fertilize lightly in February and fall. When they go briefly dormant in winter, you should cut or gently pull off the shriveled tan leaves. Keep after the weeds that are sure to sprout between the rhizomes.

As one early hybridizer quaintly put it, "The climate of California is the envy of iris cranks the world over."

Because, as one early hybridizer quaintly put it, "the climate of California is the envy of iris cranks the world over," there were once many iris growers in the state. Most moved on when land prices skyrocketed in the 1950s, but some new ones have sprung up in the last few years. Puckett's growing grounds, in Riverside, are now a part of John Schoustra's Greenwood Iris & Daylily Gardens. There you can see iris in bloom in spring and have them dug from the fields. Write or call Greenwood for a catalogue or to arrange a visit [*5595 E. 7th St., #490, Long Beach, CA 90804 (562) 494-8944; www.greenwooddaylily.com*].

At the other end of the greater Los Angeles area is Rancho De Los Flores, which also has a catalogue. You can visit the growing grounds on certain days in spring, and even arrange to have a wedding and reception held there [*8000 Balcom Canyon Road, Somis, CA 93066 (805) 529-6534*].

A FEW FLOWERS FOR LATE SUMMER

During this hot, often smoggy season, gardens look tired, if not exhausted. New recruits are desperately needed. Luckily, there are flowers that wait until August or September to bloom, and their fresh faces are a welcome relief. Of course, the time to plant these soldiers is in the fall or early spring, before the onslaught of summer, but this might be the best time to look for them at nurseries, then wait to plant in fall, so next summer's garden will look a little less pooped.

The best blooms now make the most of the orange late-summer

light. *Helianthus angustifolius*, the swamp sunflower, positively glows. A towering perennial (to eight feet), it needs room, but the explosion of golden yellow is worth every foot. In most gardens it needs some kind of support, or it will topple—though it will continue to bloom from its new horizontal position. Stake the stems or grow it in some kind of short but sturdy cage. Those cages sold at nurseries that are really too short for tomatoes work well if placed over the clump when it is just beginning to grow.

Helenium autumnale is another bright, late-flowering perennial with stiffer stems that don't tend to topple. It grows to six feet, though three or four is more common. The vaguely daisy-like flowers are autumn shades of gold, orange and red, at least in the mix called 'Sunshine Hybrid'.

Both of these perennials love hot weather and sizzling climates. Don't be surprised when they die completely to the ground in winter. Just cut them back, close to the ground, and they will return. If you can't find them at nurseries, try growing them from seed, which sprouts easily in August, though they won't flower until next summer. One source for the helenium is Thompson & Morgan [*P.O. Box 1308, Jackson, NJ 08527-0308 (800) 274-7333*]. Other golden flowers for the late-summer garden include coreopsis, rudbeckia, solidago and the annual edible sunflowers, which can breathe life into even an overworked vegetable garden.

While soft pinks don't usually cut it in the late-summer sun, infusing this color with purple makes it come alive. Though a little invasive, *Physostegia virginiana*, sometimes called false dragonhead or obedient plant, is a three- to four-foot tower of sturdy color. The most noticeable perennial asters, another group of late-summer bloomers, are also purplish pink or purple (or glistening white), and their airy stems are a nice contrast to the stiff spikes of physostegia. Nurseries typically carry perennial asters only in late summer. Cut both of these perennial to the ground after bloom.

Several bulbs also bloom now. *Amaryllis belladonna* is a strong pink-flowered, drought-resistant bulb, commonly called naked lady since it blooms before foliage appears. Nerines are similar bulbs, but smaller in all their parts.

If one late bloomer should get a medal for valor, it is the California fuchsia. Botanists haven't decided if it should be named *Zauschneria* or *Epilobium*, but nearly all have striking orange-red trumpet flowers that glow like embers in the warm late-summer sun. Now and into fall, they brighten even drought-tough gardens with flame-colored flowers, set

California fuchsias are most unfuchsia-like, blooming in the hottest, sunniest, driest places— spots that would make a regular fuchsia faint.

against cloudy gray foliage. In the wild, beside Highway 18 on the way to Big Bear and next to Highway 1 in Big Sur, they do the same thing.

California fuchsias are most unfuchsia-like, blooming in the hottest, sunniest, driest places—spots that would make a regular fuchsia faint, although they are related. Great on hillsides, they may be low and mounding or make fluffy bushes of several feet, but all spread underground. To control their spreading, keep them on the dry side. In winter, you can cut most back to ground.

I have a mounding 'Everett's Choice' growing though clumps of the dwarf burgundy-colored flax 'Jack Spratt'. In a nearby dry area, *Zauschneria septentrionalis* 'Select Mattole' makes a starched gray mound. But it is the bigger, billowy kinds I like best, the scarlet flowers mixed in with penstemons and salvias in my border. 'Armstrong', which probably tolerates the most garden water, blooms earliest and for at least two months. 'Catalina', native to that sunny isle, blooms later, becoming frothy with large flowers.

I've found California fuchsias amazingly tolerant of occasional watering (for a native plant). They add brilliant, crackling color just when gardens need it, and hummingbirds love them. If you've wanted to add natives to your garden, buy a couple of these, but wait until fall to put them in the ground.

A BULB BLOOMS IN AUGUST

A nurseryman was trying to describe to a customer just what the fat bulbs of *Amaryllis belladonna* would grow to become, but was having no luck. Until he said: "You know, it's the bulb that flowers in August in vacant lots, the one with the big pink flowers." That did it.

Everyone has noticed these bulbs, blooming when almost nothing else does, in the middle of summer, and where almost nothing else grows—in completely dry soil where even the weeds are dead. "They're amazing," says Polly Anderson, whose backyard in La Cañada Flintridge is full of these bulbs. "They need absolutely *no* water, and they grow in sun *or* shade."

The common name for *Amaryllis belladonna* is naked lady, referring to the fact that it flagrantly flowers without foliage. Later, usually in October, the bulbs typically make a bold clump of shiny dark green, strap-like leaves two to three feet across but only about 18 inches tall. This is just in time to take advantage of winter rains. In late spring, the plants brown and go dormant until the first flowers push out of the bare ground in August.

Amaryllis belladonna has also been called *Brunsvigia*. It is native to the southwestern Cape region of South Africa, which has a climate similar to our own, with a very long dry season. In the Southern Hemisphere, it is commonly called the March lily, which is when it blooms there. Belladonna lily is another common name. Anderson politely calls them pink ladies.

The *Amaryllis belladonna* growing in Anderson's backyard bloom in September, because they are hybrids she has developed over the last 40 years. They grow under a large aleppo pine and around cit-

WEEK 34

rus and eucalyptus that are about 100 years old, reminders of the previous agricultural use of the gently sloping property. In the heat of early September, most of the garden is dry and crisp, the air smells strongly of pine, and the San Gabriel Mountains rise abruptly in the distance. But it is the naked ladies that command the attention, bright pink at a time of year when most flowers are yellow or orange. In the Anderson garden, however, they are not just pink—they are pink with white throats, pure china white, white with throats of creamy yellow or apricot, and a dark pink that most people would call red. The flowers are bigger and are often on taller stems, and each flower head makes a full circle—the common pink makes but a quarter circle with most of the flowers facing the sun.

Some of Anderson's bulbs grow in full sun, others in complete (but bright) shade. Some grow from under a ground cover of cape weed (*Arctotheca calendula*) and some from a mulch of pine needles. Most, however, send their sturdy reddish brown stems from bare dirt. The bed under the aleppo pine has the most bulbs and flowers. Anderson thinks this is because she waters this bed in the winter (but not in the summer) since narcissus also grow there. The other beds get no water at all so the bulbs grow more slowly, but they too are full of blooms.

And some of her amaryllis grow in pots, but she says they don't flower well, or at all in some cases, much preferring the dry, open ground. Some also grow at the base of the taller crinum lilies, which flower at the same time with very similar flowers but with year-round foliage. In the front yard, she has a veritable field of the common pink belladonna. The flowers of the common pink and the hybrids are excellent cut, fragrant and last a week or two in a vase.

Anderson does not fertilize at all and has heard from other growers that fertilizing can contribute to the early demise of amaryllis bulbs, causing rot. So can summer watering, though they can take a certain amount. Bulbs are normally long-lived, often outlasting their gardeners and even the gardens they grow in.

In some beds she does not even bother with the weeds, which do not seem inclined or able to overwhelm the amaryllis. Anderson notes that the cape weed, a very tough plant from South Africa that looks much like a gazania, even has trouble growing into the bed of amaryllis because the ground is so dry. Though she says you do not have to watch where you step here, you do, because every square inch of ground seems to have the papery tops of the bulbs poking through. The bulbs are planted just under the ground with the very tops of the necks sticking out.

Polly Anderson does not fertilize at all and has heard from other growers that fertilizing can contribute to the early demise of amaryllis bulbs.

In general, it is best not to dig or divide clumps of amaryllis because it takes them at least a year to become re-established and begin flowering again.

She began hybridizing with a dark rosy-pink amaryllis that grows nearly wild in Santa Cruz and a nice white named 'Hathor' that she found in Santa Barbara. It has been a long, slow process because it takes five to six years from seed to flowering bulb. The seeds are easy to grow, she says. She simply sows them in the ground, in neat little rows as though they were corn, and they sprout in early fall. Even the seedlings should be allowed to go dry in summer. If she doesn't plan to save seed, she snaps off the seed heads after the last flower fades, to help conserve the bulbs' energy. The flower head breaks off cleanly with a crisp *pop*.

Several large bulb growers have shown interest in the Anderson hybrids, so someday they may be more available (Burkard Nurseries in Pasadena sometimes sells some of Anderson's extras at this time of year). In the meantime, there is nothing wrong with the plain pink ones of vacant lots, which are generally available at nurseries now or in the fall. Their return to cultivated gardens is long overdue. They will simply smile at the next drought.

STUMPED

Those who have tried to remove even a small tree by themselves don't need to take a wild guess about where the word *stumped* came from. Cutting down a tree is hard enough, but with the help of a little chain saw, small trees can be pretty quick work. Getting rid of the stump, however, is another matter.

Just how do you get rid of a stump? Those chemicals that are supposed to dissolve them don't work. I recently removed a bottle-brush tree with the help of an electric chain saw, even managing to fell it right between the flower beds without smashing the pansies. I invited a few neighbors over to see my handiwork, and my neat pile of firewood, and they were suitably impressed.

Full of confidence, the next day I tackled the stump with a mattock, which I had sharpened with a bastard file. Mattocks, or Pulaskis—part pick, part ax, part grub hoe—are the best hand tool for digging something out of the ground; you chop at the roots and then lever them out. Though the tool helped me get quickly through the upper roots, when I pushed on the trunk (one should always leave about five feet of trunk for leverage), nothing budged. It didn't even quiver.

A few more hours convinced me that somewhere under that thick trunk were some substantial roots and that I was going to have to dig a much bigger hole and then try and cut them from underneath with a bow saw. A few more seconds of thought, and I decided that I was licked. It was time to call for help. Actually, I rationalized, I had always wanted to see the machine called a stump grinder at work. This relatively new machine has made stump removal easy and a lot less costly than having someone dig it out by hand. In the phone book under Tree Service, I found a firm that listed "stump grinding." Talking to the owner, Ruben Fernandez, of All Cities Tree Service, I learned that the stump grinder would fit through my gate, had rubber tires so it wouldn't ruin the lawn and was self-propelled so it could easily make it into the backyard. The minimum charge would be $125, though it might cost more, which sounded like a real bargain to this exhausted laborer. I made an appointment for the next day and put away my mattock.

If someone had invented the stump grinder 20 years ago, the stump I have been gardening around for the past five would probably not be there. I think it too belonged to a bottlebrush tree and that someone else had given up trying to remove it a long time ago. In the old days one could buy dynamite and blow stumps out of the ground or build a fire on top of the stump and let it burn for a week or so, or spend days digging it out by hand. Now I was about to see the latest wrinkle in stump removal in action. What I imagined was something like the giant, lumbering tree-eating machine I remember from an old Uncle Scrooge comic book that the Beagle Boys used to demolish Scrooge's money bin.

If someone had invented the stump grinder 20 years ago, the stump I have been gardening around for the past five would probably not be there.

What arrived in my driveway was not quite so impressive. The stump grinder is a small machine, considering what it does. Only one man wheeled it easily through the gate and into place. A hefty 15-horsepower motor sits on top and drives a disk studded with short stubby chippers. It took all of about five minutes to set it up and about 10 to get rid of the stump, maybe less. It just ground it away, leaving behind a mixture of soil and small wood chips. These would make a perfect soil amendment if I added some nitrogen fertilizer to help them decompose. Otherwise, raw sawdust or chips rob the soil, and any plants growing in it, of nitrogen, that essential plant nutrient (packaged soil amendments already have been partially composted and have nitrogen added).

It turned out that the hole I dug was in the way and had to be filled in. The grinder digs its own hole as it goes and otherwise needs solid ground to sit on. I noticed as it chipped away that, sure enough, directly under the stump were several large roots that I never would have got to, but they too disappeared in a blur. The stump grinder removed all traces of the stump and roots to a depth of about 18 inches, which gave me plenty of room for gardening above. What an invention, and what a bargain.

GARDEN GOOFS

Everybody makes mistakes, even the best of gardeners. But it is the good gardeners who learn from them. Just listen to, and take heart from, the goofs some of Southern California's best made when they were starting out.

Although her garden is practically the first thing visiting English gardeners, notables such as Rosemary Verey and Christopher Lloyd, want to see on their swings through Los Angeles, landscape designer Christine Rosmini remembers many mistakes made as a beginner. "It's hard to single one out, I made so many," she says. These should be reassuring words to novice gardeners, coming from one of the acknowledged best, whose garden appears in many books including the recent "Gardens of California," by Nancy Goslee Power (Clarkson Potter, New York).

One of Rosmini's worst gaffes was carefully cultivating two noxious weeds "until I realized their imperial ambitions," she says. She thought false garlic (*Nothoscordum inodorum*) was a dainty little white-flowered ornamental allium, or onion, like the kind seen in

English gardening books. Then it started coming up everywhere. She regarded nutgrass already growing on the property in the same way. She finally eliminated the false garlic by painstakingly digging up every bulb, including all the little baby bulbs so easily left behind. She got rid of the nutgrass "by moving" to her present garden. (The only other way is to fumigate the soil, killing everything else, or starve the plant by constantly pulling off every leaf, which can take years.)

"You tend to forget those first fiascoes," says Jack Christensen, who developed some famous roses, including 'Mon Chéri', 'Gold Medal' and 'Voodoo'. The former Garden Q&A columnist for the *Los Angeles Times* does, however, recall not thinning fruit on his trees and

WEEK 35

vegetables in the garden. "I just couldn't bring myself to thin my first fruit trees, and so I got a lot of small, tasteless fruit and a few broken branches," he admits. Now he thins the trees around his Victorian home in Ontario so that each fruit has plenty of room to develop and no branch is overladen. As for the vegetables, he always reads the seed packets and thins to the recommended spacing. "It makes quite a difference," he says.

"I remember having all the leaves fall off a rubber tree when I fertilized it dry," says Lili Singer, publisher of *The Southern California Gardener*, garden consultant and radio host. "I soon learned to make sure that plants got watered before they got fertilized," she says. "I also sowed seed way too thickly, thinking they wouldn't all germinate—but they always do. And I discovered that watering by hand only works on new, small plants or for sprouting seed," she says. Remembering how she tried for years to grow tomatoes with only three or four hours of sun, she says, "you learn it doesn't work, even in the San Fernando Valley."

Mike Evans, who runs Tree of Life Nursery, a large San Juan Capistrano wholesale nursery specializing in native plants, remembers a truly disastrous event. In the early 1970s, he was teaching horticulture at the Regional Occupation Center in Orange County and building up a rare collection of orchids, bromeliads and other exotics in one of the greenhouses.

On one greenhouse shelf were two nearly identical white plastic gallon jugs, one filled with a very mild algicide, safe enough for use in restaurants and hospitals, the other with a potent herbicide. "There was a lot of green algae growing on the greenhouse walls and benches, so I reached for the algicide but grabbed the herbicide instead," he remembers. "I got about 100 percent kill in that greenhouse—nearly the entire collection was dead. The lesson here is to carefully read the label, starting with the name!"

In Northern California, Kathleen Brenzel, editor of the "Sunset Western Garden Book," remembers planting a young rhododendron that "looked so cute and small in its one-gallon can" in a three-foot space by the front door. Soon it "looked like an elephant in a phone booth." Planting things that grow too large for their spots was her biggest mistake when she first started gardening, she says (along with leaving shovels face up on the ground, sometimes with painful results). "It's crucial to know how big a plant will grow and then give it room," she adds, which is perhaps why that information is so easy to find in the new edition of the "Sunset Western Garden Book."

Every single expert gardener I talked to had made, or is still making, this mistake of planting things too close together. One explains that nursery plants "look so small and lonely with all that bare ground around them." But here's where patience is required, and a virtue, in gardening. I also confess to regularly making this error, ever trying to fit more into an already crowded garden. My wife says my epitaph will read: "I didn't know it would get that big."

Brenzel also remembers "pouring quantities of vitamin B_1 into every new planting hole." Says she: "I don't believe it did any good, but it sure was expensive." Tests have since shown that the benefits of B_1, supposed to encourage rooting, are mostly psychological, good for the gardener's sense of having done something, but not really helping (or hurting) the new plant.

Tom Nuccio, whose family runs Nuccio's Nurseries, the camellia and azalea specialists in Altadena, also remembers making planting mistakes—though, growing up in a nursery family, he wasn't allowed to make many. "We gardeners are always planting the wrong thing in the wrong place and then just plant too much. Way too much," he says. "Gardeners have got to leave room for things to grow, otherwise nurseries are going to have to give away a free machete with every purchase."

While you wait for the more permanent plants to grow into their allotted space, a good mulch can help keep a new garden from looking like a vacant lot, or you can try temporary things as fillers. Just remember to take them out later to make the required room.

Planting horsetail and thinking he could keep this invasive plant under control was a more recent goof. "I should have known better," Nuccio says. "I planted it here and suddenly in was over there." Several of the gardeners mentioned other potentially invasive plants: agaves, some running bamboos, Mexican evening primrose, even the

"Gardeners have got to leave room for things to grow, otherwise nurseries are going to have to give away a free machete with every purchase," says Tom Nuccio.

beautiful native matilija poppy.

"These plants are simply too aggressive for the average garden," says Gary Jones, who ran the former Hortus Nursery in Pasadena. Equally aggressive is creeping fig (*Ficus repens*), which Jones is still trying to get off his house. Though it begins as delicate tracery, it grows much larger with tough leaves and stems capable of pulling off stucco.

Jones has been gardening since he was a child (his graduation present was a greenhouse), but even with a degree in landscape architecture, he's made his share of mistakes, though he can't really be blamed for the one having to do with California's seasons. Growing up in Utah, it took a while after moving here for him to discover that there are two distinct seasons in California—winter and summer, the cool season and the warm season. "I can't believe no one sat me down and said, 'Look, you plant peas, pansies and lettuce in the fall, not in spring,'" he says. Years later, when he sees his customers making that same mistake, he tries to point them in the right direction.

Those new to the Golden State should know that spring is when we plant the flowers and vegetables that do best in warm weather, such as tomatoes and marigolds. Fall is when we plant the peas, pansies and others that prefer the cooler winter weather. The "Los Angeles Times Gardening Calendar," available every fall, suggests when to plant what, as do the planting charts in this book.

The author of "Pat Welsh's Southern California Gardening" (Chronicle Books, San Francisco) warns: "Don't plant anything that grows fast." Almost all have major drawbacks. They may be short-lived, brittle, greedy or just plain ugly when they grow up. Welsh remembers, "When my family first moved to California, my father, who was a knowledgeable gardener, planted young blue gums on either side of a picture window. Those trees eventually ruined the garden, killing the lawn, clogging pipes, even sending roots up into the drainage holes of flowerpots. Yet I did the same thing in my first garden, planting fast Monterey pines that grew too big and have been sick ever since," she says. "There are so many good trees, why plant a troublemaker?"

Welsh says, "Some mistakes still burn into my heart." Like the time she cut off all the new canes on a climbing rose, thinking that they were suckers from the roots. "A landlady had told me to be sure and cut off any suckers, but I was embarrassed to ask just what suckers were." (They are growth coming from the roots, below where the plant was grafted onto its rootstock.)

Agatha Youngblood's glorious Rancho Santa Fe garden has appeared in the *Los Angeles Times Magazine* and on television's "The

> "You can't spend enough time preparing the soil," says Agatha Youngblood. "You can't give it a lick and a promise and think things are going to grow nicely."

Victory Garden." "When I began, I thought I had tilled in enough amendments, but I had to do it over and over again before the soil really became good," she says, digging up and replanting everything in the process. "You can't spend enough time preparing the soil," is her advice to beginning gardeners. "You can't give it a lick and a promise and think things are going to grow nicely."

Youngblood is adamant that "soil amendments are all-important. That's what makes healthy plants, not the fertilizers or anything else." Soil amendments are composted bark products that physically improve a soil, making it easier to dig in, easier to water, even easier to weed. Often sold as "planting mix," they should not be confused with potting mix, though they contain some of the same ingredients.

Youngblood now adds a lot of amendment, so her soil ends up being about a third amendment and two-thirds dirt, and she digs it in by hand with a spade or spading fork, thoroughly mixing it. If you were to prepare the top 12 inches of soil, you would need to add a whopping six-inch layer of amendment, but this is only necessary for intensive flower and vegetable beds like she has.

For Jan Smithen, who teaches the perennially popular Fanatic Gardeners class at The Arboretum of Los Angeles County in Arcadia, soil preparation was also the first thing she had to learn in gardening. "I never did enough," she says. "I made the mistake of thinking that all you had to do to have a garden like those in the magazines was to sit back and choose the right plants. I got the idea it was like decorating the house," she says. "But it's not. It requires a great deal of digging and you have to do it yourself or carefully supervise others if you want it done right. Even then, plants grow and change through the seasons. The reality—what the magazines don't tell you—is that you have to get in there and dig and then keep your hands in it all the time."

Smithen believes that gardening is a matter or trial and error, no matter how good you've become, so making mistakes is part of the process. "I've killed a lot of plants through the years," she says. "But that's how you learn what does well and what doesn't. You just have to get out there, get started and then learn from the mistakes."

Actress Julie Newmar had everybody's favorite garden on a recent Brentwood garden tour, and she thinks mistakes can even be exciting. Like the time she accidentally purchased some outrageous orange tuberous begonias to plant with blue lobelia in hanging baskets, instead of her usual pink. "I planted them with blue lobelia, and they were shocking," she says. "But now I adore the combination, and the pinks look so drab." She says, "It's healthy to make mistakes. That's how I learn

"I made the mistake of thinking all you had to do to have a garden like those in the magazines was to sit back and choose the right plants," says Jan Smithen.

HOW TO AVOID MISTAKES

- Spend time preparing the soil.
- Plant at the proper depth.
- Don't plant too much.
- Give plants room.
- Beware of fast-growing plants.
- Learn how to prune properly.
- Keep on top of weeding.
- Read all labels carefully!

and I look forward to trying again next season. I bless my mistakes."

"I couldn't understand why the flowers on my roses were getting smaller and smaller and smaller," says Cristin Fusano about her first attempts at growing roses 20 years ago. She is now the horticulturist at Roger's Gardens in Corona del Mar and teaches their standing-room-only rose-pruning classes, as well as classes on Potager and Cottage Gardens.

She remembers doing just about everything wrong when first pruning roses, cutting only the tops so they produced nothing but small twiggy growth from increasingly elderly canes. "There was nothing new to work with," she says. "I didn't get it." Now she prunes to encourage strong new growth, in winter completely cutting out old, woody canes, even if it means leaving only three strong canes on each bush (though she says five are ideal). She prunes the remaining branches just above a big, swelling bud, even if it's low on the cane, to avoid that twiggy growth that sprouts from small buds. She suggests not trying to save old, twiggy bushes, like she did in her first garden. "Even cutting them to the ground doesn't work, so just take them out and plant another."

She also recalls killing a lot of bedding plants by planting them too deep. "I'd buy a floppy lobelia and plant it a little deeper to support the stems." But once buried, the plant would rot and die. "I didn't have a clue what I was doing wrong," she says. Soon she learned to "plant a little high," so the rootball sticks out of the soil a fraction of an inch and there is no way any of the above-ground parts of the plant can end up below ground.

Randy Baldwin, who has a large and varied garden at his wholesale San Marcos Growers, remembers a simple mistake—not taking off the stakes that come with vines and trees. "I still see plants tied to them in gardens," he says. "But they're only to support the plant while it's in the nursery can." Tie vines to a permanent support, and securely stake trees in the proper way—place two sturdy two-by-two-inch stakes about a foot away on either side of the trunk and tie the tree with flexible tape so it can sway and move and gain strength.

"I should know better," says landscape architect Shirley Kerins, "but I still buy way too many plants impulsively, with no idea where I'm going to put them." This can be forgiven because she runs the Huntington Botanical Gardens plant sale, where each May there are far too many irresistible plants. "Another mistake I still make is waiting too long to pull weeds. I look at them and think, 'I'll do that tomorrow.' By the time I get around to it, their roots are four inches into the soil and they're hard to get out," she says. "It's *so* much easier to pull weeds when they're only a half inch or inch tall."

She can think of many other mistakes, like planting things too close together in her own Pasadena garden, or in too much shade, but "that's how you learn." She adds, "Thankfully there are no garden police keeping tabs." All of us can be glad that nature is so forgiving and resilient and that no one is keeping tabs on our growth as gardeners.

Index

Index compiled by
Elisabeth Cheves